MIXED COMPANY

MIXED COMPANY

Women in the Modern Army

Helen Rogan

G. P. Putnam's Sons
New York

The author thanks The MacDowell Colony and the New York State
Council on the Arts/PEN Fund

Library of Congress Cataloging in Publication Data

Rogan, Helen.
  Mixed company.

  Bibliography: p.
  1. United States—Armed Forces—Women. I. Title.
UB418.W65R63   355.1'088042   81-10662
ISBN 0-399-12654-6   AACR2

PRINTED IN THE UNITED STATES OF AMERICA

To
John and Anne Rogan
with love and thanks

Contents

Author's Note   9

1. The Case Against Women   15

2. Military Customs and Courtesies:
   Basic Training   30

3. The Tire and the Toolbox:
   Questions of Capability   63

4. An Army with Banners:
   The Women of History   76

5. Perfect Soldiers:
   Peaceful Coexistence on Bivouac   92

6. Marching as to War:
   Early American Partisans and
   Patriots   119

7. "A Debt to Democracy, a Date with Destiny":
   The Women's Army Corps,
   1942–1945   129

8. Strac City:
   The Peacetime Esprit   148

9. Passing Muster:
    The Days Before Graduation   166
10. Obstacle Course:
    West Point   184
11. Small-Unit Tactics:
    Women in the Integrated Army   224
12. In the Line of Duty:
    Sixty-seven Army Nurses
    in the Philippines   258
13. The Action of the Tiger:
    Combat   272
14. In Close Formation:
    Soldiers and the Citizenry   303
    Selected Bibliography   328

Author's Note

When I first approached the Army Public Affairs Office in New York and asked to spend some time with women in training, I was met with the courtesy and cooperation that have characterized the Army's response to all my other requests for information and access over the past two years. I was initially granted a two-week visit to a basic training company at Fort McClellan, Alabama, but as things turned out, I spent close to six weeks there—the length of a basic training cycle—with the young trainees and the officers and NCOs who taught them, from first light until late at night.

Subsequently I requested, and was given, a stay at West Point, in the course of which I was free to meet and interview anyone I chose. At both West Point and Fort McClellan the restrictions placed on me were minimal. I was asked not to impede any soldier, cadet, or trainee in the course of his or her duties. The same flexibility made my visits to the Pentagon and to posts in this country and abroad a pleasure. I am extremely grateful to the authorities for allowing me this rare opportunity to study the workings of the Army from the inside, and to the following people especially for being so candid and helpful (I refer to them here by the rank and posting that they had at the time of my research): in New York, Lieutenant Colonel Patrick F. Cannan and Colonel John C. Grant; in Washington, Margaret Tackley; at Fort McClellan, Betty Kelly; at West Point, Lieutenant Colonel Miguel Monteverde. Many thanks also to Brigadier General Madelyn Parks (ret.) and Brigadier General Lillian Dunlap (ret.) in San Antonio, and to Sara Lister, General Counsel for the Army, Carol Scott from the Military Court of Appeals, Carol Parr of the Women's Equity Action League, Robert Goldich of Congressional Research Services, and Colonel Bettie J. Morden and Colonel Rosemary McCarthy of the Center of Military History, Department of the Army—all of them in Washington; and to Major Russell Fontenot at Fort Bragg and Dr. Zeborah Schachtel in New York.

I owe most gratitude to the soldiers, male and female— colonels, cadets, recruits, veterans, prisoners of war—who submitted so patiently to my questions. They let me trail around after them at work, they met me at bus stations and hotels, and they entertained me in their homes. When I asked them about sensitive or difficult issues, they were unfailingly thoughtful and honest with me, even at the risk of harming their careers. To protect these soldiers, I have changed their names. For consistency, I have changed the names of all the other soldiers still on active duty and below the rank of general. I have not, however, combined identities or altered the substance of what any one person told me.

Some civilians—Georges Borchardt, the late Henry Robbins, Faith Sale—went beyond their duty in offering shrewd advice and kind encouragement, and I am very grateful to them. I owe special thanks to my family for aid and understanding, and also to my friends, in particular Joan Arnold, Timothy Foote, Veronica Geng, Hendrik Hertzberg, Judy Hicklin Jay, Caroline Pick, James and Ann Raimes, and

Judith Rascoe. Petra Morrison cheerfully gave me many kinds of help at crucial moments. Finally, I thank Alfred Gingold for his generous optimism, tolerance, and affection.

Know'st thou not there is but one theme for ever-enduring bards?
And that is the theme of War, the fortune of battles,
The making of perfect soldiers.

Walt Whitman, "As I Ponder'd in Silence,"
Leaves of Grass

1

The Case Against Women

"Why don't they ever worry about the best use of *men* in the Army? How come they never put them under review?" These words came in a soft, angry voice from a career soldier, a lieutenant who in the course of fifteen years of service in the Women's Army Corps had worked her way up from the ranks and served in Vietnam before she was twenty-one, had learned to fly, worked as a drill sergeant and a company commander, and who sounded unsure of her place in the newly integrated Army.

We were sitting in her office at Fort McClellan, Alabama, in the spring of 1979, only a few months after the WAC had been disestablished and its members dispersed into the mainstream of the Army. The lieutenant wore pressed and starched fatigues, a white T-shirt, spit-shined boots, and a WAC ring. Also in the room were two male career soldiers, her colleagues, who studied paperwork while listening intently to our conversation.

Glancing around at her coworkers, Lieutenant Evans added softly, "In my head I know integration was the right thing, but in my heart I'm not sure." She showed me out into a torrent of spring rain, and, standing on the doorstep as drips fell on her head, she said, unwilling to end the conversation, "I wish we could have talked properly without all those people listening." We agreed to meet another time, more privately.

The All-Volunteer Force ran into manpower problems not long after it replaced the draft on January 27, 1973. The pool of available young men dwindled rapidly, and many of those who were available shunned the military, especially the Army, which had sunk low in public esteem after the upheavals of the 1960s and the Vietnam war. The Women's Army Corps expanded rapidly through the early 1970s because the planners had decided that women could replace men in many Army jobs. By 1978, it had become no longer feasible to have a large and separate Women's Army Corps, and so the two were merged. Ever since then the status of the women in the military, who at present number about 174,000, over 8 percent of the total force, has been controversial and under review.

There is no other country in the world in which women play such a large part in the uniformed military. There are only 10,000 female soldiers in the Russian armed forces of over four million. The armies of eastern and western Europe seem to have in common a lack of interest in expanding women's participation. Their governments apparently share the view expressed in confidential tones by a military attaché at the British Embassy in Washington: "These Americans do take things too far."

American women are to be found on Navy vessels and on Air Force planes and training as astronauts, but the greatest concentration exists in the U.S. Army, where about 63,000 enlisted women and 4,000 officers live and work alongside men, in missile and helicopter repair, as tank-turret mechanics, and in the elite Old Guard, which participates in Washington ceremonials. They serve with the 82d Airborne Division at Fort Bragg, they drive and service trucks, they train troops, male and female.

Approximately 28 out of 345 categories of work are closed to the women—the jobs in infantry, armor, cannon field artillery, combat engineering, and low-altitude air defense artillery. Any of these jobs would be likely to involve them in aggressive combat. Women are allowed into medium- and high-altitude air defense artillery jobs because missiles and rockets traveling at those altitudes are fired from far behind the front line. They can enter all aviation jobs except those of aerial scout and attack helicopter pilot. They can be every kind of medical specialist except a "field medic," the person who literally crawls out onto the battlefield to tag or retrieve the wounded and dying.

Individual women are to be seen every week in *Army Times*, breaking new ground. The first black female jump-master, the female star of the Golden Knights parachute team, the Army's Air Traffic Controller of the Year, the three female members of the Python Combat Skills Branch at Fort Rucker, the Rhodes Scholar from West Point.

Because the expansion has been so rapid and so recent, the women are disproportionately concentrated in the lower ranks of the Army, officers and enlisted. Young female lieutenants and captains are, however, being promoted as fast as possible. Some say they are promoted faster than men. Now that the entrance requirements are equal for both sexes, many more young women can pour in, as the men always have, to take the opportunity for possible adventure, escape, education, self-improvement, security—and, in addition, to save the all-volunteer Army.

In Congress and in the press there have been many expressions of dismay about the Army's problems, about outdated, poorly serviced equipment and a decline in the numbers and quality of recruits. There is concern about wages so low that many soldiers are forced to use food stamps or take a second job, while most leave after their first term is up; there is worry about plunging esprit, racial tension, drugs. There is talk of an Army so depleted that it is "hollow," and of serious shortfalls in the Reserves and National Guard. The over-all shortages are so dire that recruiters have bent the rules to admit illiterate or poorly educated young men and those who are simply not intelligent enough to operate the Army's complicated technology.

The women have become associated with all that is wrong in the Army; some feel that if things were going well, there would not have to be all those women around with their hair straggling out from under their caps. There would be no pregnancies, no tales of harassment. Many male soldiers see the encroaching women as part of the gradual erosion of the prestige and power of the old Army, which has fallen under the control of civilians. Congress has periodic seizures about females coming home in body bags. Conservative columnists furiously ask, like Pat Buchanan, "Do we want coeds at the Khyber?" Nervously, the military and the government request of each other more surveys about the use of women, while the public gloomily looks on, wondering to itself if anyone really knows what is happening, and how all this confusion will affect the deadly game in progress called "The U.S. versus Russia."

Because the Army is responsible for the safety of citizens, and because of this country's place in the world, feelings on military issues are bound to run high. Those who are eager to defend the Army against the women who seem to threaten its stability have a very real case. Armies are for killing, not for equal opportunity, they say. Prove to us that we need to integrate the women fully and we'll do it, but not until the case is proved.

A large majority of the administration and faculty of the U.S. Military Academy at West Point had fought the admission of women cadets in 1976 bitterly but without success. By the time I arrived, in the winter of 1980, to spend some time with the first graduating female cadets, the faculty, and the administration, and find out to what extent coexistence had been achieved, the men had learned to be evasive, oblique in their comments. I met a young captain who told me that nobody was prepared to discuss the deep and basic questions involved in the systematic integration of women into the Army, not because of a lack of interest, but, said Captain Edwards, "because people feel a sense of uncertainty about our direction, and it does not behoove them to express their objections. That is not unusual in the military, but the question of women in combat is a particularly sensitive topic, and people who speak out too freely on the subject can ruin their careers."

One day I persuaded Captain Edwards to explain in detail his objections to the women. We met in his tiny office somewhere in the labyrinthine caverns of the Academy's main classroom building. Captain Edwards graduated in the early 1970s. He was a pale young man, sharp and quick, a credit to his class. I had heard him lecture on campaigns and battle strategy to cadets who were visibly enjoying the aggressive flair of his delivery. Nevertheless, when we met and he produced a sheet of white paper covered in small, neatly penciled writing, with headings and little arrows, he seemed hesitant, and a faint flush rose on his face. He said slowly, "I have very mixed feelings, you see. So I have made a list of the various arguments. You are the first person I have ever gone over it with."

Edwards explained the premise. "The advocates here are those on the affirmative side, and so the burden of the debate goes with them. They say that there are two reasons for this change in the military: social justice and numbers. Now, numbers is not a real problem, because however short we are, there are the people out there with combat MOS's [military occupational specialties]. The draft would bring them back and fill all the quotas." Another version of this opinion was given at the House hearings on women in combat, held in November 1979, when Representative Larry McDonald from Georgia raged, "We loudly proclaim that we don't have enough men and prove it by teaching our women how to use machine guns so that the men don't need to bother. We have 110 million male bodies, 108 million of which are not in service, and then claim that we need to send visibly pregnant women to Germany to beef up our forces there."

Edwards consulted his paper and continued, "As for the social justice argument, I have three objections in the areas of, one, capability, two, military effectiveness, and three, morality. They overlap. The affirmatives have to satisfy my objections before I will buy their argument." He stopped and looked defiantly at me, then plunged on, using his pencil to emphasize his points. "Capability. They say if a woman is capable she should be allowed to do any job. How do you examine it? Person by person or on a group basis? Physical differences exist—different build, different functions. They should not be overlooked or trivialized. Advocates would say, let's look at it case by case. Where this argument breaks down is that it would be expensive, and the Army cannot afford to conduct things on a case-by-case basis. Also, there is the question of, say, thirteen to fifty-eight-year-old males. Some of them would be better able to do it than most women." "It" was combat, but not just in the narrowest sense of hand-to-hand fighting, as it is used to exclude women today. Edwards meant that kind of combat that women will face if there is a war sometime soon, and that will, most likely, kill or injure many of them.

Captain Edwards did not dwell unduly on the question of women's intrinsic capabilities. He did, however, say, "I have been very pleasantly surprised by the female cadets. I thought we'd have a bunch of Valkyries with a chip on their shoulder, but they are extraordinarily sensible and practical. I very much enjoy them in class." I had heard this too from one of his colleagues, another young instructor who conceded that while individual women were impressive per se, the others were the problem, the group en masse. Edwards' colleague said, "It's going to be rough for these women out in the Army. A lot will be expected of them, and people will set out to prove that they don't belong. Many of those men in the field won't take orders from a woman, and they'll get slammed."

Edwards consulted his spidery notes and said, "Of course women have been used in guerrilla warfare and resistance movements. Nobody can deny that when your back is against the wall you go all the way, but it has to be based on need. Things just aren't that desperate."

He moved into category two, military effectiveness. Marshaling his considerable knowledge, he asked why we had not tried other things that would improve our capability without offending our sensibilities—using women as a work force, or specialization of skills by gender, or all-female units. He said with fierce assurance that the U.S. Army today was just like the French Army before World War II—"ripped apart by social experimenting and prejudices."

"Men in a group can have this tremendous unit bonding," said Edwards, "and I'm not talking about a bunch of fags. It's camaraderie with your fellow men in the best sense, and I just don't see how that can be recreated with women. There's sex, there are personal relationships that transcend the legal. Someone has to demonstrate that the primary group experience would not be damaged, and on a consistent basis." He said impatiently, "In over two thousand years of Western civilization, there are no historical precedents for women in conventional warfare. I think the people in the Department of Defense have flung us into a social experiment, and the battlefield is not the place to conduct a social experiment. In order to train a unit to be ready to fight, you need an incredible amount of energy and time. If you divert the energy and time, you jeopardize the unit's chance of success in battle."

Edwards continued calmly, "People will talk about the right to fight." We were moving into morality. He discussed the effects on women of entering a rough, vulgar male environment. He mentioned his little daughter. "Do I want my daughter to become promiscuous and callous? Do I want her to become defeminized? And what about in war? Do I want my daughter to be taken prisoner and raped?" he said. He told me a grisly story about some NCOs whom he had overheard talking when he was a cadet. "They had shot up some VC, and one was a woman who was severely wounded. They had to drag a soldier off her. He was raping her as she died."

His tone softened a little. "I am worried about the government's reasons for legislating this change onto us. I think this is trendy, an attempt to rectify the recruiting problem, a high-visibility social demonstration. I don't sense caution." He looked bleak and repeated his point. "It seriously bothers me as an American that this whimsical plunge has been taken, and it is truly immoral to play with something so important. People have a moral twinge at the thought of women or thirteen-year-old boys or fifty-eight-year-old men going out to fight. We keep them out, which means we discriminate by sex and by age—*but we are keeping them out of the meat grinder*. What use is it to defend a nation that sends its women to the meat grinder? What are we defending? And what right do people have telling me I need to be resocialized, change my ideas? I say, Sez who, *and why are you so certain?*"

Most of the opponents of women's advancement into "nontraditional" areas of the military—helicopter maintenance, truck driving, engineering, and other jobs that involve greasy, dangerous, or unesthetic work—have over the last few years softened their views on women's inadequacy. The diehards may not have changed their minds, but they seem to have realized that it is more useful to talk in terms of military effectiveness. Nevertheless, perhaps the most outspoken and articulate opponent of women's approach to combat is General Elizabeth Hoisington, a former director of the Women's Army Corps, and she is particularly outspoken about capability.

I attended a West Point seminar that General Hoisington was scheduled to address. The female officers who attended knew what her pitch would be and were a little nervous. One, looking immaculate in a newly pressed Class A green uniform with pants, said, "The word went out that we should wear skirts if we didn't want to upset her. When she came to my office I had my feet on the desk and a copy of the NOW newsletter lying around. Linda here hid it under a pile of notes." There was stifled laughter, and we moved into the airless conference room, which, in the manner of all such rooms, was overwhelmingly color-coordinated, and which contained about seventy-five people in uniform, all women except for ten male cadets.

General Hoisington is a sprightly person, with gray hair and an open, quizzical expression. She wore a flower-patterned dress with a big brooch, and from the first moment she had the cadets rapt and delighted with her feisty manner. "You can all go home and sigh and say she was just horrible," she said, wagging a finger, "but for now you can just listen to me." She did not mince words on the reality facing the women. After an introductory history of the Women's Army Corps, as seen in terms of her rise to the top—the general is known for her acuity and articulateness but not for her humility—she said, "You men and women are going to have the shock of your lives outside in the Army. And as for the women, some of the things that will be expected of you will lay you low." She added, "You must stick together and help each other, because you don't have anyone to look after you now that the WAC is gone."

"How would you feel," the general asked the stunned audience, "if you were in a chain and every other link was a weak one? Well, you are, and the weak link is you." Silence fell. I looked at the cadet sitting beside me. A bright dot of color was visible high up on each cheek; she sat erect, neat and polite, with a look of intense bewilderment in her eyes. An officer stood up, cleared her throat, and planted a potentially helpful question that the general could use to clear up any misunderstanding: "Are we *really* a weak link or just perceived as one?" General Hoisington, as it turned out, did not need any help. She said firmly, "You're really a weak link. There may be one or two Amazons here, but you know there are things you can't do."

It was here that the tire and the toolbox made an expected appearance. Some officers sitting nearby sighed. There is an Army toolbox that weighs fifty pounds, and women supposedly cannot handle it very easily. Also, there is a heavy tire on the biggest trucks that is said to be difficult for them to change. It is a well-known fact of Army life that the puniest soldiers with a truck-driving specialty will be assigned to the heaviest trucks. If they are men, the men help each other, but if the women need help, letters are written to the papers. (Often the women may not need help, but they get it anyway.) General Hoisington said, with a frown of concern, "Think of the poor GI who has to help you. The greatest thing you can get out of the Army is job satisfaction, and you can't feel good about your job if you're not qualified to do it." She concluded, "When the day comes that our women and children do not come first, our country is down the drain." I glanced around the room and saw stricken faces, and a dawning surreptitious pleasure on those of a few males.

At the end of the seminar a group of female cadets clustered around the general, perhaps hoping for some reassurance. General Hoisington was addressing one of them with great vehemence: "You say you want to go into the infantry, and you think you should have the right to—but you can't, and you have to accept that. So you'd better live with it, sweetie!" The cadet abruptly excused herself and rushed from the room with tears in her eyes. An officer went after her, saying, "Oh, dear, I thought that would happen to Janet. She wants to go into combat."

Many of the capability arguments against women are centered on the female lack of upper-body strength and on women's inability to sustain for any length of time the footslogging, grueling nature of war. These arguments compel largely because they are spoken by people who have been in combat, and they have a way of silencing everyone else. General Westmoreland testified before the House hearings on women in combat that the battlefield, "primitive and dirty, . . . extends to the utmost one's physical endurance, fortitude, and emotional resistance." He made the point that in a combat zone you have to be flexible, "performing a specialty one minute . . . doing exhaustingly hard labor the next minute." As General Hoisington has said on many occasions, "In my whole lifetime I have never known ten women who I thought could endure three months under actual combat conditions." She too gave testimony on the Hill, and she said, "We should listen to the men with knowledge and experience in such matters. They alone know the endurance and stamina required. They alone know the reaction to hand-to-hand combat, to bodies and minds being blown apart or crippled forever."

Soldiers usually confine their arguments to what can be proved or, at least, to the subject with which they are familiar. However, there are times when they speak with more damaging prejudice than logic. A deputy chief of staff for personnel, announcing an Army decision taken in the spring of 1981 to "hold the line on the number of women in the Army" until their effectiveness had been evaluated, said that 40 percent of the soldiers in some medical units were female and they encountered "just simply physical problems of lifting litters and so forth." When asked if the figure of 40 percent was correct, he said, "I don't know, but I have a gut feeling it is."

Civilian critics of women's new importance in the military are less restricted in their suppositions. Lionel Tiger, author of *Men in Groups,* is the foremost proponent of male bonding as a major force for social cohesiveness. His case against women is that they do not have the capacity to bond, whether in social groups, in sport or work, in hunting, or, most important, in what is called the "primary group," to which the fighting soldier owes true allegiance, whatever the concerns of the country. Tiger said in a magazine interview that the male bond was one way in which men retained power, by resisting women, and added, "The reason men resist women is likely to be something deeply rooted in our biology . . . something very useful to us in the hunting-gathering phase of evolution" (which in turn is so useful to anthropologists examining the reasons why twentieth-century Americans behave as they do).

Other arguments range from the mystical to the highly logistical, and most have in common a distaste for civilian control of the Army. Richard Gabriel is the coauthor of *Crisis* in Command, a controversial book about the decline of the military, the premise of which, crudely expressed, is that management is not leadership and it is ruining the Army. Gabriel argues that an army is effective only when it can properly do its job as a killing machine. He says it is a grave mistake to overestimate the importance of technical skills. The military, unlike a business, depends on unit cohesion, or, in the fashionable sociological term, "primary group cohesion," or, in the original term, "male bonding." Like Tiger, Gabriel believes that women are incapable of that bonding and by their presence prevent men from bonding among themselves. The evidence suggests that the complete integration of women will be a disaster. The numerous instances of women fighting as partisans and guerrillas are not, he says, useful as an argument because there is no comparison between fighting units of that kind and a large modern army. The Israelis tried the experiment and it failed. Many critics join him in worrying that our enemies will see the importance of women in the U.S. military as a sign of weakness at the very least, and possibly as an invitation.

Gabriel says that the resistance to women's advance is greatest among the lower classes. The all-volunteer Army is primarily made up of the lower classes, and these men will either refuse to knuckle under to Army policy or will not join up, because the prospect of working with or under women fills them with dismay. In the next conventional war many women will face combat in integrated units, with the risk of capture or death. Combat readiness will be severely hindered by the large number of pregnant women, who will have to be evacuated, and by the sole parents, who might have to make arrangements for their children and would be reluctant to abandon them. The distress of the actual battle would be heightened because the modesty of both sexes would be compromised by their degradations, mostly in matters of hygiene. The men would instinctively help the women, think about protecting them, and be oversolicitous toward the wounded. At the same time they would *never* under stress take orders from a woman. There would be sexual contests for the women's favors.

James Webb, a Vietnam veteran, author of a novel called *Fields of Fire*, and an Annapolis graduate, wrote in a passionate magazine article that if a man and a woman were put together in a foxhole at the front, "many aggressions would be directed inward, toward sex, rather than outward toward violence." Other critics worry that men in war, with their animal lusts released, would rape their female comrades; one writer in *The New York Times* referred to "the roar of the hormones." Webb makes the traditional and persuasive argument in favor of a warrior elite, deploring the policy of training women to be combat leaders, which, he says, is what training them at the academies amounts to. Men can fight at their best only when women are not around. The presence of women has "sterilized" and "eviscerated" the atmosphere in which officers are trained, and has lowered the standards.

Throughout the Army, from basic training companies to units overseas, career soldiers are worried about the decline in standards, about the softening of training and the drop in physical achievement. The Army is not effective in the ways it used to be, and the reason is that it is no longer a man's world. As Webb sees it, good soldiers are "competitive, often vulgar, and tough." The best soldiers are created in a harsh, cruel, and stressful environment that represents a rite of passage into manhood. The arrival of the women has robbed these young men of their manhood in the interests of some ludicrous travesty of equal opportunity. This is war, he reminds us. And, as General Westmoreland says, "No man with gumption wants a woman to fight his battles."

The morality question looms here, for war is not simply hell, but a man's hell, where women do not, should not belong, partly because they are the ones who have the children, while men go off to fight wars to protect them. People like Webb are concerned about the effects of rugged training on the women who struggle through. Others feel, like Captain Edwards, that the rough and tough atmosphere of the Army will rub off on the women and turn them into promiscuous, easy-living creatures, even homosexuals. The pregnancy figures for soldiers are alarmingly high, which shows that the Army is a very bad place for a woman.

Because of feelings like these, the women are observed, studied, and reviewed. In recent years they have been in the headlines: when the first female cadets entered the academies, when President Carter announced his plans to register women, and whenever the House Armed Services Committee debates the draft or combat readiness or harassment. The debate has a one-dimensional quality.

One raw November day I visited Fort Dix, New Jersey, with other journalists and a television crew. We drove out to a bumpy, blasted heath where male and female trainee soldiers on bivouac sat shivering among the gorse bushes and picked over their C rations. A free-lance male photographer, who was later discovered to be working for a men's magazine, was heard to say to their commanding officer, "I'd like a blonde, a brunette, a black girl, and a redhead," whereupon a weary one of each was found and taken aside to be photographed. Whenever women like these are photographed or discussed or taken up by one lobby group or another, the debate about their purpose and effectiveness remains one-dimensional, because the women themselves are never really consulted about their views or asked for the benefit of their experience.

This book presents the women: veterans of both world wars and women soldiers in history, ex-Wacs and Army nurses, prisoners of war and colonels at the Pentagon, young troops and cadets fresh from training and seasoned officers who have served all over this country and abroad. Today's female soldiers find themselves in a man's army, and they have complicated feelings about the conditions of their lives, about their colleagues and the possibility of war. Their opinions are varied, and to that extent typical. They are also important. Just by being in the Army in such large numbers and so widely dispersed, military women are the catalyst for questions about the purpose of the Army, the relation of military service to citizenship, the morality of a selective draft, the making of perfect soldiers.

The modern Army is a laboratory where the results of differences in gender can be observed. Military women are exposed more directly than civilians to the effects of society's prejudices about appropriate male and female behavior. Because the Army is authoritarian, behavior can, and must, be controlled in a way that cannot be achieved in the civilian world. Army women are required to become effective soldiers, in just the same way that the men are, and the process leads us to question all our traditional ideas about masculinity and femininity.

We owe it to the women to hear them out, to benefit from the loyalty and expertise of the career soldiers with years of experience, to understand the pressures on the young troops starting out in the Army—and to appreciate the dangers they face. We owe it to them, not just because they are our daughters or sisters or friends or wives. With a peacetime draft unpopular and impractical, the All-Volunteer Force must survive—but it cannot survive without successful integration. Military women have become vital to our national security.

2

Military Customs and Courtesies: Basic Training

The young men and women are called "rainbows." Their bright clothing distinguishes them as civilians when they step, pale and nervous, with cigarettes clutched between their fingers, from the ramshackle green buses that have brought them in from the airports and bus stations. One may have come from halfway across the country, to arrive at a deserted post in the middle of the night, after rattling around with a suitcase, like an evacuee, in a freezing, cavernous bus, its driver taciturn, sleepy, and hardly older than the passenger. A female trainee told me, "A whole bunch of us came in together from Birmingham Airport. The boys in the back took out a joint and started smoking furiously. None of the girls did that, none of us even took a puff. It was as if the guys saw this as their last moment in the world, as if they were going away forever, while the girls were much more— well, *enthused*. It was as if the guys were escaping and the girls were going to an adventure."

Fort McClellan, Alabama, is a small, quiet post at the bottom of the Appalachian chain. It sits in hilly woodland just north of Anniston, a genteel little town with a theater, a natural history museum, and a lifeless town center. Fort McClellan's buildings are white and cool, with red-tiled roofs. Torrential rainstorms wash away the golf course every spring; when I arrived the first dogwoods and daffodils were appearing in the woods. The reception station is a modern building, square and impersonal. Processing of new recruits takes three to four days in facilities designed to process up to 440 people at a time. However, only a trickle of trainees arrived during the first week of April 1979. They slumped on brightly colored chairs, waited on line, filled out forms, and sat through lectures on life in the Army. There was little chatter. One day they sat through numbing film shows—on military justice, on the amenities of the post—staring numbly at the screen while soft rock music accompanied harshly lit shots of the sauna, the PX, the swimming pool. I looked around at the expressionless faces, wondering what they were thinking. Some might never have seen a swimming pool. A captain told me later that some would arrive from backgrounds of inconceivable destitution, their hair crawling with lice and their bodies malnourished.

Fort McClellan in 1979 was one of only two posts in the country where women were trained, the other being Fort Jackson. Because it had been the headquarters of the Women's Army Corps since 1954, Fort McClellan was commanded by a female general, and throughout the post there were women in senior positions. Today women are trained alongside men at most posts, and the numbers of women at Fort McClellan have dwindled, so that the proportions there more closely reflect those in the Army, where women make up 8 percent of the total.

In the company that finally took shape out of the clumps of jittery young ex-civilians huddled in the reception station, there were 87 men and 76 women. Twenty-two of the women had some college experience, as opposed to 7 of the men. Only 7 of the women had a GED (General Educational

Development) diploma instead of a high school diploma,
whereas 36 of the men had neither. The women tended to be
between nineteen and twenty-two years old, the men a year
or so younger.

At its peak the Women's Army Corps, founded in 1942,
was 100,000 strong, but after the war, numbers decreased
sharply, and it was not until the seventies that the women's
services were expanded. When the Women's Army Corps
was disestablished, in October 1978, women began, with
much hoopla, to be moved into the so-called "nontraditional
MOS's," such as parachute rigging and truck driving. Despite all the fuss, the actual number of women going into the
newly opened fields was small. In this particular cycle at Fort
McClellan the majority of the men were going into helicopter
or missile repair or work with radar and ammunition, while 64
of the women were going into medical jobs or psychiatry or
social work, and 6 more into other jobs that were also obvious
for women, such as clerical work or photography. Only 6 out
of the whole group were venturing into unusual fields. Two
had chosen parachute rigging, one helicopter repair, one
veterinary studies, and two were on their way to OCS
(Officer Candidate School). So these women, as well as being
consistently older and much better educated than the men,
were more interested in acquiring skills that would serve
them later in a civilian life than they were in a pioneering
future.

Between lectures at the reception station, there were
cigarette breaks. Clumps of people stood outside, shivering
in the spring cold, scuffing at the gravel and wet grass, and
tentatively exchanging confidences. The women in their
denim skirts or corduroy pantsuits seemed warier than the
men as they searched for a way to open conversation,
chatting stiltedly about the soap operas they were missing.
The men joshed each other, nudging their neighbors as
officers went by, although they could not tell an officer from
an enlisted man, and were wont to spring to attention for
anyone who walked by in a uniform. Gradually the women

relaxed a little too and began to fish out photographs from their pocketbooks, pictures of their families and boyfriends. Soon female war stories were exchanged.

"Listen, honey, I was married and divorced twice before I was twenty-one, and I'm *never* getting married again," drawled a pretty, pale young woman with curly blond hair and slim build. Her name was Elizabeth Brady, and over the next few weeks she told stories of life in Dalton, Georgia, that were as full of violence and treachery as a country song. Elizabeth announced that she was first married at fourteen, and added wryly, "In my town, if you weren't married before fifteen, you were on the shelf."

There was a sympathetic, knowing ripple of amusement among the little group, and more of the women volunteered details of such experiences. Telling these stories of divorces and hysterectomies and the jobs they had held, they sounded much older than their years. Standing quietly to one side was a seventeen-year-old from Vermont, small, shy, and delicate, and one of the few not to chain-smoke. Her name was Claire Hayes. She grimaced awkwardly and said, "I feel out of this. I wish I was at home with my boyfriend." She said, tailing off, "My father hated to see me go. He said I was too young to leave home."

The women seemed dazed. Unlike the men, they had absolutely no idea what to expect, no familiar ideal. A sergeant informed them that each trainee would be given a chance to drop all forbidden items in his or her possession— candy, knives, magazines, drugs, alcohol, assorted weapons—into a padlocked amnesty box behind a closed door while nobody watched.

A couple of young black women, friends from Newark, looked particularly sullen and terrified, and whenever possible they sat by themselves, away from the others—a pattern in which they would persist throughout the training. Some of the black males, annoyed, started to needle them. One sat down beside them and said vehemently, "We all got to be friends. We's cool. We help each other." He said that in

New Orleans, his hometown, if somebody said hello, you would answer back and be friends. Lynne Hunt, who had a ferocious, self-contained elegance, stared at him with a thunderous look and said slowly, "My friends are my mother, my sisters, and my drill sergeant." She continued, "And my God. That's *all* the friends I *need.*" She shrugged on her field jacket, a special issue because of the cold, and stiffly walked off to the bus that was to take them to the finance office, where they were to receive their first pay.

Standing outside the finance office, waiting, the men whispered and passed cigarettes, but most of the women stood impassively, in silence or else talking without moving their heads. Elizabeth said several times, "You have to laugh, or else you'd cry." New female soldiers passed by on the other side of the street and yelled something jocular while the trainees looked back at them with a glum mixture of resignation and alarm.

One of the first things they learned was to stand at attention and yell "GOOD MORNING, SIR" at the required volume. I was surprised that the women seemed to have no inhibitions about yelling as loudly as the men. I mentioned this to a friendly plump trainee, who looked older than the others and told me that she was in fact twenty-nine. "I'm amazed at these girls," she said, "how different they are from the way I used to be. They're so *like men.* They don't want to get married and settle down, they want some excitement. The one in front of me dumped razors and a knife in the amnesty box!"

Basic training is still conducted on principles familiar from World War II. While the trainees trundled through medical tests and filled out forms, I went to see Colonel Grimes, who was, after twenty-eight years of service, a couple of months away from retirement. She was in charge of basic training for the whole post—that is, for the military police school, where they had fourteen-week training that incorporated Advanced Individual Training (AIT), as well as for ordinary basic.

Colonel Grimes was highly respected, a quiet woman with curly, graying hair and a reflective manner. She explained training as a system of building blocks, starting with PT (Physical Training) and the basic skills, such as marching and cleaning and upkeep of uniforms, before moving into weapons familiarization. She said, "In the early stages, the Army is so new and unfamiliar that the trainees do not get impatient or create problems." In the fourth week they prepare for bivouac, which follows in week five, the field trip that requires the trainees to sleep in tents and integrate everything they have learned with offensive and defensive techniques. The sixth and last week is for testing, refreshers and inspections. During that week, traditionally, everything falls apart.

Colonel Grimes told me, "Seventy-five percent of trainees can get through without assistance, twenty percent need help, and five percent cannot do it." She emphasized that Fort McClellan was not self-consciously rough and tough. We talked about the notorious recruit deaths at other posts. She said, "We have very hot weather here, you know, and six weeks is not a long time in which to acclimatize them. However, there have been no serious heat cases, ever." (Subsequently, in 1980, there was one. A young woman collapsed after exercising in the sun, was misdiagnosed, and died of complications from pneumonia three days later in the post hospital.)

Colonel Grimes continued: "We're not training combat soldiers, infantry, here. Our training is demanding, but we haven't experienced any serious abuse here. That's because Fort McClellan was WAC Center, and the drills here have always been dedicated to ensuring that individuals *learn*." Fort McClellan was the training center for all WAC recruits until disestablishment, and WAC basic training was a restrained affair, mostly restricted to cleaning, drill, and classroom instruction, with a one-week bivouac, when the women learned map-reading and other military skills. However, as Colonel Grimes wrote in a memo, "at the slightest

indication of inclement weather, the troops were returned to
the company area."

The first male drill sergeants arrived in 1974, and also in
that year voluntary weapons training was introduced. "The
pressure for change came after Vietnam," Colonel Grimes
said, "where everybody was drawing combat pay." Or, as
another colonel put it, "The bullets did not come in pink and
blue." A test was instituted at Fort Jackson to see if young
women could undergo the same training as the men did.
Colonel Grimes told me that two battalions participated,
about eight hundred men and eight hundred women. "I was
amazed at what the women could do," she said. As a result of
this test the training for women and for men became almost
identical. Today's basic training is not the same as it used to
be when it was all male and called basic combat training.
Because it covers only 6 weeks instead of 8, some subjects
have been eliminated and others abbreviated. Today's recruit receives only 57 hours of rifle marksmanship instruction
instead of 72—but does have classes in contraception and the
prevention of rape.

"Today's recruit is different, more aggressive than in the
old days," said Colonel Grimes. "You shouldn't kick and
shove them; these days you do more counseling. This has
nothing to do with the arrival of the women, although people
think it does." She reminded me that everyone in today's
Army is there because he or she wants to be, so that there is
no case to be made for unreasonable bullying. The Army has
always been based on teamwork; today it is essential.

The issue of female uniforms took place in a long, low
building crammed with all uniform items in almost every
size. The women wandered about in slips and bare feet,
carrying piles of clothing, adding new items at each stop.
Kind, abstracted women of middle age, their mouths full of
pins, smoothed and tucked and pulled at the clothes as the
trainees stood on boxes, walked to test new shoes, and
grinned faintly as they tried on the more unattractive items—

for example, the box-shaped black raincoat that, although intended to be up-to-the-minute, made every young woman look like a prison warden. Most of the women came off the conveyor belt in olive-green fatigues, white T-shirts, black combat boots, and a green baseball cap, thrilled to be taking on a new identity at last. Until now they had only felt themselves to be moving out of their old identities, relinquishing their freedom to have a soda when they chose. The only difference between a male and a female uniform was that the females had to wear the jacket top of their fatigues loose instead of tucked into their pants, so as not to incite the males. Those women whose bodies bore little relation to the shapes of the fatigues had to put their civilian clothes on again. On the bus back the others lounged and grinned cockily, trying to look battle-scarred. "These pants are *so comfortable*," said one.

That night I accompanied the trainees to the barracks where they slept and where they would train. A posse of male drills was waiting as the trainees stepped cautiously from the bus. The drills were impatient after the wait, for before this company was assembled, there had been a months-long hiatus, in the course of which they had painted the hallways and stayed at home, irritating the spouses who were forced to alternate between their fretful presence or their continuous absence when the cycle began. They stood, very self-consciously assured in their big Smokey the Bear hats, known as "round browns," and watched their new charges with intimidating grins. Then, shouting jovially, they herded the trainees onto the wet grass; it was dark now, and spring nights in northern Alabama are cold and heavy with dew. There the trainees did their first push-ups—male push-ups for all. The women without fatigues were hanging onto their white handbags, sinking into the ground in their flimsy espadrilles, gasping in shock at the unaccustomed strain on their arms—and trying not to collapse in the mud and ruin their civilian clothes. The ground was littered with dropped keys, lighters, cigarette packets, candy, change.

In the dark the trainees were marched off—it somewhat resembled marching—to the PX, where they wandered around in a daze looking for something on which they could spend their newly earned hundred dollars. They carried a list of items, "required and suggested," that ranged from soap case (plastic) to dog tag protector and edge dressing (shoes). The women, who had an extra allowance for "black pumps, brassiere, panties, nylon hose, slips," gazed at the well-upholstered bras and greeting cards, automatically dropping items, useless or forbidden (candy and magazines are called contraband), into their wire baskets, looking like the Stepford Wives.

The drills stood by the door, rocking on their heels, joking, laughing heartily, so that the trainees would start and nervously glance over. Sergeant Fogle, a short, bluff infantryman from Fort Benning, Georgia, told me with a grin, "I like 'em integrated, but it was a real shock to me to have a female commanding officer." He said more seriously, "You have to hold the men back. I would push them to go faster on the marches if there were no women along, with their little legs." Another sergeant, Stokes, an MP, told me, his eyes gleaming behind spectacles, "I used to work with prisoners. When I first arrived I kept treating the trainees like prisoners. But I hate it when the women cry. I just stare at 'em and hope they'll stop." He sucked on his toothbrush mustache and laughed wildly, looking around at his colleagues. Then he said, leaning confidentially closer, "Cussin' is not big these days. Hollerin' is OK, but not cussin'." He added, "I myself prefer to speak real quiet and serious. But you should see the folks at Fort Jackson—they stamp on heads, they think we're easy." Everybody laughed then and set to work rounding up the trainees.

The Alpha Company barracks was a three-story white building on top of a grassy hill, consisting of ground floor offices and sleeping bays on the upper two floors: males on the third, females on the second; first and second platoon to the left of the stairs, third and fourth to the right. The women I had met at the reception station were all in the second platoon. They and the women of the first platoon—thirty-five altogether—would share the long, low-ceilinged room, with two rows of iron beds on either side of the central aisle and a gleaming blue linoleum floor. The white walls were bare except for fire drill notices. The room was divided into two, half for each platoon, by a ceiling-high row of lockers. The women flounced around, swapping beds and mattresses, investigating the lockers.

A former sorority sister at the University of Kentucky sat on her bed picking through her uniform. She held up a resplendently unfashionable pair of regulation low-heeled black leather pumps between two fingers. "Well, my Lord, isn't this just the neatest thing, girls?" she said. The others, intently hiding candy and magazines behind the asbestos ceiling panels, guffawed and shrieked, on the edge of hysteria.

Elizabeth Brady, one of whose husbands had been in the Army, had a self-contained, grim air as she unpacked, smoking steadily. Periodically one of the women would be summoned to the drill sergeant's office down the hall. Sergeant Lester, a medic from Walter Reed who had been zeventeen years in the Army and had served in Vietnam, was the drill sergeant for Alpha 2, and Sergeant Stokes, the MP, was responsible for Alpha 1. As a result, jurisdiction over the women in the bay was always confused, so that often the lines were unnecessarily crossed. The more paranoid trainees came to believe that it was deliberate, a version of brainwashing. "They messing up our minds," said one young black woman dourly.

The grumbling and chaos were particularly marked in the Alpha 2 side of the bay, where the women were, on average, younger than those on the other side of the lockers. The disaffection increased considerably when a tiny Korean, Patty Sharp, came back from Sergeant Lester's office with squad leader stripes on her sleeve. Patty had been the object of curious stares ever since her arrival at the reception station—she was tiny and sticklike, with hair cut short and standing rakishly on end like a rooster's. She had been regarded as an eccentric, faintly amusing, until she got the stripes. They made her monstrous. She looked around the room with an expression that was a mixture of alertness and total noncomprehension, then started to march around the bay, shouting from her thin little frame what was to become an unbearable irritation before it finally turned into a joke. "ALL RIGHT, YOU GUYS, NOW LISTEN UP, EVERY-BODY, LISTEN UP." She stood beating a clenched fist against her hip, notebook and pencil akimbo, yelling more loudly as people muttered between their teeth or simply ignored her, pushing past on their way to the latrines and lockers. Lynne Hunt, who had been so aloof with the men in the reception station, heard a platoon of troops marching by, and she rushed to the window, her face rapt and excited, with all the lowering tension lifted out of it.

I arrived at the first morning of training just before 5:00 A.M. The dogwood blossoms gleamed through the darkness. The air was damp and chilly; motionless, the trainees stood in T-shirts and fatigue pants at the edge of the parade ground, ankle-deep in mist. The birds struck up their dawn chorus in the woods, and the shivering trainees began PT, some of them taking strenuous exercise for the first time in years. For an hour they strained, rolled, toppled with their bottoms in the air or on the wet grass, keys bobbing from the chains around their necks, faces flushing from the cold and their racing circulation. They learned that in a pause it was mandatory to shake their hands, growl violently, and clamor, "MORE PT, DRILL SERGEANT, MORE PT, WE *LIKE* IT, WE *LOVE* IT, WE *WANT MORE OF* IT," and then growl again. In response, they were taught the squat thrust, the knee bend, the leg circular, and other elements of Baseline PT, the Army's current training enthusiasm. That day they ran nearly a mile, and several—males and females—faltered. Those who still had not received their uniforms had to put their purses in a neat pile to one side and dive into the dew with everyone else.

Male sergeants in hooded sweat suits demonstrated the exercises. A little to the side, staring closely at the trainees, stood their commanding officer, Lieutenant Pamela Myers, twenty-seven years old, from Chicago. She is disarmingly pretty—five feet two, with large green eyes, a pointed face, and a curving little body. The trainees barely noticed her, she was so small and quiet. As dawn broke she and I walked to the mess hall for breakfast. We had been formally introduced the previous day by the female colonel in command of the battalion, who had established the protocol by referring to me as "Miss Rogan." We were to be "Miss Rogan" and "Lieutenant Myers" until graduation day. Lieutenant Myers was once a schoolteacher and she wears authority well. The oldest child and the only girl in the family, she was encouraged to be competitive "from the day I brought home my first speech trophy from school." She told me that she and her husband of seven years had joined together; he had decided to be an Army helicopter pilot and told her she "absolutely was not going to join the Army." Lieutenant Myers mimicked her reaction, half-laugh, half-gasp of shock. "And I said, *never* tell me that."

In the mess hall most of Alpha Company's female cadre were seated at the top table, their trays piled with orange juice, toast, Danish, eggs and bacon, waffles, bananas. The cadre consisted of Lieutenant Myers, her young male training officer straight out of West Point, one first sergeant, one senior drill sergeant, five drill sergeants, and other assorted part-time NCOs—a total of fifteen. Out of the fifteen, eight were women, and among their number were not only the commanding officer but also the first sergeant and the only female senior drill on the post, Sergeant Gayle Bell, a thirty-two-year-old black woman from Columbus, Ohio, with fourteen years of service. She was an attractive, muscular woman, with a reserved manner and the most natural authority in the cadre, male and female. The women were stowing away large quantities of baked goods, and as soon as the one male present went to his duties, the conversation turned bawdy.

A hefty, cheerful sergeant in her mid-thirties, who drives a pickup and scavenges from the post dump, leaned across the table to Sergeant Bell, calling her "Senior Drill," and started to tell her about a fishing trip up in the mountains the previous weekend, when they had got drunk and gone skinny-dipping in the river. Crude jokes flew. Then Lieutenant Myers, who spoke in a crisp, low voice, began to talk about the naked bodies she remembered from the showers in high school. Her eyes widened, and she said unself-consciously, "One girl had hickies *all over* her body." They laughed, and she continued, "I didn't like to stare, but I just kept looking."

During those first few days the female cadre members told me how integration had been achieved and how they felt coeducational training was working. Alpha Company had been the first at Fort McClellan to integrate. Lieutenant Myers, a highly organized woman, had calculated the likelihood long in advance. "I thought, we're going to get them," she said, "and I was really excited." They were told to integrate one platoon and otherwise left to their own devices. I asked her what preparations they had made. She said with an amused smile, "Absolutely none. Oh, a couple of people went over to the MP school and talked to them, but that was about it." She added, "Of course we were in a goldfish bowl, although they had promised that would not happen, but still, we decided not to get that excited about it all."

Lieutenant Myers told me, "There was one great surprise, something we hadn't anticipated. The men overloaded the washing machines, because they didn't know how to use them, and so all the laundry rooms were flooded. I really would have to say that there were no other differences," she added. Whenever I asked other cadre members about differences, they would puzzle over the question, then say with polite regret, "Well, I can't think of any at the moment." General Mary Clarke, the poised and intelligent commander of the post, said, "The only real difference is that women are used to their privacy. So for them we have put up shower curtains and partitions in the johns."

The first sergeant, Sergeant Reilly, was a wiry, quizzical-looking woman in her fifties, who sat in her office inside a cloud of smoke, puffing on her cigarette, talking on the phone, and looking up to address acerbic remarks to the visitors who came in a steady stream, officers and NCOs, to flop down in a chair and tell horror stories about trainees. She said, "The men make more noise at first, but after that they're the same. I've found men who will take advantage of us females, trying to get our sympathy." She grinned at me. "I was frightened of what I'd do when a man cried in front of me, but I didn't mind at all. I just gave him a Kleenex." She was more likely to reveal her soft heart to the male members of the cadre, she said. "Sometimes when my young men do something outstanding, I have a tendency to kiss them on the cheek, and they don't know what to do about that!"

Ultimately the women all seemed to agree with Lieutenant Myers, who was a social scientist at college and loves quantifiable data. She said, "Everyone keeps telling me there are differences, but I don't see them. They say the men can't march and the women can; the men can't houseclean and the women can; the women can't fire well and the men can. But that first group came out surprisingly equal. Some men and women couldn't run; some men cried and were scared. It was the same with taking orders. The variations always had more to do with the drills than the trainees."

Alpha was run on that assumption—that the most important differences were between people when it came to training soldiers. I asked Lieutenant Myers about her drill sergeants. These days they are chosen from volunteers and nonvolunteers. The assignment is prestigious, considered to be good for anyone's career, and so a good sergeant, however reluctant he or she may be to leave a specialty for three years, is unlikely to turn down the invitation. In these days of the integrated Army, drills have to be educated not just in the steps of Baseline PT, but also in the correct way to fold female underwear. Lieutenant Myers told me, grinning, "It's hilarious—the men try to back out of teaching all that right-cup, left-cup stuff." Many are infantry- or artillerymen, to whom the very idea of women roughing it is hallucinatory, and they have to learn how to deal with a sobbing woman, a flirt, or someone who refuses to do PT because she is getting her period.

The monstrous and brutal drill sergeant is a familiar image, and I asked Lieutenant Myers if that presented a special problem with female trainees. She said, "Sometimes the men will take advantage of female trainees, but the women did that too in the old WAC days. Drill sergeants *always* give you problems. They're a unique breed of egomaniacs. They have to be to survive the hours and the emotional strains of the job." She said that many of the problems arise with drills modeling themselves on their old drills, and added, "That's females too. I've worked with female drills so brutal that you have to keep restraining them—they're imitating their old drill sergeant."

Lieutenant Myers had no disciplinary problems with trainees, and neither did her NCOs. The atmosphere in the company was orderly and relaxed for the most part. There was a minimum of bellowing, and those males, and females, who overdid it—"Hollerin', not cussin'"—were not well regarded. Only one of the three female drills had a visible temper. Sergeant Pace was tiny, no more than five feet one or two; she looked ravaged and older than her thirty-three years because of past illness and alcoholism. She was too small to gain much sartorial benefit from the female drill sergeant's hat—a gray Stetson worn with one side pinned up—but she had its status. Sergeant Pace would occasionally creep up behind trainees and snarl at them with a ferocity so unrestrained that they would jump and drop their glasses of chocolate milk.

The other women expressed their authority in ways that I

was told originated in the Women's Army Corps. Their manner seemed to have its roots in civilian life—cool, crisp, efficient, and reminiscent of an excellent school principal, but with the starch and impersonality of a dental hygienist. It took a while for the troops to notice it. Early in their training they might not see Lieutenant Myers when she walked into a room to address them. Even as she began to talk, there would still be a low buzz of chatter at the back of the room. I asked her what she thought about this, and she said, choosing her words carefully, "I don't believe that you have to shout, and my voice is soft unless I make an effort to raise it. So I think it takes a while for them to realize that I mean what I say. Most of the men have a hard time believing that I really am their commanding officer, because they have that image of the classic male drill fixed in their brains."

The routine during much of the first two weeks was dominated by meals, the high points of the day, and by cleaning followed by inspection, PT, drilling, and classroom lectures. The meals were enormous and very good, even if trainees did have to bolt their food, stand rigidly in line for a long time before receiving it, and run double time back to the barracks after finishing. There was an abundance of wholesome food—fruit, vegetables, cottage cheese—as well as cafeteria reliables and an endlessly recyclable tureen of chopped beef in various forms. The drills would eye their charges from the top table and appear on fleet and silent foot behind the left shoulder of someone busily chowing down on cake and ice cream and whisper, "You wear your hat to the table at home, sweet pea?" and a beet-colored trainee would whip it from his head, too late to avoid twenty push-ups. "Knock 'em out, sonny," the drill would say cheerily, strolling from the hall with a fudgesicle in his hand.

Cleaning was the hardest part. Elizabeth Brady said to me sagely at one time, looking up from her task of applying ammonia to the lower half of the corridor walls, "This is all psychological, you know. They want to see if we can stand it. They want us to make a team." It was probably the only time

that they felt themselves to be achieving nothing—they were
not learning anything, becoming stronger or more limber,
they were not cheering themselves up with food. It seemed
an inspection was always imminent, whether by a drill
sergeant, the company commander, or the battalion commander, Colonel Allen. The trainees were meant to have at
least seven hours sleep a night, and none of the cadre would
keep them up late deliberately or postpone bed check.
Nevertheless, basic was intended to instill the ability to
organize. Those who had not learned to organize—and the
women had not—would get up at 2:00 and 3:00 in the
morning to have the bays ready for inspection at 5:00. I
arrived one typical morning at 4:30 to find that they had
already been up for two hours. Their faces were tense and
their tempers ragged. They lined up in formation outside,
Baird, the sorority sister from Kentucky, surreptitiously
applying Lipsmackers in the back row while pretending to
stand to attention. Sergeant Fogle, pacing slowly up and
down with the measured stateliness of an infantryman, said,
"The place looks like a pigsty. We're going to cancel PT so
you can get it squared away. You better get it squared away."

Racing back upstairs, complaining bitterly, the trainees
tore off their hats and started to bicker. A thirty-one-year-old
from first platoon, who was called "Mom" by everyone from
the moment she stepped off the bus, had been forced by the
weight of years to take charge. She had them mopping and
scraping wax off the floors in order to reapply wax. They
were crawling along the top of the lockers, wiping down
skirting boards, scrubbing scuff marks, replacing broken
curtain hooks. Mom told someone sharply to use her brain,
and the person promptly burst into tears.

In the other half of the bay Patty, the Korean, was
wandering around waving her notebook. Badly rattled, she
had lost her composure, and tugged at people's sleeves,
asking nervously, "Hey, what should we be doing?" The
impatient answer was "Oh, *find* something." So she crept
miserably around with wet paper towels wadded into a bunch
and dabbed at the ends of the beds. Elizabeth crawled under

the beds to clean the springs. On her way to get more detergent, someone said to me wearily, "All this just to call my mother." The women had had no phone privileges since they arrived, no contact with the outside world at all, except what they could see about half a mile away, namely, a highway, a row of ramshackle stores, and a bar with a hand-lettered sign in the window that said BAIT and PAWN.

Someone took the electric clock off the wall and cleaned behind it. The sorority sister, a well-bred twenty-one-year-old whose idea of cursing when she fell off the horizontal bars was to say "Oh, zippedidoodah!!" said, "I can feel my background falling apart. Listen to the way I talk." Indeed, she was acquiring the Army's all-purpose Southern accent. Elizabeth said viciously, "Goddam this fuckin' shit. You do everything you can and still you don't do it right. I ain't ever doin' no more of this fuckin' shit." This kind of free-form, free-associated monologue came to sound like poetry, the poetry of drudgery. A small black woman, the best female athlete in the company, said as she passed, "I didn't know basic would be so hard and cruel."

They had bleach in their hair, and their hands were rubbed raw with the Comet, which left a greasy film on the window ledges. They were putting black shoe polish on the banisters. A funny, freewheeling Californian who had been a landscape gardener and was going into the National Guard doggedly held the plug of the buffer in the wall socket so that it would not be jerked out by the movements of the machine as it lurched over the floor. She looked up, wiped her face with a dusty, sweaty hand and said, "I would love for that guy on *Fantasy Island* to walk up to me and say [and here she adopted a Montalban accent], 'How was your treep on Fantasy Island? Now—eet ees time for you to go home.'"

A male timidly entered the bay, carrying ice cubes in his bare hands. The women jumped to seize them. Elizabeth said, "Hey, imagine these are margaritas." She added wistfully, "I used to be a cocktail waitress in Dalton, Georgia, in one of those fancy nightclubs. We wore hot pants. It was one of those joints that served rattlesnake and whole pigs to businessmen.''

As the chaos continued, two of the women literally fell on each other's necks, hugged and kissed and cried. People walked distractedly by with mops and small, precious rags while these two stroked each other's hair, murmuring, "We will not let this place get to us." One said to me, "Forty-three more days, and write that down." (This would not be true for her. Two weeks later she broke her neck in a fall from the horizontal bars.) The inspection was a disaster. Colonel Allen proclaimed forcefully, "It stunk."

These scenes were repeated throughout the six-week cycle—sometimes less lacerating, sometimes punctuated with sentiment. For example, a trainee would stand up and say, "Hey, you guys. You see we can do it, we can work together. And I just want to say that we should remember what a difference it makes when we do." Then the women would grin shyly and clap, they would hug each other and fish out some contraband candy from Kotex boxes or from behind the ceiling panels. More often people would slam their locker doors or fling themselves on their beds in tears, muttering, "I'm going to lie here an' have someone punch my head for joining up."

The trainees moved numbly through it all: the briefing from the Roman Catholic chaplain who spoke to the "gang" and jovially advised them not to slit their wrists with a Trac II; the instruction in the science of boot polishing; the muscle-tearing PT, which, for many of them, was their first experience of serious exertion; the inspections. They learned to cry, albeit in a ragged and desolate way, "Alpha Company leads the way. Hey." It was a bumpy beginning for the women, who protected themselves with bitter jokes or slipped into an exhausted trance. Late at night, however, as they starched and ironed their uniforms, they were too exhausted to keep their guard up. That was when they would stop for a moment, smoke a cigarette, and tell me a little about their lives.

The women, it seemed, had come into the Army for the same classic reasons as the men: a decent job opportunity, the chance to train and get an education, escape from a stifling small town. They wanted to serve their country or to travel or to meet different kinds of people; they were optimistic or desperate. A few, mostly from the South, had joined up with an idea of service; some were on the run from bad fortune, hoping that, in addition to the three square meals, a roof over the head and job security, they would find emotional stability and a chance to alter the patterns of their lives.

There was a former nude dancer from New Orleans, the mother of a two-year-old. As a child she had been beaten by her parents, and so she had run away from home at fourteen and had been raped by the man who gave her a lift. There was a divorced former meat wrapper, whose small son had been stolen by his father. There were jilted fiancées and women from the ghettos and the mountains. One was a legal secretary who had tired of her stable life. Two had had hysterectomies by the age of twenty-one.

An early moment of melodrama was provided by Joan Clark, eighteen years old, from Kentucky. Clark was small and nervous; she would bluster to hide her terror. At the Armed Forces Induction Station, on her way to Fort Mc-Clellan, Clark had met a boy, Jimmy, who was on his way to the Navy. He had given her a ring, and they wrote to each other every day. One night, when all the trainees were cleaning, complaining about their aching feet, which were sore and blistered from running in combat boots, Clark collapsed to the floor with pains in her legs. Two men carried her downstairs as she wept loudly and called out, "Tell Jimmy I love him." An ambulance took her to the hospital. The others, subdued, began putting in their pink rollers. Late that night Clark returned, pale and hobbling. The doctors had diagnosed her pains as muscle spasms.

By the second week, the trainees were exhausted, cantankerous, and succumbing to colds and flu, despite the

rising temperature. The women were nervous about handling weapons, which they did for the first time on a sultry,
airless day out on the asphalt square at the foot of the hill.
Some of the women seemed to be adapting to drill, the
uniform and all the military tackle less readily than the men.
Whenever the company was outside en masse, there always
seemed to be one woman at the back, scarlet face contorted
with effort and strain, breasts bobbing, gear flapping, arms
and legs flying out, running fiercely in an uncoordinated way
to keep up.

On this particular afternoon the trainees were wearing their
steel pots and web gear and were close to dropping from
fatigue and the 81-degree heat. The women handled their
slender black M-16s gingerly. Sergeant Lester was helping
an overweight trainee, who would get so nervous before the
early-morning PT that she would visibly shake. Sergeant
Lester said with a genial, warning tone, "You'll blow your
head off if you do that, old thang," as the trainee fumbled
around with nerveless fingers. To defuse the tension, which
was carefully not admitted but nonetheless vibrated there in
the soggy air, the drill sergeants made jokes. Sergeant
Carroll, a tall and kindly black who is a military policeman by
training, said with a slow smile, "DO NOT point the weapon
at anyone, especially your drill sergeant, even though you
might want to." There were dutiful, appreciative yocks all
round, the trainees realizing somewhere inside their strained
and aching bodies that the joke was a kindness.

Later they lay on their stomachs in the grass, in a large ring
facing inward, and learned how to zero the M-16. They
learned about the Canadian Bull target and the eight steady
hold factors as swallowtails fluttered by. The next sergeant to
speak was Sergeant Johnson, tall and intense, a devout
Mormon, whose belief that women should stay home and
raise a family fought with a perfectionism so strong that he
would spend many extra hours with his platoon laboring to
get them through. As he started to speak, people fidgeted
with the straps of their weapons, eyed each other. He said
seriously, "Now I'm going to talk about trigger control. If

you breathe while you shoot, you may miss." Every time he mentioned "trigger control" a couple of the younger women spluttered into their hands. Johnson looked puzzled; two of the other drills strolled over to explain, and he, stiffly smiling and irritated, muttered "I see—they think that's funny, right?" That night Claire Hayes from Vermont, polishing her boots, her face white, told me that she could barely concentrate through the afternoon. "The M-16 was killing my back because it's so heavy. Did I tell you that as a child I was allergic to milk and so my bones aren't strong?"

Sitting nearby and organizing her locker, Sue Jarrell talked about her ambition. Jarrell was nineteen, from North Carolina, and a beauty—tall and slim, with high cheekbones and a new, cropped boy's haircut, through which she constantly ran her fingers. She had given up a botched love affair and a job pairing stockings for a life of adventure. She was the company guidon carrier, whose pride was visible whenever the company prepared to march and she hoisted the guidon and ran to her place at the front, trying to look like a soldier. She said, "I'm going to do helicopter repair, which means going airborne at Fort Bragg. I want to be a crew chief eventually." I asked if she was worried about the week of rifle training ahead and she said calmly that she was looking forward to it.

Before 1977, the limited rifle training course for women had been voluntary; then, when it became mandatory for women to qualify on the M-16, no pictures were allowed to be taken for fear of the effect this would have on the sensibilities of the public. However, there was as little fuss about women using weapons as there was about the integration of basic training. Since October 1978, women have learned how to use the M-16 rifle, the Claymore mine, the grenade launcher, and the LAW (antitank weapon); they fire an M-60 machine gun and throw a live hand grenade. I asked Colonel Allen, the battalion commander, about the rationale for arming women when there was no intention of putting them into close combat.

Colonel Allen is in her fifties, a thin, poised woman, with

neat curls, spectacles, and a calmly impersonal manner. We talked in her cool, dim office while outside trainees panted around the track under the pine trees or hung and then dropped like lemmings from the horizontal bars. She said patiently, "If we put women in units that were previously all male and that may have a rear-area security mission should the enemy come, they must know how to handle the weapons. We can't have *part-time* soldiers." She spoke more forcefully. "It's not an attempt to defeminize the women or demasculinize the men. We are trying to develop in these women dimensions of their womanliness they never had. We are forcing them into adventures."

There was no gainsaying the mystique of the M-16. Some in Alpha Company squinted down their weapons that day in the grass with ease and confidence. They were the country and mountain girls from the rural South or Midwest like Joan Clark from Kentucky, who told me, "My daddy first let me handle his Smith and Wesson .38 when I was six years old," or Elizabeth Brady, who said, "We used to shoot squirrels from the bedroom window. You never went into the woods without a gun." They were the ones whose brothers and boyfriends had probably taught them how to shoot. On the other hand, there were women who had never come near handling a weapon, city people mostly, who had never even fixed a puncture on a bicycle tire. Maybe they had handled one piece of machinery—a sewing machine or a typewriter— but maybe not. They were the ones the sergeants most liked to teach. Sergeant Stokes said, "The men get blocked by feeling they know it already. They think they're Audie Murphy or John Wayne, so they won't listen. But the women don't know the first thing; they're nervous and they listen. And then they do it *right*."

Sergeant Fogle, the little infantryman who had seen combat in Vietnam, and not from a desk, was in charge of the classroom lecture. He took off his hat, picked up the rifle, and began to rattle through a speech on its history and design. "The Vietnamese used to call it the little black gun. . . . By the way, remember to call it the 'Vietnam conflict.' We never did declare war on the people over there." Dazed with data, the trainees scribbled in their notebooks. Sergeant Fogle reminded them, "In the Army, we don't talk of killing people, we talk of producing casualties." They frowned, trying to make sense of so much unfamiliarity—how to clear the weapon, how to assemble and disassemble it. It was not like an ordinary classroom lecture, there was urgency mixed with the drowsiness in the long, gloomy room. The males were on their mettle; this was the first time they would be able to prove that they knew manly things, that they were intimate, nonchalant with the bolt carrier and the pivot pin. Sergeant Fogle said, "If you have no pencil, borrow one from your buddy. Or girlfriend." He stopped, temporarily at a loss, and added with a slight smile, "Or your sister, or whatever . . ."

Each weapon rested on a chart, reminiscent of the placemats in a cheap restaurant that illustrate the birds and flowers of each state. This chart was of a disassembled M-16—large bits, like the handguards, and small bits like the slip ring. The women stared at it with some dismay and began. Assembly was the hard part; they had to work in pairs, standing up, to get a purchase on the handguards. Several men were helping women; some women were helping men. Jarrell and Baird worked side by side, cool and concentrating, both clearly having decided that any sensible person could do it, just like driving a car. Jarrell looked excited. Wiping her nose with the back of a grease-covered hand, she said, "This is fun. I love it." Her neighbor was wearing spectacles suspended from a chain, and she frowned in concentration, like a maiden aunt at her needlepoint.

Once the weapons had been reassembled, there was a four-point safety check, which finishes when the bolt goes forward, with a loud clunk as the bolt clicks. The order was given, there was the noise of many bolts, then a pause, and then, sporadically, more. Sergeant Fogle resignedly repeated the order, and more isolated, tentative bolt-moving-forward sounds were heard, like the last popcorn in a saucepan. Lieutenant Myers walked casually up the center aisle.

Trainees glanced up and almost unconsciously sat higher in their chairs, like schoolchildren who had been passing notes. She came over to the table where I was contemplating my own reassembled M-16, leaned down to my ear and said, "Some of the guys at the back are really screwing up, putting the charging handle in upside down," and wandered away.

Out on the range that afternoon all the information that the trainees had received was repeated by a very peppy young lieutenant with a neat chignon and lots of makeup. Women in the Army often wear heavy makeup, in particular bright emerald-green eyeshadow. *Yes, I am a girl,* it says. This woman was abrasive; she took odd deep breaths and made sudden faces. "Think 'BRAS,'" she said in a part-stewardess, part-Sweet Briar voice. "Breathe, relax, aim, squeeze."

Range 21 is in the middle of the kind of wilderness found only in the Army, with orange clay, pine trees, and willow herb. The range itself was dusty and bare, with no shelter. People get "range burn" from being outside all day when a hazy layer of cloud has deluded them into thinking that there is no sun. The trainees filed awkwardly past, picked up magazines and targets, and found their foxholes. Lieutenant Myers looked crisply Cuban, with sunglasses, rifle, canteen, and a flat Ranger's hat. A voice boomed instructions from the spindly frame tower.

The women in the foxholes—deep circular pits buttressed by sandbags—experienced at first hand the dimensional problems that afflict the female body when adapting itself to weapons built for men. The configuration of shoulders, head, neck, cheek, elbows, and weapon came to seem immensely complex; to achieve the simplest posture of comfort and steadiness for firing, with weapon tucked into the shoulder and cheek against the stock, seemed almost impossible. The women distractedly shifted. Some asked for crates to stand on; the smallest ones could not see over the top of their battlement, but once they were elevated and leaning perilously out, elbows planted awkwardly on the piled-up sandbags, they could not see out from under their helmets. They were allowed to take the helmets off, releasing their full hair, which fell around their flushed faces and over the collars of their fatigues. One young Californian flashed me a grin and, shouldering her weapon with muscular poise, said, "Wow! This is great! I feel like Patty Hearst!" She waited a moment and then said, "Not really, though."

Weapons training lasted for an interminable week, and it was conducted at desolate ranges as rickety and derelict as a military Coney Island, where targets would pop up randomly, if at all. Once the women got used to the feel of the weapons, they enjoyed it all. Julie Drake, the youngest, shyest trainee in the company, who was very pretty, with big violet eyes and a tiny whispering voice that had earned her the name Marilyn, would seek me out in a cigarette break or at lunch and say, "I thought I would hate shooting because I dislike loud noises and getting dirty, but I *loved* it! Look how well I did," and she would point proudly at the rumpled score sheet.

The record fire mattered; the scores out of forty would determine which little pin each trainee would wear after today—marksman, sharpshooter, or expert. Julie Drake was with her best friend, Ann Schulman, who was going into the National Guard. Schulman was a sturdy, serious woman, and she made a point of loving weapons and manly things; she had worked as a meat wrapper and an armed guard. Her weapon jammed on the first fire. She and Julie waved furiously, the splattering crackle of firing all around them, but no drill sergeant was near. Claire Hayes in the next hole, as pale and thin as Eurydice, had about 50 percent nonfunctioning targets. She looked up from under her wobbly helmet and said in a soft, polite voice, "I feel very discouraged." Schulman, still unable to attract a drill sergeant's attention, became so enraged that she took the steel pot off her head and banged it in fury against the side of the foxhole. Julie, despite the temperamental targets, did very well. Her cheerfulness seemed to make her less inclined to panic. As she climbed in the foxhole she said to Schulman, "Got my, er, cartilages, Ann?" and chuckled. Every time she hit a target, Schulman, intently penciling in her score, would give a little exclamation, like "Aw right!" or *"That's* my friend!" A small black woman, usually composed, jumped up and down, squealing, when she was told her score, just like a contestant on *Let's Make a Deal.*

Only a few managed to score more than twenty-five. Most passed, by scoring seventeen, and went to the bleachers, where they sat talking quietly, almost dazedly, because it was a rare occasion when there was nothing they should have been doing. As for the others, inching their scores up from six to eight to nine, the scorers were trying everything possible to push and pull them into qualifying, by praising, warning, saying, "Next the fifty—look, over there." Some were practically astride the trainees. Lieutenant Myers took charge of one. "Quick," she snapped at another trainee, "get off your can and get us another sandbag. Quick!" The bespectacled second lieutenant, just out of West Point, poked at the ground with his rod and said ironically (he always spoke ironically), "Oh, yes, we're lenient and fair. We give them every opportunity." In fact, they had five opportunities, and only eight out of the whole company failed to qualify that afternoon. On the way home in the bumping bus there was a tepid, exhausted singsong, with Lieutenant Myers leading her trainees in adapted versions of WAC songs. The men who did not do as well as they had wished to kept quiet or muttered obsessively to each other about their malfunctioning scorer partners. After chow there was sheet exchange—laundry—when Joan Clark provided a moment of high drama by fainting as she stood in line draped in her sheets like a ghost.

The ritual of weapons cleaning took place every night after chow, and as the women grew less intimidated by their weapons, they learned to halve their original time at the chore. Down in the basement of the shadowed classroom building, through the swing doors, an entire company of a hundred and thirty-six people would be as busy as immigrants in a New York sweatshop. The sodium lighting gave their faces a horrible ashen color (they had not yet acquired their tans), which accentuated the exhaustion they showed.

They sat crowded on long benches at metal tables on which at intervals stood cans of cleaning fluids and boxes of pipe cleaners, toothbrushes, and rags. The struggle for possession of these items came to be an outlet for the trainees' tensions.

They scrubbed furiously, those who wore spectacles squinting through the ugly black Kissinger-like frames that they had been issued. They had seen a cartoon film starring Rust and Carbon as small bad people, so they knew the principles. By this stage of the day, I found that, as weapons cleaning became a habit, the trainees were tired enough and glad enough that the unfamiliar aspects of the day were over to talk and swap jokes in a weary, friendly way. As they scrubbed and scraped, and the room filled with the odors of metal and grease, you could hear a couple of lines of a marching song softly sung, or a bawdy innuendo about rods and holes and tips would cause a burst of laughter, which in turn would cause a drill sergeant to look up from inspecting a bolt and stare carefully in the direction of the noise.

I talked to the two black women from Newark. Lynne Hunt was polishing methodically and in a self-contained way. She said, "Sure, we had a nice time. But I was scared to begin with. I closed my eyes." I asked about her family and she said, "My sister, who's twenty-one, is like a housewife, even though she's not married. She just likes to go home from work and watch TV. I like to experience things and have adventures."

Schulman had calmed down after her tantrum on the range, and she offered to help the man next to her with his cleaning. He had earlier been complaining about the Army, saying basic was too soft. He studied her, his thin, angular face crowding with suspicion, and said, "Well, okay." Across the table was another I-hate-the-Army man, who, when politely asked, would neither relinquish any rags, a commodity with which he was very well equipped, nor pass the solvent so that the two-thirds of his table without it could have some. A black male trainee sitting next to him talked him into doing it. Trainee No. 1 was furious, beetling and scowling, and he said to Trainee No. 2, "You'll *never* get it back without fighting for it, you'll see." Five minutes later, when they did ask for the solvent, it was handed to them at the first request. Thereafter they passed it back and forth.

The redheaded girl sitting next to Trainee No. 1 on his other side asked for the rag that he had near him on the table. Putting the rag deliberately in his lap, he smiled conspiratorially at her and said, "I need it. I fought for that rag and I'm not giving it up." She looked at him and said with irritation, "Why d'you have to be so huffy-puffy about it?" He said darkly to himself, for the question had begun to bore the others, "You can say that, all right, but you should have seen yesterday when those women wouldn't help me out and I had nothing to clean my weapon with."

The next day it was pouring out on Range 18, where the trainees were to learn automatic fire, and night fire complete with tracer bullets. They were as excited as children allowed to stay up late to watch a comet. They arrived at lunchtime, and sat in the mud, under dripping, brilliantly green trees, eating spareribs and corn. A blushing young man in the chow line approached Sergeant Lester and asked if he might wash his hands before lunch. Sergeant Lester turned wearily to the squad leader he had been berating and said, "That's what is wrong with this platoon—you're all PUSSIES." The squad leader and the hygiene-conscious trainee, rain dripping from their shapeless ponchos to their boots and forming puddles in the red clay in which their feet were miserably planted, agreed, wretchedly. Sergeant Lester finished his ritual berating, turned to me, and said, "The women are easier to work with, I find. Men kick and complain, and you can spend a lot of energy trying to bring them into line. But you don't have to do a great macho number with the women."

One day I had asked Julie Drake how she and the others felt about having male drill sergeants order them around. I wondered whether they preferred to take orders from a woman. Julie looked up and said in her whispery voice, "That Sergeant Ferris should be a man! She looks just like one! You know, she frightens us; we cower when we hear her coming." This particular sergeant wore steel taps on her shoes so that you could indeed hear her coming. She was tall and young, and she looked like a gawky adolescent boy in fatigues. Julie paused and furrowed her brow, then said, "The ladies can yell so sharp, but the men, when they yell, it's sarcastic and you somehow know that they're laughing." I heard similar comments from other female trainees, who would tell me that they felt shown up or seen through when a woman criticized them because that woman was like them, or like a mother, and so if she shouted she must really know that they had done wrong. They accepted males in authority more phlegmatically, even when they considered them harsh or unfair. It was still something familiar and manageable. The male drills would stroll around with a quizzical and faintly menacing air, eyes shadowed by the brims of their hats. Sergeant Stokes would coo benignly to a flustered female emerging bareheaded to join formation, "Where yo' hat at, sweet pea?" and the stiff lines of trainees would shiver in pleasant anticipation of the fury or sarcasm that would be staged if the delinquent female did not move quickly enough to get her hat. The youngest women, who were liable to hurl themselves on their beds giggling hysterically at vulgar jokes, were quite giddy in the face of authority and humor combined; they would flush scarlet when their attempts to get attention were rewarded. Inevitably the male drills reveled in this admiration. Sergeant Lester said on his way out to take a PT test, "I'm not going to take my shirt off; the girls would go crazy at the sight of my muscles," and winked.

We waited for nightfall in the torrent. This part of Alabama is visited by nature's violent melodrama in the spring, and just a few days before, there had been a tornado watch accompanied by rains that drowned the golf course and prevented a scheduled ride in the Huey. As night fell, the wind rose. Shivering, the trainees sat in the bleachers, peering at the ever more indistinct form of an instructor who said that it was almost never so dark that you could not see anything. They learned to look around the target, not at it, and to aim low. Each drenched trainee lined up for two magazines, each containing ten bullets, one of the ten a tracer. It took a very long time for them to be cleared to start, because no NCO wanted to trip over an armed, nervous trainee. There were odd distant shouts, flashlights bobbing white and red. Then as the trainees fired, the tracer bullets seemed to float up from behind. The intermittent flickering light in the targets was meant to represent a match lifted to a cigarette, but it was very dim—you felt you had imagined it—and by the time you blinked and looked again, it was gone.

Two aspects of military life were very hard for the women: the uniforms they had to wear and the physical training that had become crucial by the third week.

It was not that they disliked the uniform; most of the women loved the way they looked in fatigues, despite their endless complaints. The white T-shirts and the high-waisted green pants accentuated the curves of their bodies, which every day became stronger and more supple. Nevertheless the women felt themselves to be discriminated against. At that time the female fatigues were not made of a synthetic wash-and-wear material like the men's. They were cotton, so they had to be pressed and starched, which meant that the young women spent hours slaving in the laundry rooms when they could have been cleaning, practicing their military customs and courtesies for a test, or just resting. As a result, the laundry room was where most of the chatter and tension occurred, with the women smoking incessantly as they waited in the humid atmosphere for their clothes to finish spinning around and kept a wary eye on the people near the ironing boards they had managed to reserve.

Colonel Allen said, with obvious exasperation, "I have worked in and around the clothing problem for seven years now, and the issue of the fatigues was raised back in 1972. There was emotional controversy over the idea of a unisex fatigue, which was an impediment to getting anything done." This was one of the most visible signs of a paradox that haunts today's Army women: they are admitted, but not really perceived as soldiers.

The problem with the boot was similar but worse, in that it caused permanent injury. The female boot was designed for nurses standing on concrete floors and not for the vigorous life of a trainee in the integrated Army. Running in the boots causes shin splints, fallen arches, blisters, stress fractures, and muscle spasms—all of which I observed during my visit. I saw fit and willing trainees drop out of runs, sobbing in pain and frustration; Baird, who would rather die than admit she was beaten, would hide twice a day in order to cry about her feet.

Simmons, who was overweight and twenty-nine, and therefore at a disadvantage on two counts, fell and sprained her ankle. Then, because she was made to wear the boots too long when she should have been put in more accommodating shoes, the condition lingered and deteriorated, ruining her entire training. Today, two years later, she works at Fort Sam Houston, Texas, with a profile that excuses her from any PT. At Fort McClellan she was called "the crip."

Colonel Allen, being careful to preface her remarks with the reminder that this was just her own point of view, said, "The boot just angers me no end. There is plenty of info in the hands of the authorities to prove that it is improper for the tactical training environment. I've turned in I don't know how many reports on that. We finally, in desperation, asked the people at TRADOC [Training and Doctrine Command] to permit us to issue the women one pair of male and one pair of female boots."

The women began with physical handicaps because of the way most of them had grown up. Every week they were tested on PT, and before the test, tension in the bay would be high, with the women anxiously inspecting their blisters. The most alarming word was "recycling." People were terrified that because of weight problems or a sprained ankle they might be pulled from training and put back into the cycle behind. The two who were going airborne doggedly practiced push-ups between the beds, preparing for the more strenuous test they would be taking. Jarrell looked as if she would never manage—her arms were childlike and her back collapsed on every push-up.

Some women were so determined to make it that they refused to give up when they felt themselves failing. If they dropped out of a march because of foot injuries, the men, who did not understand the boot problem, would jeer or complain, so the women often kept going until they were dangerously vulnerable because they had lost all their strength. When Nancy Miller fell from the monkey bars, she cracked two vertebrae and broke her neck. She was in traction, and they expected her to stay there for three to five months. It was feared that she would be permanently paralyzed, but within a week she had regained some sensation. Sergeant Stokes told me subsequently that they had been trying to get women off the bars for a long time, because most of them did not have the upper-body strength to stay on, and suffered serious injuries when they fell. The monkey bars were not used again in that cycle.

3

The Tire and the Toolbox: Questions of Capability

"The first time I failed miserably, so I had to do it again. I was just dying. I thought, *What am I doing this for?* There's no point. I'm not going infantry, I'm not going to be out in the woods like this. They'd never put a woman in charge of an infantry platoon anyway." This was said plaintively by a female cadet at West Point, class of '80, who was describing her poor performance on the greatly dreaded "enduro run," which takes place in the course of summer field training, when cadets have to run up and down hills in full uniform, with pack and weapon, at a certain speed.

If the Army is a gender laboratory, West Point, in its obsession with the tangible, may be the place to observe the most controlled part of the experiment in comparing the physiology of young men and women, and the limits of their strength and endurance. West Point treasures the ideals of physical prowess and competition. There are two occasions on which the women and the men are directly visible in competition, usually with disappointing results for the females. These events are the enduro run and that part of the PT testing known as the "obstacle course" (O.C.), which takes place once a year in the spacious high-ceilinged old gym, up a flight of stone steps. The gym has dark beams, sloping skylights, and the ubiquitous stifling reek of sweat.

The course is an aerobic exercise designed to put maximum strain on the constitution. It involves climbing ropes, running, swinging along bars, shinning up vertical walls, squirming along the ground on elbows and knees at high speed, and so on. Men hate it too; occasionally the male cadets cry before the test. An instructor standing with me as we watched them forming into a long line that snaked halfway around the gym and then out into the corridor, pointed out the tension in their faces, and the nervous joshing and backslapping as, holding their cards, they waited for their turn. Friends and tactical officers were watching, with the inevitable reporters, wondering where the women were. The women were somewhere down the hall, at the end of the line, where they are placed because their speeds are so much slower than the men's that they hold up the exercise.

As the men of the class of '80 sped off in fours, the atmosphere heated up. The gym echoed with screams and cheers as people watched with gleeful anticipation for the first sweating, straining body to drop from a rope or get stuck on the bars. Hundreds of cadets went through over an hour or so, and then twenty-three women appeared at the end of the line, huddled and awkward, their pale bodies in marked contrast to those of the beefy males. As they began, the yelling stopped, except for a few ragged shouts from a loyal boyfriend or two.

The women were noticeably slower. Some showed the jerky lack of grace that betrays extreme fright. With grim faces, they forced their bodies through tires, up ladders, and between bars. They faltered badly on the bars, holding themselves erect and quivering with the strain on their muscles, unable to move an inch forward, hanging on, and finally dropping to the floor. By the time they reached the ropes they were in despair. They would make it halfway to the top and then drop, with slow finality, like a textbook diagram of upper-body strength deficiency. That night they would experience the "O.C. cough," brought on by doing aerobic exercise in a room in which the oxygen had already been used up by the hundreds of young men ahead of them. Puffing and flopping, the leaders ran the obligatory three circuits of the track on a gallery around the top of the gym walls, while others tried to take a run at the vertical wall, hit it with a mighty thump, and fell back. Most managed to finish, by which time the room was empty except for instructors. The men had averaged over three minutes, the women over five.

The obstacle course gave life to some of the statistics of difference between the male and female body, as measured meticulously through surveys undertaken by the Academy's physical education department and Dr. Jim Peterson. The female plebes were typically found to have one-third the upper-body strength of men, two-thirds the leg strength, and the same amount of strength in the abdomen. The figures also confirmed that men have more power and power endurance, leg power and leg-power endurance, dominant hand-grip strength, nondominant hand-grip strength, lean body weight, body weight, and height. In short, men tend to be bigger (by 10 percent), heavier, and stronger.

In specific ways these differences affect the military performance of many Army women. I had noticed at Fort McClellan that the women with small hands found it hard to negotiate the handguards of the M-16, and that the smallest women could not keep up with the marching because of their short legs. While most women can, with proper training, learn to lift the requisite variety of heavy objects, their lack of upper-body strength makes it hard for them to lift heavy things to shoulder height or to change position at that height. Air Force women find this hardest, because so many of the Air Force jobs entail lifting objects to wing height. However, that is only part of the picture. In September 1980 a female ROTC cadet became the first woman to score a perfect 500 on the ROTC Advanced PT test, which demands all-round physical excellence. The test has been conducted since 1975, during which time 2300 women have attempted the perfect score. Cadet Alice Barry, the first to achieve it, said afterward, "You'll be seeing more women like me in the future."

Young women all over the country are benefiting from the changes in mores, and the resultant expansion of athletic programs for them is proving old ideas to be either wrong or not as important as once thought. When Grete Waitz won the women's section of the 1980 New York marathon, her time was 2 hours 25 minutes 41 seconds. If she had run that time in 1974, she would have won the race over both men and women. Each year her time improves. When the women of the class of '80 arrived at West Point, most of them could not do more than one pull-up. When the class of '83 arrived, they managed, on average, two and a half pull-ups. When the trainees of Alpha Company, Second Battalion, Training Brigade, first sank into the muddy grass on the orders of their drill sergeants, most of the women could not do one single push-up, and by the end, even Mom, overweight, thirty-one years old, and formerly sedentary, could muster ten or fifteen push-ups if someone yelled at her. The data are usually seen in the wrong context. The constructive way to measure military women's performance and their potential is against either their own past performance or that of other women.

One day I watched the West Point women's basketball team pulverize one of the best teams in the country. The cadets were so authoritative on the court that they seemed to outnumber their opponents, who became rattled at 12-22, one-third of the way through, and, in the classic female response, they froze and adopted a safe and plodding game. They hardly ran with the ball; they hardly even passed it. Obviously they were frightened of the Academy team, which played a rough game. "Not dirty," said Jim Peterson, "but they certainly play rough." He said, "When the men see the women in a competitive sport against other women, they realize that as women go, ours are tough, but they are hardly ever made to realize that."

These days, the data on women's potential proliferate with bewildering speed but do not indicate that abdominal skin folds and upper-body strength are, in the long run, more important to the competence of soldiers, even those in the front line, than attitudes and training. Furthermore, attitudes affect both the search for facts and their interpretation, which makes the truth even more elusive.

Menstruation is a classic example of a phenomenon that has for centuries been regarded with alarm or revulsion, and one that has been assumed to incapacitate most, if not all, women for a number of days in each month, as well as disposing them toward all kinds of irrational, even violent behavior. Medical experts talk about severe bloating, breast swelling, massive temporary weight gain, and emotional swings. Now, however, the emphasis has changed. The physical and emotional aspects of what *can* happen are not overlooked, but they are no longer considered crucial, mostly because of the evidence provided by more and more women athletes and women who became more and more physically conditioned. Their periods cease or else become so light as to be no real bother. Such evidence is almost a vindication, because military women are judged by their biology and found to be failed males.

Scientists are hard to convince. Until recently it was thought that women had so little cardiorespiratory efficiency compared with men that it severely limited their abilities in sustained physical activity. However, a West Point study established that the women's cardiorespiratory capacity improved to a far greater degree relatively than did the men's in the course of the initial phase of Cadet Basic Training (Beast)—to a point where it was much less of a handicap than anticipated. The authorities did not believe the results and carried out a follow-up test, at the end of which they said firmly that men's and women's cardiorespiratory capacities were not the same (nobody had said that they were), but that the women did indeed seem to have improved at a greater rate than the men, which indicated the need for a change in the training.

Recent research seems to show that many of the old ideas about female deficiencies vis-à-vis the physical vigor of men are inaccurate. The anthropologist Ashley Montagu, in a pioneering and polemical work, *The Natural Superiority of Women*, stated that women endure starvation, exposure, shock, fatigue, and illness better than men, that they suffer less from baldness, gout, and ulcers, and that they have superior sexual responses. Montagu's intention was to prove that women were better equipped to survive. Other research goes further.

Women have more acute hearing than men; their ovaries, being internal, are far better protected from injury than men's testicles. Studies of female athletes indicate that the female combination of a low center of gravity (in the hips) and leg and abdominal strength comparable with a man's means that in leg wrestling an average woman could defeat an average man. The layers of subcutaneous fat on the female body make women more buoyant in the water and better able to withstand cold. Women are more efficient marathon runners than men, less likely to hit the "wall of pain," because their bodies can burn up fat and thereby increase their staying power. There is also the question of heat tolerance. Women have been supposed to succumb to heat more rapidly than men because they appear to sweat less than men do, having fewer sweat glands. Recent research suggests, however, that women do not sweat as *visibly* as men, because they have sweat glands all over their bodies and not in dense concentration, so that, in fact, they sweat more efficiently.

There are two important things to remember here. One is that the significance of physical data seems to change frequently, and the data are open to varying interpretations. The second is that the use of "men" and "women" as definitive terms is misleading in a discussion of physiological differences. The overlap in functioning between the majority of members of each sex is far more significant than the differences between those at the extremes of the spectrum. Army women know this, and it makes them furious to see a puny or overweight or beer-swilling Army male talking about the inadequacy of the female soldier.

In all the voluminous Army data on women's capabilities, information about sex differences that seem to give women the advantage over men, or at least parity with them, is rare, maybe understandably, because the thrust of the research is toward establishing whether or not women have the potential to be front-line infantry soldiers who can overpower a man in sustained hand-to-hand combat. With intensive training, some have; without it, most have not. The superintendent of West Point, General Goodpastor, said to me that this was not the crucial issue, adding, "The women's shortcomings are not that important outside of the infantry, the combat part of the engineers, and a few other branches that have front-line combat. I believe there has been an exaggeration of physical prowess as a component of leadership. The main run will have all the leadership strength and capability that's required."

A somewhat impromptu test was conducted by the Army's Human Engineering Laboratory in 1979. The lab, situated in Aberdeen, Maryland, is an interesting establishment where much time is spent on questions of male and female dimensions and what they mean for the design of everything from helmets to tanks. In this test, fifteen women were taught to fire 105-mm and 155-mm howitzers to see if they could serve in field artillery units. A physiologist at the laboratory said that while the test did not address the question of whether or not women could sustain the work for a typical battle day, it did prove that the rounds were not too heavy for them.

I sat in on the self-defense class at West Point—where the ratio was one woman to nineteen men—with Sue Peterson, a civilian instructor, who had developed the class based on work she had done teaching aikido to males and females at the University of Illinois. She said, "It all seemed much more normal than here. Here the men are the kind who look at women as mothers and sisters and girlfriends, and not as peers, which makes this kind of instruction particularly difficult." We sat at the side watching them engage in the rear strangle takedown. The lone female battled her opponent with a set face; he was cheerful and punctilious. Subsequently the instructor talked about the fist in the nose, cutting the air with his fist and arm. "Thrust that nose *right up* into the brain," he said. Sue Peterson leaned closer and said quietly, "He's doing it wrong for the women. I only teach women to go for the eyes, throat, groin. They shouldn't have to get down to the ground with a man. They should be taught to work with leverage rather than power."

The women often complained about the self-defense class, even though Sue Peterson was clearly a good teacher. I asked one of the physically confident cadets about it. She sighed and said, "I think it was the aggressiveness. Women who were scared to kick or hit another woman really had a hard time. We were all pretty good friends, and it was like wrestling our best friend. Some of the women were *so big* it was like brute strength; there was no technique at all." She laughed as she remembered. "I had this big girl on top of me, just strangling me, and I was saying, 'Get off, *get off* me'—but it was funny when you look back on it, how you could hate people. I hated that class, I hated *her* because she was going to choke me."

It is no longer easy to define aggression, particularly when discussing male-female differences, because the term has become so leaden with resentment and old prejudice. John Money, a professor at Johns Hopkins, talks of "adventurous exploratory roaming, assertiveness and aggression, and the defense of territorial rights" as all of a piece, and says cautiously that while the male has no "exclusive prerogative" over these traits, "there does seem to be a sex difference in the frequency with which these patterns of energy expenditure are manifest." "Energy" is an important word for psychologists, who have retreated into it because the idea of a male monopoly on aggression has become too charged. As the extent to which culture determines behavior appears to grow, so, in direct proportion, scientists search for a shrinking, neutral definition of aggression, and may be obliged to fall back on biology, seeing it as just the release of the tension that the male musculature accretes.

Despite the touchy nature of the subject, scientists insist that there is a hormonal basis to "aggression" or "energy." Administering large doses of testosterone or estrogen to pregnant mothers affects the behavior of their children in ways that may make girls "tomboyish," boys "less stereotypically masculine." The results are very variable; researchers work with small numbers in such projects, and their operating assumptions are firmly rooted in the culture, as phrases like "stereotypically masculine" show. Scientists will acknowledge that boys wrestling in a yard may not be feeling more aggressive than girls who are fighting in other ways—for example, through spite or coldness—and add that society determines appropriate ways for the two sexes to express emotions. That is no reason to deny the influence of hormones on behavior.

We are left with a tendency in more males than females to express more obviously than most females an aggressive approach to the world around them, aggressive being here defined as energetic, or assertive, or dominating, or physically active. Scientists are very reluctant to go further. Certainly they would not be ready to say which, if any, particular aggressive trait makes a competent soldier in the modern Army, whether in peace or war.

Those who oppose women's importance in the Army use the idea of aggression to try to prove that women have no place in fighting wars, and, furthermore, no justification for disturbing the balance maintained through two thousand years of recorded history. Adducing evidence from tribal society, primate society, mythology, and prehistory, these people postulate that biology dictates the patterns of history, in particular, the "taboo" against using women as soldiers.

There are opposing points of view, not confined to feminist scholars. Briefly, the arguments go as follows: the polarization of our society in recent times is, to quote one Stanford professor, "a caricature of the biological foundation." For those who like to use animals for proof, Freda Adler, the sociologist and author of a book on women and crime, explains that while men may, overall, be bigger and stronger than women, and in early societies physical strength was crucial for leadership, it is only in the lower animals that males are clearly more aggressive in a way that is directly linked to their male hormones. It is only in these simplest and least socially developed species that androgen equals aggression and estrogen equals nonaggression. Adler says that even here aggression is not exclusive to males, and that mature females can rout low-status males. Female elephants are the dominant ones in a herd; female lions and tigers are more aggressive than males; female rats fight less often than males, but when they do, they attack viciously without any preliminary rituals. In the higher primates, the ones anthropologists love to study, there is "hormonal-behavioral detachment"—that is, the characteristics of status and dominance that are present in all societies are defined by the culture and not by biology.

As for prehistory, some anthropologists counter the argument of primitive man's domination by saying that the idea of man as provider has been overemphasized, that while men undoubtedly did the hunting, the gathering done by women provided 80 percent of the food. This is not a new idea. Robert Briffault wrote in his classic book *The Mothers*, published in 1927, that since there were no economic factors in less developed cultures, hunting and food preparation were regarded as of equal importance. Furthermore, he wrote, "There is not among primitive men and women the disparity in physical power, resourcefulness, enterprise, courage, capacity for endurance, which are observed in civilized societies and are often regarded as organic sexual differences." Childbearing made women sedentary for some of the time, but it was possible for women to drop babies and be working again within a few days.

There are various explanations of the process by which a simple division of labor ended up as a quasi-biological truth. Feminists refer to male jealousy of women's childbearing function, which turned pregnancy and childbearing into a "handicap" and led men, on the one hand, to restrict women with clitoridectomies and the taboos surrounding menstruation, and, on the other, to overcompensate through war. In this argument, the aggressive instincts leading to war are far from biologically determined. Other anthropologists say that because females are more essential than males for the survival of the species, they have to be more cautious, out of self-protection, and not because they lack aggression.

Sue Mansfield, a professor at Claremont College, in California, participating in a Congressional Research Services seminar on women in the Armed Forces, held under the auspices of the Library of Congress on November 2, 1979, said that war was assumed to have been first institutionalized in the Neolithic era, among tribal people who had a "mythopoetic and dualistic world view. They equated war with death and women with life." Both life and death were supernatural forces that had to be controlled and kept separate. This theory was carried to extremes: men who had recently married, had sex, or become fathers were regarded as a potential danger on the battlefield. So, Mansfield concludes, the taboo has nothing to do with gender, but still it has become institutionalized to the point where it is a proof of manhood, and, by extension, of full citizenship. It was during the Vietnam war that eighteen-year-olds were given the vote.

Margaret Mead summarized her findings on male dominance as biology by saying that all the tribes she studied had different ideas about the sources of power or status, the only constant being that whatever the men do is the important occupation, "even if they cook, weave, or dress dolls, or hunt humming birds." Mead found societies in which the females are aggressive; other anthropologists have found societies in which men just sit around and do their hair while women lug water and hoe. There are also cultures, though very few, where women fight alongside men. Why so few? Because, the theories go, warfare was, in the past, one of the only ways in which men could use their size and strength to show their superiority and maintain real power.

So that is how anthropologists tend to see the origins of the current belief that women are gentle and intuitive, and natural parents and spouses, while men are violent, rough, and marauding. Centuries of hardening tradition fostered this belief. Ideas of size and strength became abstracted over the centuries, expressed as wealth, status, class, or expertise. The organized armies that have dominated the history of recorded warfare came into being with the idea of property, and they were as different from old tribal battles over grievances as they are from today's wars. The circumstance of two people facing each other with blunt objects has become increasingly rare in war, and may be absent from the next war, in which women may be able to perform just as well as men in all respects. However, the idea is still deeply rooted in our minds that men fight wars, and women would hinder them.

Professor Mansfield says firmly, "Neither sex takes naturally to battle." She cites "physical ineptitude, fear, indiscipline, inhibitions against killing" as barriers that can be overcome only by proper training and leadership. Contemporary statistics seem to support her argument. An item in *Army Times*, February 1980, read "Combat arms troops reenlist out of their military specialties at a far higher rate than noncombat soldiers." The figure for first-term soldiers was 46 percent. Special benefits are now offered to recruits who choose certain unpopular combat specialties.

War literature, especially that of World War I, is full of men who hated, feared, and were revolted by war—and so are the wards in the VA hospitals. There is no reason to think that has changed, whatever men might proclaim on a Saturday night in the taverns off post.

A Chinese military strategist, Sun Tzu, wrote in 500 B.C. that even the palace courtesans could be turned into effective warriors if the right training were used. Whether or not this is true, theories about macaques or the Bronze Age are of limited use, and the best way to resist them is to present the record of women in war, as leaders, auxiliaries, heroes and killers, from the earliest days, setting it against the experiences of Army women today.

4

An Army with Banners: The Women of History

"I am come amongst you, as you see, resolved in the midst and heat of the battle to live or die amongst you all, to lay down for my God and for my Kingdom and for my people, my honour and my blood, even in the dust. I know I have the body of a weak and feeble woman, but I have the heart and stomach of a King, and a King of England, too, and I think foul scorn that Parma or Spain or any prince of Europe should dare to invade the borders of my realm. . . ."

Prehistory and mythology are rife with precedents for Elizabeth I of England's famous speech at Tilbury. The Greek goddess Pallas Athene, who was to become the symbol of the Women's Army Corps, was the archetypical warrior goddess born out of a man—out of the head of Zeus in fact—"fully armed and brandishing a sharp javelin," as the *Larousse Encyclopedia of Mythology* has it. Athene was a virgin, dedicated to battle, and in Libya there was an annual festival in her honor, during which two camps of girls would battle each other with sticks and stones.

Many other Greek goddesses and heroines had warlike

tendencies, and they were devouring females who struck terror into men. In Sparta the beliefs were held in everyday life. It was a society of strong and well-nourished women who had dresses slit to the thigh to facilitate movement rather than for seducing men. The more fit and determined the women, the better their sons would be. The heroines of Greek drama were not retiring. Medea said she would rather stand in the front line of battle than give birth to one child. The warlike women of mythology range from the Avenging Angel to the Valkyries, from the Eumenides to the Erinnyes, sometimes known as "the dogs of Hades," black goddesses who would appear, their hair bristling with serpents, torches and whips in their arms, to punish parricides and those who had violated their oaths. The Assyro-Babylonian Tiamat was a feminine presence representing the blind forces of primitive chaos against which the intelligent and organizing gods struggled.

Some of the famous warriors of earliest times were purely mythological, some are thought to have been real—but most were probably actual women whose lives served as the basis for legend. Queen Semiramis of the Assyrians built Babylon, founded Nineveh, and led the Assyrian armies as they conquered Ethiopia, Bactria, Egypt, and Libya, in the second millennium B.C. Hatshepsut, the fifteenth-century B.C. queen of Egypt, dressed as a man and commanded the fleet. In the Book of Judges there is reference to Deborah, a judge of Israel who led the Israelite forces to decisive victory over the Canaanites. Judith, and Queen Zenobia of Palmyra, Agrippina, and Cleopatra—the queens and heroines continued through the legendary Maeve of the Celts to two female Celtic generals who faced Caesar: Bridget and Rhiannon.

One of the most famous women to challenge Rome was Boadicea. She was queen of the Iceni tribe in Britain, and led them in revolt. She even managed to keep a coalition of tribes together until they were routed in a decisive battle against Suetonius and his troops. As Tacitus described it in his *War with the Germans*, the battle took place in A.D. 61.

Boadicea drove around all the British troops in her chariot with her daughters and cried, "We British are used to woman commanders in war! I am descended from mighty men! But I am not fighting for my kingdom and wealth now. I am fighting as an ordinary person for my last freedom, my bruised body, and my outraged daughters . . . you will win this battle, or perish. That is what I, a woman, plan to do!— let the men live in slavery if they will." Two paragraphs down the page a great Roman victory is recorded. It turned into a massacre, and, says Tacitus, as he says with regularity throughout the book, "The Romans did not spare even the women." There was no reason for them to. Fighting women were to be found throughout the tribes of Ireland, Germany, Britain, and the Iberian Peninsula, defending their countries against the Roman invaders.

With the rise of feudal power in the Middle Ages, women inherited baronies, duchies, and kingdoms on the death of their husbands, and this gave the more resourceful and power hungry among them a chance to go to war, steal property, and dispatch their rivals. Eleanor of Aquitaine; Jane of Flanders; Agnes, Countess of Dunbar; Philippa of Hainault; Margaret of Anjou—the list is long, and I mention the names because, quite simply, they are not often mentioned together. People may think of Elizabeth I, or of Joan of Arc riding at the head of her army in shining armor, but as isolated instances they are just tales from school, adventures from library books. The volume, the statistics, are more important than the individual acts of daring or heroism. It should not be necessary to mention these names—to say in effect, yes, women can be warlike and brave, cruel and cunning. Nevertheless we are accustomed to pass over the names with some impatience because they seem so few. On the contrary, there were Mary of Hungary and Joan Hackette, Queen Margaret of Denmark, Catherine the Great, Isabella of Spain, Christina of Spain, all of whom commanded men, changed history, led armies in war. There were many who overcame the restrictions of pregnancy, childbearing, and convention, and the numbers attest to their spirit. The numbers also make irrelevant the arguments about the marked physiological differences that stamp one person as male, another as female.

Although the Amazons are probably the most famous of the female warriors, they are as mysterious as they are familiar, a mythical all-female band of fighters, references to whom occur over and over again in legend but whose actual existence is doubtful. Supposedly they lived in Anatolia, or farther away in the mists of the barbarian world. They resorted to men of the neighboring tribes for sex, and they sent away or crippled their male children, to be used as servants. Herodotus states that they were related to the Scythians. The story that they cut off their left breasts to facilitate the pull of the drawstring on their bows is, apparently, just a story, based on a misunderstanding of the derivation of the word "amazon." The Amazons are the only such band known from ancient times. There are of course, and increasingly so these days, people who believe in matriarchies as the original structure of all human societies. Despite the evidence of powerful queens and belief in potent goddesses, scholars have not yet discovered convincing proof of matriarchies in any formal or widespread sense.

In India, just after the death of Alexander the Great, a ruler apparently kept a bodyguard of strong and tall Greek women. There are other reports of isolated units throughout history—in Africa chiefly, but in fragmentary revolts in Europe as well. During the wars between Dutch and Spaniards in the sixteenth century, a female unit commanded by a widow, Kenau Hasselaer, fought with great endurance and bravery at the siege of Haarlem.

No account of female fighting units is complete without the obligatory mention of the female regiments of King Gezo of Dahomey, in West Africa. Army historians, from whose work most of this information comes, wince at the mention, because it is so much a staple of the textbooks. For the record, these bands were formed in the middle of the nineteenth century, and they are frequently mentioned in the memoirs of explorers and missionaries. These women were the products of a society in which women were accustomed to doing the hardest work, suffering physical labor and hardship the most stoically. This made them excellent material, and King Gezo and his committee carefully selected the absolute cream. In order to qualify, they had to walk through fire and over thorns; in order to remain, they had to abstain from sex and fight to the death. There were three regiments, with a thousand women in each, redoubtable warriors. The heyday of these regiments ended when the king mistakenly sent his women, who used spears, to take the fortress of a neighboring tribe armed with cannon and guns; when they stormed the walls they lost a thousand. Bitter and terrible hand-to-hand fighting ensued, and the Egba, the neighboring tribe, enraged to discover that their heroic opponents were women, went after them with grim relentlessness. This was a phenomenon to be repeated a century later when Arab troops fought all the more bitterly against their Israeli opponents once they found out that they included women. A female unit is alleged still to exist in the army of Dahomey (now called Benin).

No other female units rivaled those of Dahomey in fame or prowess, although the kings of Siam used women for their bodyguards at about the same time. Interestingly, although the women were an elite and renowned for their precision in drill and competition, they had a taste for duels of such seriousness that elaborate funerals became frequent. Just like the Libyan worshipers of Pallas Athene, these women chose to fight each other, so imbued were they with a warrior ethos, or so we suppose. Social psychologists say that girls very seldom engage in mock fighting; these two examples of grown women involved in ritual fighting against other women are tantalizing glimpses of another truth, all the more interesting because they are so incomplete.

The most recent all-female unit to go into combat was Kerenski's Brigade of Death, formed during the Russian Revolution. The unit was famous all over Europe, and Madame Bachkarava, its commander, was visited by famous suffragettes, including Mrs. Pankhurst, from London. The unit was never very successful and was disbanded. Since 1917 there has been no all-female combat unit used in the manner of a conventional force. The much more traditional pattern of women's involvement in war or violent strife has been as a motley, disorganized parade of individuals. Warriors, leaders, heroines, adventurers, poisoners, conspirators, murderous queens and robber baronesses, soldiers, partisans, guerrillas and gunrunners, terrorists, revolutionaries, spies, nurses, raped civilians, camp followers—women have been no strangers to war.

Some disguised themselves as men and ran away to the war, either because they were following their loved ones or because they wanted to fight and it was the only way it could be done. Often they were not discovered until they were wounded or killed. In the seventeenth and eighteenth centuries some of the famous ones were English—Kit Welsh, Hannah Snell (known as James Grey), Trooper Mary. (There were, of course, notable American examples and I shall mention them later.) A sergeant wrote after Waterloo: "Many females were found amongst the slain. As is common in the camp, the female followers wore male attire." There were, in reality, many women around the battlefield anyway, providing the logistical support, the billeting, meals, washing, mending, nursing; often they outnumbered the men.

One of the most famous women to fight alongside men in battle did not have to camouflage her sex. Flora Sandes was a gently brought-up Englishwoman who, like many others, went to Serbia during the First World War to work with a St. John's Ambulance unit. She spent the war there moving from nurse to private to sergeant in the Army, into a Serbian uniform, commanding men, and was severely wounded in action. She described how it started: "The soldiers in the ambulance seemed to take it for granted that anyone who could ride and shoot would be a soldier." She weathered long campaigns in the mountains, scrambling and plodding through rain and snow, sleeping in foxholes full of water. She wrote: "For some reason prolonged shelling always made me feel sleepy. The louder the racket, the more soundly I slept."

Sandes was severely wounded in action by a bomb, but, patched up again, she returned to the front for the rest of the war. She remained in Serbia, honored as a national heroine, and it was only when she became old and frail that she returned home to England, where she wrote two books of memoirs, their tone vivid and spirited. She wrote: "Sometimes now, when playing family bridge for 3d. a hundred in an English drawing-room, the memory of those wild jolly nights comes over me, and I am lost in another world. . . . Instead of the powdered nose of my partner I seem to be looking at the grizzled head and unshaven chin of the Commandant, and the scented drawing-room suddenly fades away into the stone walls of a tiny hut lighted by a couple of candles stuck into bottles and thick with tobacco smoke, where 5 or 6 officers and I sit crowded on bunks or campstools. For evening dress, mudstained, bloodstained khaki breeches and tunic, and for vanity bag a revolver. The camp table was covered by the thick brown folds of an army blanket, and before each was a pile of Serbian bank notes and gold, and a tumblerful of red wine. Then came a batman with another relay of little cups of the thick, sweet Turkish coffee, which he brought about every hour. But here comes a trim maid with tea, and I return to the prosaic drawing-room with a start, and the realization that I am a 'lady' now, not a 'soldier and a man.'"

Flora Sandes discovered why it is that men may dream of the war in which they served. It changed her, filled an ordinary life with terror, comradeship, esprit, and gave her a cause. La Pasionaria was another such woman. She became the heroine of the Spanish Civil War, but she had been a peasant wife, used to terrible poverty and the deaths of her babies. She began to study Marxism, she watched her husband struggle to make a living, and together they began to make bombs and to conspire. The process filled her with doubt, and she wrote: "I saw how difficult it is for a mother to devote herself to a revolutionary struggle . . . did I have a right to sacrifice my children, depriving them of a secure and warm home, of a mother's care and affection? In my life as a communist," she continued in her autobiography, "this has been one of the most painful aspects of the struggle, although I have seldom spoken of it, thinking that the best way to teach is by example, even if I had to shed tears of blood."

For the most part, women's involvement in war and civil conflict has been more acceptable in revolutionary, underground, terrorist, resistance, or partisan movements, where they can be most effectively used. Women do not need to dress as men in these kinds of wars; often their success depends on the extent to which they look like helpless females. Working as spies and informers, as messengers, with weapons carried in their shopping baskets and under their shawls, these women risked death and many paid with their lives, from the Ladies of the Covenant in Scotland, who in the seventeenth century led the movement against the imposition of English rule in the shape of the English Church, to the Russian terrorists of the mid-nineteenth century.

The Russian revolutionaries of the 1870s were often sheltered, middle-class young women who went to study at Zurich University and there came into contact with revolutionary ideas, each other, and possibilities they had not previously encountered in their young lives. Vera Zasulich shot at point-blank range a tyrannical provincial governor; Vera Figner was one of the band that killed the czar with bombs that she helped to make, for which she spent twenty years in prison. Sofia Perovskaia was executed; Olga Liubatovich spent twenty years in Siberian exile. For Liubatovich, learning to live like a male revolutionary meant abandoning her newborn baby when she began to live underground. She wrote: "Yes, it's a sin for revolutionaries to start a family. Men and women both must stand alone, like soldiers under a hail of bullets." The child died at six months. Armed women such as these were intensely conscious of their mission. They made up one-quarter of the Russian revolutionary movement.

Throughout the world there have been others like them, whose courage and ruthlessness gave the lie to any idea that females are intrinsically less able when it comes to fulfilling the ends through violent means. Also in the 1870s, for example, thousands of ordinary Frenchwomen came to the barricades of the Paris Commune. One observer wrote that they were "like the men: ardent, implacable, frenzied." Another wrote of some women at the time of their arrest: "Many had powder-blackened hands and shoulders bruised by the recoil of their rifles." As punishment, they were shot or otherwise executed, imprisoned, or deported to the Cayenne Islands.

In the Taiping Revolution, a Chinese peasant revolt of the mid-nineteenth century, thousands of women fought in all-female divisions. In the violent revolutionary turmoil of the early years of this century, women who chose to confront the regime suffered terribly, particularly those who flagrantly showed their revolt with unbound feet and cropped hair. Agnes Smedley, an American journalist who spent a considerable portion of her life in China during those years, interviewed one young woman who told her that she had been a medical corps member of the Chinese Communist party, with her hair cropped and a military uniform. She said, "We were among those that captured Hankow and Han-yang, and we laid siege to Wu-ch'ang until it fell. My body was now strong and tough, and there seemed no limit to my ability to work." She took up a rifle when the White Terror began; she fought "with hard hatred," and she told how the reactionary troops treated girls like her: "every girl with bobbed hair who was caught was stripped naked, raped by as many men as were present, then her body slit in two, from below upwards." Often the girls were no more than fifteen or sixteen. Officers, giving interviews to British journalists from Hong Kong, said, "The bobbed-haired girls are the worst; they are very arrogant and talk back defiantly. We have had to kill hundreds of them." Over one thousand women were killed during the White Terror.

Throughout this century the numbers of women involved in war have increased; they soared during World War II in Europe, most strikingly in Yugoslavia. The Yugoslav Army had been destroyed so early in the war that the country was defended by an informal army of partisans, in which the women were vital. About 100,000 women were partisans—one-eighth of the total force. They fought from the hills with the men, and were organized into units that were either static, living at home, or mobile, moving at night and hiding. They served in their customary roles, as nurses and spies, and so on, but also as radio operators, combat soldiers, and snipers. They would shoot their German prisoners without a qualm. The women were in all respects equal with the men. They fought, lived, and died together. Because of the high standard of discipline, there was no sexual tension. Husbands and wives were separated, and anyone disobeying the rules was severely punished. Too many of the women were apparently killed at the beginning, because, to quote Vladimir Dedijer, a former partisan, "They are not accustomed to fighting and do not know how to take cover." They made up for their lack of experience with unflagging bravery. President Tito said in 1975 that of the 100,000 women who fought, 40,000 were wounded and 25,000 died.

It could be said that a guerrilla war is better suited to women than a conventional war, but in this case the distinction is meaningless, since the conditions the Yugoslavs faced were as grueling as those of the front line and were distinguished from those of the front line only in that the soldiers did not constitute the official Yugoslav Army, there being no Yugoslav Army.

There was a strong partisan movement in Italy too. It is estimated that 25,000 women fought officially as partisans, of whom 4563 were arrested, tortured, and finally died, 624 were killed or wounded, 2750 deported, and 15 awarded Italy's Gold Medal for Military Valor. Most of these medal winners had refused to give information to the Germans and had been tortured to death.

In the French Resistance movement there were women at all levels, most of them young girls or housewives. Unlike the women of eastern Europe who were fighting alongside the men, these women took on a more traditional role, smuggling weapons, working as cipher operators, couriers, clerks, drivers, telephonists. Nevertheless the danger was as great.

Contrary to popular belief, the Germans did not single out the women for special brutality as a general rule, but neither did they show them special mercy. Fifteen of the exceptional women who had been parachuted into France to work with the Maquis were captured; of these one was tortured, others were killed with poison injections or shot or starved or left to die of disease. Only three survived, but none of the fifteen had talked. These were the visible heroines: they bore such famous names as Nancy Wake, who led 7000 Maquis in daring commando raids; Pearl Witherington, who took charge of 2000 men; Marie Fourcade, who was in charge of intelligence for the whole of France and who wrote in her autobiography that when she was given this assignment she said, "I'm only a woman; who will obey and follow me?"

Since the War, women have continued to fight in unconventional wars throughout the world, in Vietnam and Cuba, in Nicaragua and Iran, or with the PLO and the Provisional IRA. The descendants of the nineteenth-century Russian women are the revolutionaries of the Red Brigade and the Baader-Meinhof gang. However, the most effective use of women in underground warfare took place in the Algerian War of Independence, and their classic role was discussed by Frantz Fanon in *A Dying Colonialism*. He wrote: "The Algerian woman is not a secret agent. It is without apprenticeship, without briefing, without fuss, that she goes out into the street with three grenades in her handbag."

At first it was only the married women who were involved.

As the conflict grew, divorced women were used, and then every woman who would risk her life. Since the first days of the uprising they had helped the guerrillas in the mountains and tended the wounded, but by the middle 1950s they were used in broad daylight in the cities. A deadly game was played with the veil. Fanon maintains that the French had already mounted a major attack on the veil as a way to destroy the Algerian way of life and thereby hinder the country's capacity for resistance. The Algerians retaliated by using those "Europeanized" women.

"Carrying revolvers, grenades, hundreds of false identity cards or bombs," Fanon wrote, "the unveiled Algerian woman moves like a fish in the Western waters . . . that young girl, unveiled only yesterday, who walks with sure steps down the streets of the European city teeming with policemen, parachutists, militia men." As the women who looked Europeanized were regularly arrested and tortured, the veil returned, as a covering for weapons bound to the women's bodies, so that the bare hands looked vulnerable, empty. As the French realized this, they would push every veiled woman in the street against the wall and run a metal detector over her. Some of the women went unveiled again. They became more militant; the female cells of the FLN had mass memberships.

The Algerian women fought in what had become an enduring tradition. Women had become the cornerstone of underground warfare, with their gender a ready-made disguise. However, a new precedent was set during World War II, when for the first time women were used en masse in conventional uniformed armies. Two countries besides America took this step—the USSR and Great Britain. In Britain the women were essentially used as auxiliaries, as they had been since Waterloo and earlier, except that this time they were closer to combat and present in larger numbers than ever before. Russian women fought in combat. Both examples are pertinent, so it is worth going into a little detail.

All the accessible information on Russian women comes

from Army documents, the authors of which state carefully that their information cannot be accepted fully at face value because of the propaganda element that is inseparable from the Russian historical sources. However, most authorities agree that even if the women's achievement is exaggerated, it was nonetheless substantial, the result of active participation in the war of one million Russian women—partisans, soldiers, pilots, and many others. Women had always been involved in the great Russian wars, but the universal military service law of 1939 provided for massive drafting of women with some useful training. At the outbreak of war, women volunteered in their thousands but were taken mostly for nursing and support jobs, while the majority stayed at home to replace men, just as they did in England.

As the war progressed and the plight of the USSR became dire, conscription was extended to childless women between the ages of eighteen and twenty-five, but others volunteered. Young girls and older women from all classes and regions served. Special youth-training units had by the end of the war trained 102,333 rifle sharpshooters, 15,290 submachine gunners, 7796 automatic riflemen, 6097 mortarmen, 4522 machine gunners, and 49,509 signalers. (In addition, hundreds of thousands of women were training in various medical specialties.) The first women's air regiments were planned as early as 1941, just after the German invasion.

When the women of the 588th Air Regiment arrived at the front in May 1942, the men in the division did not take them seriously. Between June 8, the date of their first mission, and October 1, the regiment had made more than 3000 sorties, which was not an unusual record. The 586th Air Regiment, for example, participated in the air defense of Stalingrad and made sorties as far as Vienna. It carried out 4419 missions, fought 125 air battles, and shot down 38 and damaged 42 enemy aircraft. Several star pilots were shot down, others achieved feats of daring and skill. Some women served in predominantly male units, and Valentina Grisodubova commanded a regiment, the 101st Air Regiment, in which she was the only woman. She earned this position by her flying skill.

Other women were in ground combat operations, in tank units where they served as engineers, technicians, radio operators, turret gunners, drivers, and mechanics. There is some doubt as to whether or not women actually were commanders, but there are many tales of their valiant exploits. Thousands also served with the infantry, where they held command positions over men, since there were no all-female infantry units. Several won the title Hero of the Soviet Union—not for bandaging wounds but for inflicting them. Nina Onilova, who commanded a machine gun crew, died in action at Sebastopol, having killed about 2000 Germans. Then there were the snipers; there was even a special sniper school, which graduated more than 1000 women.

Participants in the defensive battle of Odessa included 3200 women, and thousands more were active in the defense of Moscow; thousands fought and died in the battle of Stalingrad. These numbers do not take into account the medical personnel, the partisans, the women in the Russian Navy.

The partisan units were said to have faced one problem that is much in the minds of today's U.S. Army personnel. There were, according to reports that were captured by the Germans, too many pregnant women, "who reduce the combat readiness of their men and are a burden to the regiment in combat." Some of these women fought in all-female partisan detachments, but still they shared quarters with male officers, and there were many abuses of the anti-fraternization policies. The Russians could not seem to manage the discipline that the Yugoslavs achieved.

There are those who would sigh and say that this particular culture under those circumstances is too removed from our own to represent a useful example. The British women, however, do. In April 1941 the first of them were registered, with no public outcry. By 1945 more than half a million

British women were in uniform, backed up by nearly five million who worked as fire watchers and fire fighters, in the Land Army, in munitions, and elsewhere. Thirteen hundred nurses were involved in the evacuation of Dunkirk. One soldier who was there said, "I saw one party of them dressing wounded who were lying out in the open. A plane began bombing. They just lay down by their patients and continued bandaging." Many died, in Europe and the Far East, and during the Blitz.

By the end of 1941, 170,000 women had joined the antiaircraft batteries around the country, where they were exposed to mortal danger. They maintained barrage balloons and they took over the searchlight batteries. As the war continued, they dominated this field, and they did everything done by the men, except for loading and firing the guns. This work was the closest Allied women came to organized combat, and despite its extreme danger, the public felt it to be somehow acceptable, because the women were in a defensive role, keeping the enemy away from the homeland. The women were all volunteers, and they formed a dedicated elite.

There were initial problems: generational tension between young women and the older men, friction between the female leaders and the male over the command of the women. The top brass in the government and the Army fretted about the women working alongside men under stress, or alternatively, about those living in isolated all-female tent cities in a sea of mud, armed only with pickax handles. All the worries proved groundless. The mixed batteries performed better in every way than the all-male batteries, and there was no promiscuity. At one terrible post in the muddy Essex wheat fields the CO assembled the thousand women who worked there and said that any who wanted to could leave. Only nine women, all of them clerks, accepted, even though the conditions under which they were living amounted to trench warfare. Testimonials to the women's cool control and quick thinking abound. Furthermore, it was reported after the war that in the most heavily bombed areas of the country almost 70 percent more men than women had suffered nervous breakdowns. The medical examiner reported of the women that "they perform the job in hand with calmer deliberation than men." He continued; "Men get through the job all right, but they work in a state of mental excitement—often consciously suppressed, which, in time, takes its toll." The extent of female endurance under stress, pain, and bereavement has not been a secret, but the strength it lends women in war deserves to be recognized.

5

Perfect Soldiers: Peaceful Coexistence on Bivouac

The Army is the most traditionally masculine of all this country's institutions. By adopting the uniforms, the rituals, and the authoritarian structure that dominates military life, boys are made into soldiers who are men. One of the most predictable rituals facing the young male recruit is the Army haircut, which takes place during the first couple of days at the reception station.

The young men had pretended to be dreading the visit to the barber, but their furtive, gleeful anticipation was quite apparent. However in this cycle, only the third coeducational cycle in Fort McClellan, things did not go quite as planned. The PX barber gave them a choice: regular short back and sides or headshaving. Almost everyone returned with a bald head, grinning sheepishly and running his hands over his smooth skull. The men looked embarrassed but proud, because they had been planning this. It was the masculine thing to do.

The women looked up at them with slight amazement, and then with some derision. "Now, what did you go and do that for?" drawled Elizabeth Brady. The men were at a loss.

Suddenly, pleasing women seemed as important as being macho. They muttered and shuffled a little, and lit cigarettes, while the women giggled softly.

The integrated Army is full of such surprises. In the particular basic training cycle I attended, traditional ideas of masculine or feminine behavior were turned upside down. Many of the men had enlisted expecting their basic training to follow the patterns of privation and stress that they felt would make them men. Confronted with women, the last people in the world they expected to see there, they reacted first with bewilderment and then with a distinct bias against the women. The young men came mainly from the ghettos of big cities or from the rural backwoods, like the women, and they had clear ideas as to women's place. "I have nothing against them," said a charming man from Oklahoma who subsequently had a sweet and courtly romance with one of them, "but I feel they have caused basic to be too soft." The men learned to keep such opinions to themselves as the women became more vocal and began to complain about the lyrics to one of the marching songs: "They say that in the Army, the girls are mighty fine/They walk like the Wolfman and look like Frankenstein."

A lecture on the role of the Army featured a film that referred to the citizen as "he" throughout, the soldier as "he." For a lecture on the responsibility of the soldier, Sergeant Pace used ancient slides featuring exclusively Wacs, plump and cheery, as they demonstrated saluting. During a film about rape the women looked restless, but the men sitting near me seemed to be fascinated and horrified. Their eyes never left the screen as a weeping victim described her experience. In the subsequent discussion a young woman stood up and said quietly, "I've been there, and I can tell you, you're treated like a criminal." Nobody knew how to react; the next question was quickly taken. The sex education class was conducted as never before, with an instructor telling the young women that the best way to check a man's condom was to bring your own, because you could never trust a man. This remark amused the women, and the men too, who felt roguish—the moment in the classroom was playful, provocative.

Later, during a discussion of VD, led by a brisk, abrasive female lecturer, one young black man, asked to describe symptoms, shyly referred to genitals as "you know, the family jewels." The lecturer harangued him, saying he was evasive and afraid to name the parts of his own body, whereupon another male trainee stood up and said, "Ma'am. He knows the street names, but he don't like to use them in polite conversation in front of the ladies. That don't mean he's stupid."

On weekends the trainees had some time to relax, which made them wistful. They would play volleyball, or snooze up in the bay. Mostly they would have to iron. However, there were islands of quiet and stillness, when the women would sit at the picnic tables struggling over letters home to parents or fiancés. One Saturday afternoon, at a company picnic for which they had all chipped in for hot dogs and sodas, some of the women sprawled in cut-off shorts and talked about combat. Inside the building the male trainees, looking very young with their shaved heads, lined up for their turns at the phones. Two out of the three phones were equipped for collect calls only. They would dial and lean against the wall, watching the traffic in the hallways, then smile sheepishly, turn toward the wall, hunching over the phone. One man who had been squatting in the grass, methodically sifting through it, came rushing over to the drill sergeant in charge to announce that he had found a patch of four-leaf clovers. The drill sergeant was at a loss.

Meanwhile a little group listened to some of the top forty on the radio in the dayroom and then wandered out to write their letters. Jeannie Fisher, a shy, gawky young woman from Florida, freckled and fragile-looking with her newly spiky red hair, chewed on the end of her ballpoint for a time, then said slowly, "It's *so hard* to write home and tell people what it's like. There's no way they could imagine what's going on with us all, how long the days are, how much we're all changing. It's just a different world." Two of the others agreed, looking a little stricken as they sensed how far behind they had left their civilian identities. It was not that they were being defeminized; they were being turned into soldiers. It looked as if the women could learn soldiering in accordance with the traditional model, which had, up till now, been applied exclusively to men. Therefore they were becoming more like men, which caused complications in sex and love.

Sexual bragging and ribald jokes have always been part of the soldier's life. Often the talk served to cover up a lack of experience, the bragging to romanticize a few minutes with the cheapest whore in town. Whatever the reason, the talk was the currency. A drill sergeant standing next to me in the rain one day carefully put a plastic cover over his round brown hat. It looked a little silly. He said, knocking at the felt softly with his knuckles, "I press this hat every night, treat it better than my wife."

The men, many straight from school, became giddy in this atmosphere that included women as active participants. The women were of two minds. They would tell me with exaggerated horror and disgust that when the order was given to dress ranks, the men would brush against the women's breasts with their fingers or outstretched arms. The women meanwhile would revel in their own crudeness, the dirty songs, the macho swearing, and occasionally a fight that ended in a moment of violence, whether a slap or a punch.

During the first week or two, before the trainees went out into the field, there was very little real flirtation or romancing—most people were too tense and disoriented. Those who did contrive to meet each other on the fire escapes tended to be giggly eighteen-year-olds who fell in love every few days and would race passionately to their drill sergeant with overcooked *Sturm und Drang* about how, for example, "the other drills are picking on us because we're in love." Lieutenant Myers said that romances would not become the norm, because many of the women felt superior to the men—which they were, in years, education, class, or all three. Already one or two had intimated that the men were nice as friends but—. Besides, the men had little scabs on the tops of their heads where the steel helmets chafed.

For the men, the desire to make out or to have a girlfriend became desperate as training wore on. Cindy Hopkins was an ungainly but determined young woman with a crush on the Miami Shores Police Department. One night she showed me an album with photos, clippings, and mementos of them, even a photograph of a cake she and a friend had made for them. She also showed me a note she had received. It read: "I would like to go with you if you are not going with anybody. Please let me know at supper. My name is ORVILLE HOLMES. I have a ring if you want it." The men began to look better, with the fuzz of hair growing back on their heads like leaves in spring. People were making reckless assignations for the laundry room, the latrines—and despite the stringently enforced rules, they were managing to make out. As the women became less and less "feminine," their sexual behavior seemed to be fluid, susceptible to change.

Female homosexuality became visible and openly discussed. Women in the Army have traditionally been labeled dykes and whores. The term "dyke" is a weapon, not simply an insult, because homosexuality is forbidden in the military, and a mere accusation may be enough to ruin a soldier's career. Walters, the young woman from California, who had a powerful body and was known for her sardonic wit, told me one slow Sunday afternoon that she was gay. The conversation had grown out of a bragging session when three or four people started to talk about being drunk, who had been arrested, and how many times. She turned to me and said with a reserved smile, "I was arrested in Mexico for kissing on somebody I shouldn't have been kissing on."

Walters had worked in construction and landscape gardening. Her complaint about basic, which grew louder as the training wore on, was that it was too soft. She wanted to be more physical and muscular. She loved to clown and joke;

she sprawled confidently in her fatigues, and several of the other women were fascinated by her. It was rumored that one of her special friends had "turned gay." Certainly the two became inseparable, always bursting into wild laughter at secret jokes and mock wrestling.

Schulman, the quiet former meat wrapper from Phoenix, told me she was bisexual. Schulman looked strong; however she had cried bitterly when the PT scores were read out and her score was low. She said her helmet sat so low on her head that, with her eyes in shadow, she could stare at the crotches of the men, which she enjoyed. She also said she was becoming too close a friend to Julie Drake and had to watch out in case Julie realized and ran off. She looked sad, then gestured across the half-deserted bay, saying, "There are other gays here. Those two black girls, they're cool."

Bivouac week, which actually lasted four full days, was a frightening prospect to many trainees, particularly those who had grown up in cities and had never gone to summer camp. They worried about snakes and bugs. On the night before, Joan Clark succumbed to melodrama on her bed. Her fiancé had just been discharged from the Navy with a knee injury. "I have to leave so I can be with Jimmy!" she moaned, thrashing a little, gearing herself up for hyperventilation. She was taken off to see Sergeant Lester, who managed to calm her only by offering to arrange for a wedding on post the day of graduation. She plunged into euphoria. "Helen, will you be my matron of honor? Oh, please say yes."

Julie Drake was methodically organizing her possessions. In a low voice she said, "I'm not really looking forward to camping out, but Schulman has psyched me up by telling me all the good things about it. We're going to pretend we're soldiers." She showed me the signatures on her platoon photograph, and so did the others. "Drive on sweet thing," said one. "To a nice lady and a hardworking soldier," said another.

The young men and women had been in training for more

than a month, and they seemed to have adapted to the process in some crucial way. They had stopped studying their drill sergeants like Tarot cards, hoping to understand why their moods or edicts changed so swiftly. The baroque horrors of intimidation they had anticipated and for a while thought they were experiencing had been reduced to prosaic hours of cleaning and scrubbing. They knew that for punishment they would have to write an essay or cut the grass instead of being bashed to a bloody pulp.

Outside, men and women were running together in the cool evening air, pacing each other. Jarrell and Schulman came racing over—they were so full of adrenaline they ran everywhere—wet from pouring water all over themselves. With their clothes sticking to them and their short hair slicked back and gleaming, they looked coltish, confident; they had a physical poise that is rare in women, but they did not look like men. On the way out of the building I bumped into Elizabeth, who was scrubbing the floor in a downstairs office. She looked up to tell me that Sergeant Lester had persuaded her to replace Patty Sharp as squad leader. I asked how she was feeling. Wringing out a cloth, she said with enthusiasm, "I can't believe the things we're all doing. I used to take thirty minutes to iron a blouse, and now I can do everything—iron, spit shine, polish, clean the bay—in that time! And just look how far we've all come. We quarrel, but we're running on three or four hours' sleep. We learned all about the M-16 in four days! Four days is all it took!" She added triumphantly, "I ran two miles at eleven-thirty this morning when it was eighty degrees. I never thought I could do it, but I just kept telling myself I had to." Turning back to her office floor, she said, "It's all true, just like they said. You know, we all enjoy it, we *really like it here*. It gives us such a feeling of accomplishment! I think I'll go OCS."

The bivouac began with a march. After breakfast the trainees clumsily smeared themselves with camouflage and then set off, with twenty-pound packs on their backs and the

6.5-pound M-16s slung over their shoulders. The total weight, with steel pots, boots, and other paraphernalia, was close to thirty-five pounds. They giggled and groaned as they put the packs on; many of the women had trouble even getting the packs on their backs. As they tottered off, with helmets askew, their faces were flushed and there was a great deal of hysterical, gasping laughter.

Within minutes six women had begun to trail. Sergeant Johnson, the devout Mormon, said with quiet vehemence, his dark eyes snapping, "You see, all women. *All women.*" The genial black MP said with some cynicism, "Now we see who's been cheating on PT. Come on, you women, what's all this about being equal?" Johnson pounced on the only lagging male (one of his) and forcibly double-timed him, by the scruff of the neck, back to his place in the column. The first woman broke down. The MP said crossly, "Move, girl," and with tears running down her camouflage she muttered, "I'm *working* on it, Drill Sergeant."

Fortunately for the women's self-esteem it was only a three-quarter-mile march to the bivouac site. By the end they were scarlet and panting. After a cigarette break they applied much insect repellent and prepared for the ten-mile march. ("We tell 'em it's ten," said a drill sergeant, grinning, "but by the time we're through, it's more like twelve.") Simmons was put "on guard" at the camp, leaning on crutches, her face a study in depression and suppressed rage.

Sergeant Stokes started the march; he ordered silence and then dispatched the trainees down the hill in twos, evenly spaced, with a swift gesture of his hand. Joan Clark tripped over a cable on her way out of the clearing, somersaulted, and collapsed in choking pain. She did not continue with the march.

Sergeant Carroll, the black MP, marched with me for a while. He said, "The women don't do so bad once they stop crying and complaining." We had started out not long after 8:00 A.M. in order to miss the day's worst heat. By this time of year, May, the days would be burning their way into the eighties by noon, and in the afternoon the air was like a hot sponge over the post. Sometimes the tree-covered mountains were obscured by low clouds, but more often they just loomed, quivering in the heat haze. In the height of the summer, when temperatures routinely reached the nineties, marches began at 4:00 or 5:00 in the morning, so that the worst would be over before it was too hot.

The narrow roads wound through forest and past abandoned ranges and patches of swamp. Butterflies swirled through the sunlight. The young lieutenant out of West Point was heading the march, and he set too fast a pace, so that the body of the troops slowed down on their way up the stony, steep hills, and then almost ran, packs banging, down them. Over a column of a hundred and fifty people this creates mayhem with "proper intervals," and it means that some people have to concentrate or push themselves to catch up. A jeep rattled by with four inert and collapsed females, including Patty Sharp, whose face was gray and pouring sweat.

I ate lunch with the NCOs, who spent most of the time sorting out C rations so that they all found something they could stand, often in the strangest combinations—like canned apricots and crackers. The trainees were sitting off the track, ostensibly in an unobtrusive posture. Resting in the shade of the trees, a group of women from the first platoon shouted cheerfully, "Patty's the only one of us who fell behind!" A serious young man called Price, who was known for his churning temper, accosted me and chatted for a few minutes. He said, "I've been feeling sorry for Patty, you know, because everyone teases her, and that's not too cool. So I'm helping her with running and with getting her breathing right."

The march resumed across a sandy heath dotted with flowers. Patty abandoned her pack—just left it by the side of the track—and wandered off disconsolately. She was found leaning against a gate and staring at some cows with an expression of distraction and grief, but she could not be persuaded to talk. Fortunately there was only a short distance to go; the trainees sensed it because of the people coming out to meet them from the bivouac site—like sea gulls indicating land.

Standing at the gate, I watched them limp in. It had been over twelve miles in suffocating, windless heat, and for some of the march they had been ordered to carry their M-16s in front of them, so that they could not swing their arms to help themselves along. Several women were in real trouble. One was a small round black woman from Chicago, Private Jones. In the bay she was very cheerful and giggly—Sergeant Stokes had said of her fondly, "We always have a little black girl like that," while I wove my brain into knots trying to determine whether that was a racist remark—but out here she labored under a major disadvantage, namely, her too short legs.

In today's integrated Army the thirty-inch marching step is becoming a fossil, even though the average-sized female can manage it without difficulty. However, Private Jones could not even match the modified step they used at Fort McClellan. In addition, she and all the other women were in routine agony from their boots. However, the men could not bear to see them give up, and they would push at them, carry their packs, shoulder their rifles, yell and curse—in short, do whatever was required to bring them in. Private Jones was literally carried in by two men, one propping her up on each side, while two others carried her pack and rifle. Tears and sweat were pouring down her face, the men were panting, but they were all thrilled. "I'm going to stick with those men more," Jones said afterward, "they're real nice."

By this stage of training, nobody seemed primarily male or female. With the novelty long gone, the trainees had learned a routine of constructive coexistence. There was sexual electricity in the air, but as people ate lunch and did sit-ups and learned how to treat snakebite and stormed foxholes, they were behaving more and more like a team that happened to be made up of individual men and women, not opposing, polarized groups. When Elizabeth Brady made sharpshooter, and when she was chosen as "supertrooper" for the way she looked on guard duty, the men in her platoon slapped her on the back and teased her with genuine pride and pleasure. The men who carried Private Jones in from the march were not laughed at by even the most recalcitrant of their fellow trainees. It all just seemed to make sense.

Female tent pitching was an example of unreconstructed female behavior of the worst kind, with Patty as the catalyst. The pup tents could accommodate two people if neither one was a restless sleeper, and the trainees had organized themselves into pairs. Couples were busily anchoring their tents and digging little drainage moats around them with entrenching tools. No one had wanted to share with Patty, and so she had ended up with Purcell, another young woman nobody wanted, a noisy redheaded trainee who had recently been wished on Alpha by another company. Various reasons had been given for her transfer. She was supposed to have fallen behind because of illnesses, but within a few moments of her arrival, when she loudly harangued the bay about matters of no consequence and took many Polaroid photos, everybody guessed that somebody over there at the other company had finally said, "Enough! No more! Get her out of here!"

To her great credit, Purcell was going at it with the trowel and the tent pegs while Patty sat like a collapsed string puppet, her eyes closing and her head falling forward onto her thin chest. Lynne Hunt, the especially belligerent black woman from Newark, looked over, got up, went over to them, and punched Patty hard in the shoulder, shouting, "You just trying to get out of your work, just like you always do." Purcell yelled, flushing beneath her freckles, "Why don't you leave her alone? Can't you see she's not well?" Patty looked dully around at the angry, sweating faces and began pathetically grubbing away in the earth, while people argued the merits of letting Someone Like Her in, let alone Pushing Her Through. Walters, the California trainee, and Jarrell, setting up their little home, chimed in that nobody should punch anyone else, and people should help Patty instead. Three of the black women huddled seditiously, and then Lynne emerged to yell at the top of her lungs, "SHUT THE FUCK UP." A trainee known as "U-alphabet" because of her unpronounceable Polish name grumbled, "I'm tired of helping Patty. I've been doing it long enough." Encouraged by this shred of support, Lynne whirled around to Walters, who was busy troweling, and screamed, "MIND YOUR OWN BUSINESS, YOU WHITE BITCH." Walters' face grew somber. She said coolly, "Don't let's go playing those little race games," and after a pause, added softly, almost to herself, "Take me back to California."

This moment brought into the open the racial tension that had previously been more imagined than real. The Army as a whole has had racial equality legislated upon it; in such an authoritarian system, behavior can be controlled in ways that civilian behavior cannot. Whatever military people may *think*, racial equality is a fact in job opportunities, salaries, housing. Nevertheless, despite a general sturdy willingness to work together, the superstitious prejudices remain on each side. I saw it in the furious scowls of Lynne and her friends. In the early part of training, groups of friends were mixed, black and white. As Lynne grew more disaffected she gathered around her most of the blacks, and they set up a murmuring campaign about racism whenever something displeased one of them. The whites would look askance at the blacks and say that it must be something in their past that made them so awkward.

Mail call is one of the great moments on bivouac. At the faint shout, people yelled excitedly to each other and jumped out from the unnecessarily huge moats to race over the pine needles to the dark-green bleachers, where they sat in patient rows like pets at dinnertime. Lynne had a letter, but she was so upset that she took a while to raise her hand when her name was called. So she was dropped for push-ups. Instead she walked, erect and outraged, back to her tent, fiercely muttering that no letter was worth push-ups. Shortly afterward Sergeant Bell talked to her in a quiet voice for a long time. "Your attitude has returned, has it not?" she began. Lynne listened without moving as tears streamed down her expressionless face.

After mail call the trainees resumed their homemaking, males and females eyeing each other across the deep abyss that separated them. The sorority sister and her tent mate had, in a parody of housewifery, plucked especially large branches of camouflage and planted them like a shrubbery by the front flap of the tent. This was much admired by the males, who began to vie with each other in uprooting or pulling off the largest boughs and saplings they could find. As evening fell on the diminishing woodland the midges came out, and the war paint began to streak down the trainees' faces. Patty came up and tapped me on the shoulder, her face ravaged and grim. She said with a weird, unclear intonation and a dark glance, "Forgive and forget is my motto."

The lineup for chow, on the top of a hill, where the air was less heavy, was a torpid, silent affair, announced by the lumbering arrival of the Maggot Wagon. The trainees filed exhaustedly by the food, taking everything they were offered, and sat outside in the dusk at the long tables, remaining for as long as they could after finishing without being noticed. Some of them dreaded the dark, others secretly wondered how to brave the communal latrines and rudimentary showers.

Afterward I sat with a group of men in the bleachers. They were smoking and reading their mail. A skinny blue-eyed fellow who was going into helicopter repair said, "My dad's in the Marines, so I knew what to expect. In a way, though, I'd like it to be harder, and I'd like the women to do their own basic." He slapped at a midge. "A lot of us think the women slow us down—but still, it helps a *lot* just having them around. You can talk to them in a way you can't talk to men." They all nodded and murmured agreement, looking over at the women's encampment, where there was bustle and the odd shriek of laughter, and a pair of shocking-pink panties drying on top of a tent.

Another man said to me, "In the bays we talk about sex all the time—and about how the day went and about graduation. . . . The females are worse than us, though. They have guys all picked out. They say what they want and they go for it. Men just hint." Another trainee agreed. Scuffing the needles with the dusty toe of his boot, he said, grinning, "I've had three offers, and only one I have accepted. But I'm shy," he said confidently, "and I like to have women come to me. Times have changed, you know." He added with pleasure, "Every girlfriend I have ever had has picked me up." Then the conversation took a more emphatic turn as they started to boast about girls and drugs, telling me it was easy to get joints and speed if you wanted. One of them said with a conspiratorial wink that tonight "some of the guys" would go visiting across the abyss.

Over on the women's side of the abyss an intent little group of women sat on the pine needles cleaning their rifles, with camouflage still on their faces. I moved closer to hear what they were talking about and heard the word "corsage." Joan Clark, busy with the firing pin and the cleaning fluid, was planning her wedding.

On Day 2 of bivouac I went over to the company, where it was quiet and smelled of disinfectant. The first sergeant, holding court from inside a cloud of cigarette smoke, said gaily, "See how lovely and quiet it is when the kids leave home?" Out in the field the trainees sat in the bleachers, white and glazed. I could see at a glance that they were as comatose as children in a civics class. Sergeant Carroll, the black MP, was teaching them how to form a company, how to stand in formation, and the like. Those who began to nod, like the Goofy Drinking Bird, were taken off and made to stand with their heads leaning against a tree. The genial black MP saw me coming and announced to the class, "I'm being liberal today." He was telling them how to assemble in formation. "Everyone fall forward on the base-person. I will say 'person,' not 'baseman,' like the manuals say."

Julie caught my eye, blushed and giggled. On the way to

formation she told me that the previous night five of them had taken showers at the same time. She said hesitantly, "You have to lose your modesty. They're trying to teach you to become a family and use teamwork. Why," she added in amazement, "we had a girl from A-3 in the shower with us last night and she didn't mind. With the latrines I don't mind anymore either." The latrines contained just a row of holes covered by a board with seats. As the week progressed, a terrible smell hung and eddied there.

The day out at Range 17 was the one day in all of the training that the young soldiers enjoyed the most. They were there to learn everything from camouflage to the low crawl, and the day would culminate in defensive night fire up on the hill, "Virgin Mountain." At some ranges the instructors would push people through, glance at their watches restlessly when it approached 4:00, because they wanted to close down and go fishing, and they were, as a result, very cursory with the slow ones or the second tries.

Range 17 had esprit, and its instructors used a robust patter that kept the trainees awake and cheerful. In the introductory briefing the men lounged around the perimeter, grinning, murmuring amiably to each other, while the sergeant in charge, a handsome, tall Indian, cracked such jokes as, "Don't call us drill sergeants, we have people for parents who know each other," or "As for latrines, we have two: 'Women' and 'Men.' And on that tree there's a sign that says 'Other,' and if any of you are from California, you will know what I mean."

The trainees split up into four groups for classes. The sergeant at camouflage class said heartily, "I know some of you are thinking, I don't have to learn camouflage because I'm a medic and I'm not going to be firing in combat. If somebody told you that, they're lying." He looked around in the impressive, expectant silence he had just created, and then, expertly, defused the little pricking of anxiety: "All you women should know what camouflage is anyway. You girls with the long fingernails, and some of you guys from

California." Soft, gratified laughter ran through the troop. Nobody before had set out to keep them entertained in this way; it relaxed them. They split up into twos and very carefully applied the two shades of green to each other, taking great pains at the hairline and around the eyes. Males painted each other; those painting women seemed especially serious and careful as the women grinned saucily, "puckering up" when instructed.

All got up in war paint, they looked like children playing in the woods, full of embarrassed delight at being dressed in the real stuff, complete with little bits of foliage stuck in their helmet covers. They looked as if they were thinking on the one hand, Wow, this is the real thing, it's what we came here for, and on the other, Gee, it's like playing at soldiers—the same double-sided pleasure that people experience when they move into their first apartment or open a bank account, the feeling that this familiar adult ritual means you *must be* an adult, but how can you be, because you still feel the same?

The use of the Claymore mines was taught by a young blond Vietnam veteran, who said to me subsequently that integrated training annoyed him because all the way through class he would see the men eyeing the women, or, at the very least, having some part of their minds concentrated on them. However, he genially played along with the spirit of the range, setting off crowd-pleasing flares by remote control when no one was expecting it. He said, shaking his head, "This place is like summer camp," and added that there should be more weapons training in basic because it was the only sustained weapons training many of them were likely to get. The trainees loved it, scraping their elbows raw as they struggled through the high and low crawl, watching intently as they were taught how to dig a foxhole.

At the next station, Sergeant Rickey, a bulky infantryman, taught them about fire sectors, how to fire at people in the woods, how to use foliage for camouflage. He led them down the hill a little, where, in a dense growth of saplings and bushes, they became aware of dummy Russians, inconspicuous, motionless, the shapes of torsos without any features—

oddly sinister in the shifting leaves and moving patterns of light. Past the dummy Russians and into the bleachers, where Sergeant Thomas, looking as handsome as an Indian scout in a Western, said with a grave smile, "Now I am going to choose twelve aggressors for the assault on Virgin Mountain." The trainees jumped up and down, waving their arms in their wild eagerness to be chosen. Joan Clark, who had developed an immediate fixation on Sergeant Thomas, shrieked, "Choose me! I'm very aggressive—and I would be to you if you weren't a sergeant!" The sergeants looked disconcerted and amused. Clark was chosen, and so were Elizabeth Brady and Claire Hayes. The impatient blond Claymore instructor said in scorn, "All twelve are women!" to which Sergeant Rickey replied, "Listen, I used to teach here in the days of WAC Center, and *everything* here was built or done by women, so *I know* they can do it."

Clark, digging away at foxholes with the little group of aggressors, rushed over to grab my arm. "Drill Sergeant Thomas reminds me of my daddy. He looked a lot like him," she confided. Looking sidelong at Sergeant Thomas, she said coyly, "You come to my wedding, Sergeant Thomas?"

For night fire there was a brilliant moon and a warm breeze. I walked with Sergeant Stokes on the paths circling the mountain, and he said quietly, "I'm really proud of my women, the way they've changed." As we came upon one foxhole after another, each containing a pair of jumpy trainees, we would startle and scare them by poking them from behind or whispering in a threatening manner. The wait seemed to be the best part, the unexplained rustlings in the leaves, prickings of fear at the thought of Jake the Snake at the bottom of a foxhole, under the leaves, maybe in eighteen inches of water. When the firing started, raggedly, at the bottom of the hill, the defenders peering down the barrels of their rifles into the buggy darkness, the crackling sound seemed very far away. Flickering spots of white light from flares were visible through the trees; the running figures of the aggressors, silhouetted against the light, together with eldritch screeches, gave the impression of a witches' Sabbath. The firers up on the hill fired for only moments, and then had to wait while everyone was cleared, and checked, and shepherded out, in such a way that nobody sprained an ankle by stumbling in the darkness. The trainees were dismayed that it was so anticlimactic. No storming of the foxholes, no sudden rushing through the undergrowth, no rolling over and over in the mud, hanging on to a fistful of fatigues.

The company sat in the bleachers, in the warm air under the enormous white moon. Sergeant Thomas made a surprise speech about Alpha, saying it was the best company to visit Range 17 this year, "with a high level of motivation and a good nature." Everyone was quiet and still. He went on: "You worked so willingly, particularly my aggressors, and you laughed and talked so pleasantly that it made the day go by fast." I sensed imminent tears around me, but then he said, "I think a great deal of credit for all this must go to your cadre," at which everyone jumped up and yelled "HOO-RAH" and whistled and clapped so fervently that Sergeant Stokes winced and said softly, "Don't overdo it." "I can honestly say," Thomas the Indian concluded, "that I hope to bump into some of Alpha in other corners of the world."

The trainees went trudging back to their bivouac tents full of dreamy optimism about their future as soldiers in an Army populated by people like the sergeants on Range 17. The trainees, males and females, most of them very young and impressionable, had become dependent upon the structure of Army life. The imprinting process of basic had worked. They were malleable, eager, dying to learn, and fixated on their sergeants. When I left at 9:15, Sergeant Lester was racing around in the shadows hurling firecrackers and imitation grenades to keep them on their toes.

In peacetime training there is little talk of killing, and at a noninfantry post such as Fort McClellan, no hand-to-hand fighting. When Sergeant Lester called Cindy Hopkins from formation to say crisply, "I'd be happy to take you to war with me," he was congratulating her because she had the top score in the company for night fire. Hopkins blushed with delight, but she knew there would be more to it than marksmanship. The training in offensive and defensive techniques was conducted in so orderly and undramatic a fashion that it was more like athletics than combat. The night war games contained more potential to frighten, but I saw the trainees truly alarmed only twice.

The devout Mormon had double-timed the trainees to the machine gun range and had taken them the long way round. It was hot; many dragged behind, and far at the back a black male squad leader tackled Patty. With the steel pot wobbling on the small head and her web gear and equipment dangling, she looked pathetic, her face gray and anguished. Manshell, who was steady and patient, had dropped behind to be with her. He walked at her side, keeping up a monologue of bullying and encouragement. He said, "Come on, *run.*" She flapped her arms in agitated movements. He said soothingly, "You're not running. You're walking. Open your eyes and then you'll see the road." She said, with hate in her gaze, "I am." He said, "No, you're just thinking how much pain you're feeling; you're just feeling sorry for yourself." They trundled on, arguing, as the column receded into the distance ahead of them.

The drill sergeants had tried to calm the nervous trainees of both sexes. Nevertheless, as they watched a sergeant demonstrate the machine gun, many grimaced and put their fingers in their ears, flinching at the overwhelming noise. They worked in pairs, most of the firers so nervous that they jammed the weapons by loosening their grip on the trigger too soon. Their assistants, surrounded by the deafening, terrifying thunder of fire, the smell of cordite and the smoking barrels, flung themselves into a fetal position on the ground, stuffed their fingers into their ears, closed their eyes, and waited grimly till it was over. They hated it, and said so. I wondered what the Joint Chiefs of Staff would have made of it.

The gas-chamber exercise took place on a sweltering

afternoon. By mid-May the afternoon temperatures were routinely in the high eighties and nineties. The trainees sat in bleachers under the trees, with the smell of honeysuckle and pine, a red dirt road winding by, saplings, butterflies, swamp, and the sound of rifle fire in the distance. Dressed up in the Chemical Protective Overgarment, a huge padded baggy green suit containing a charcoal filter, the trainees looked like very hot, very young astronauts. The lecturer explaining the uses of the protective mask and the procedures to follow in a polluted environment talked on as the young soldiers, flushed, drowsy, fought off their apprehensions, which mingled uneasily with the desire to sleep, a desire that they had to fight off too, for the drills picked them off, one by one, as their eyes closed.

The instructor put his speech into higher gear. "Check out your mask," he said. "Here in Alabama they have a lot of bugs and snakes and maggots that like to live in masks. They screw their way up your nose and into your brain. And then you die." This was like school and the one about the girl with the beehive hairdo. They perked up, just as they had in First Aid class when an instructor said, "When using mouth-to-mouth resuscitation techniques on a baby, do not blow too hard. It will, literally, explode."

The company stood at attention on a dusty beige square of ground, out of the shade. In their gigantic suits, they were loaded with rifles, web gear, and the bag containing the mask and other equipment. Then the order was given: "Females, let down your hair." A young woman in A-3 had a great fall of blond hair that cascaded and rippled halfway down her back, over the uniform. The menace evaporated; everywhere there were Rapunzels. Many trainees looked helpless because they had to take off their spectacles, so they were fumbling gingerly around like moles. As they practiced masking, they propped their helmets on the ends of their rifles. Most dropped the helmet or the rifle or both. The male drill sergeants, very gently forcing the masks on over the females' hair, had an almost clinical delicacy.

Masked up, they stood in line, waiting outside a small hut.

People attempted to smile reassuringly at each other with their eyes. The hut was small, wooden and low-ceilinged, with stone chips on the floor; only dim light filtered through the small windows. In the middle of the gloomy little room stood a brazier and beside it a man dressed in a suit and mask like theirs. As the trainees shuffled into the room and took their places around the edges, their boots grinding on the chips, he talked in an eerie, booming, and indistinct voice, less distinct than the sound of their breathing. It was claustrophobic—like being under water. The man at the brazier reminded them that the package he had emptied onto the coals had been burning for a few minutes, and that the small plume of gray smoke drifting up from it was lethal. He said in his otherworldly, booming voice, "So this means that if your equipment had not been working properly, you would be dead by now."

Lynne Hunt bolted out of the back door and had to be brought back. The trainees were told to walk around the room, and then each trainee, on reaching the sergeant at the door, was to take off the mask and recite name, rank, and serial number before being allowed out the door. "Take off your masks," said the sergeant. In a nervous reflex, as soon as they took off their masks, one by one, they inhaled deeply before speaking. Bent double and choking, they were kept there until they had forced out the required words. Then, whirling and beating the air, they were passed expertly by the drill sergeants from hand to hand, and they lurched through two sets of doors and out into the fresh air again.

A couple of them slapped into a tree, like cartoon characters. The members of the cadre outside stood grinning and pointing at the spectacle, while bleary trainees staggered the obligatory two circuits of a dirt track in clouds of fumes to get the worst off their clothing. "DON'T RUB YOUR EYES!" Sergeant Bell shouted, one of the rare occasions on which she raised her voice. People began surreptitiously breaking into sheepish, proud smiles.

The mood at evening chow was benign. People were accustomed to the stench from the latrines now, the endless flies circling around the dumpster. They had sensed and adopted the relaxed mood of the cadre, several of whom had confided to me that bivouac was their favorite part of training because most of the pressure was off, and out here, with no floors to wax, no humid classroom to doze in, they had a chance to be truly helpful and friendly toward the young trainees, tell them war stories and cadre jokes, watch them flirt and sneak up on them at night.

The night war game had once been a major event. Lieutenant Myers must have told me at least three times, her voice heavy with nostalgia, about the old WAC days when she and her trusted Sergeant Cooper, who was a little like Myers' younger sister—tomboyish, sharp, and fiercely military—used to have elaborate plans for bivouac and especially for the night war games. She said, wistfully sighing, "I guess we should've known cherry bombs weren't allowed. We did have to drive across the state line to get them."

After evening chow Lieutenant Myers briefed the company on what to expect in the war game. The premise: twelve infiltrators, led by Sergeant Stokes, were out to storm the camp and take the commander prisoner. Lieutenant Myers looked around at the trainees. She said, slowly, for effect, "They let me be captured one time. *[Pause]* You're probably wondering what happened to them. Well, I assigned them to First Battalion." There was easy laughter in the stands. Sergeant Bell, standing next to me, whispered, "I see she has her confidence stick." Lieutenant Myers was holding a carved stick, one of the precious few whittled as favors by Sergeant Stokes, and as she talked and gestured, she tapped at her extended right leg with it.

Watching the drills and trainees as they listened closely, I realized how ordinary it had come to seem to have women in the top positions. This was not simply because there were (relatively) so many women with power at Fort McClellan.

The cool, assured model of authority presented by Lieutenant Myers and her senior female sergeants was instinctive, not chosen, but it could not have been better chosen—so unobtrusive, so sensible a model that the male NCOs fitted into it without loss of pride. Against it their burly joviality looked reassuring. The men sometimes grumbled, just as males all over the post continually grumbled about General Clarke, or the men in the battalion grumbled about Colonel Allen, but it was standard Army griping and differed very little from the complaints made by the women.

Most of the sergeants were military policemen, who were not products of the old, harsh style of the Army. Some told me with obvious sincerity that, yes, they would follow Lieutenant Myers into combat if that was required. They were undeniably tickled to be working with a small, attractive woman who was competent.

The most obvious resentment was expressed by Captain Dixon, who worked at Battalion HQ. He was a graduate of Virginia Military Institute, who loved to quote Kipling and dreamed of going off to fight in the Rhodesian war, an impatient, highly strung young man with a smooth, freckled face that flushed easily. He had wanted the company commander's job and was reportedly furious that Lieutenant Myers, who was younger, smaller, a reservist, and only a first lieutenant and a female, had snapped the job up from under his nose. I saw him suffer the further humiliation of being shown up by a female NCO.

On the morning of the march to bivouac a young male trainee had lost his nerve. Lieutenant Myers had warned me of this, saying, "Basic sends a number of people over the edge. They start talking to themselves, swallowing a bottle of vinegar, compulsively looking for things in corners. There was one of mine I went to visit in the hospital, and she was sitting upright in her bed cramming palmfuls of food into her mouth, with her eyes staring straight ahead."

Private Osborne, a somber young man who wanted to leave the Army and had threatened suicide, had climbed the tall smokestack by the kitchens, and clung to the rung of a metal ladder about forty feet from the ground. He was preparing to jump, saying in lugubrious tones, "It's the only way out." He looked as if he would do it. Captain Dixon strode by and glanced at me angrily. "What page will this be

on?" Then he decided to use his authority and end this
fiasco. "Get your ass down here, trainee," he snapped,
looking irritably up at the doleful private. Osborne shifted,
muttered something unintelligible, and prepared to loosen
his grip and drop. Sergeant Bell, who had deferred to the
captain's rank and stood silently at one side, quickly moved
forward and said in a firm, low tone, "I don't think you
should talk to him like that, sir." She moved to the base of
the smokestack and, looking up, began to address the trainee
in a soft, calm, decisive voice. She told him that nobody had
hurt him yet, and nobody would hurt him if he came down,
but that he did have to come down, because until he did
nothing could be resolved. "So please, Private Osborne,
come down, and we'll talk things over and see what we can
do." Osborne considered, then began his slow descent. (He
was subsequently discharged.)

With the briefing over, the company dispersed into the
darkness, some to form a reconnaissance team, most to move
into a double row of defenses ringing the top of the hill,
facing downward and out, there to wait nervously until a
crackling of twigs or a surprise bang or flash quickened the
heart and announced the enemy. Lieutenant Myers moved
to one side with a small, dark female trainee, slightly toothy,
very curvy, and began to coach her in a couple of recogniz-
able Lieutenant Myers positions, most particularly the extended leg with hand on hip. They changed clothes, and
Lieutenant Myers explained quietly, "Now I shall spend the
duration of this game up a tree, without moving, and nobody
will find me." With that she slipped from the dim light cast
by the storm lantern and was not seen again.

Night settled in. I was taken on a tour of the defenses by
two drill sergeants. We crept in and out of the moonlight,
coming up behind people, who would gulp, recover, and
stammer urgently, "Halt, who goes there?" or, losing their
wits entirely, "Er, is that you?" Someone attempted to storm
the front gate in a truck, with headlights blazing, and he was
stopped once, twice, as the defenders peered into the

darkness, aware that this might be a diversionary tactic.

The actual assault was long in coming—at least forty-five minutes—which showed admirable control on both sides and kept the tension high. Most of the infiltrators were attractive women. The peculiar relish of the men who captured them, one after another, was partly, I am sure, related to their sexual attractiveness, and it reminded me of fears men in power express on the subject of women in combat—namely, that when captured, they will be singled out for rape and sexual torture. One of the captured women at one point had her legs raised and held against a tree by a drill sergeant, who was half-jokingly menacing her with lurid, nonspecific threats. She joked nervously and stoutly refused to divulge her secrets. There was enough anxiety, enough hint of a sadistic impulse, to remind me that this game would never be played in such a way that it would truly resemble war. The young males persistently behaved like teenagers, preoccupied with "searching" the female prisoners. The females responded with shrill, overexcited demands for another female to be present. They knew their rights.

The West Point lieutenant was taken; he came in struggling and yelling about fascists. When Sergeant Stokes was captured, he fought and screamed and yelled rape as his female captors attempted to keep him secure by taking off his trousers. The rest of the operation was mopping up. In the woods, just away from the clearing and the bleachers, I overheard the men arguing. "I killed you and you wouldn't die." "But I saw you first—and I threw a grenade at you." "You did not—I shot you from behind, and you were dead, you know you were." Lieutenant Myers appeared, neat and composed, down from the branch where, just a foot or so above the heads of her would-be captors, she had spent the entire exercise. She said that the attack had been swift and convincing, that the defenders did well.

Late the next day, out on another range, as the heat faded, Sergeant Butler addressed the grimy, sunburned trainees through a microphone. A small wiry man, not afraid to be sentimental, he read with high emotion his poem called

"Private Littlebit." First he made a short speech about the strengths of the Army: "It's the fellows in the Army that make it great," he said, adding gingerly, "and the *ladies*." One of the black women from Newark shook her head, smiled, and said, "Yaay!" Then he talked about patriotism: "Maybe there's some respect left for Old Glory. Maybe some people still feel our country's worth fighting for. If you think so, next time you see that old flag out there flying, don't run behind a tree or behind the house. Get out there and salute it!" The Californian groaned "Oh, no" at the mention of Old Glory; everyone else stood and clapped and cheered, truly softened up for this moment by Private Littlebit. A couple of final lines from the long poem: "But when my time comes and the candle for me is lit/I hope to see an American fighting man and I will even salute Private Littlebit." Lieutenant Myers said to me, "He's famous for this. I made sure he was going to do it today." Elizabeth said later, *"Sure* I cried."

When the troops returned to the bivouac site, in an excited and boisterous mood, they were given a fifteen-minute break. Some of them began to shout as they ran down the hill to their tents, and in moments this had turned into a spontaneous eruption of noise, screaming, singing, yelling, hooting. The noise built to a crescendo and held there for five, seven, ten minutes. Some of the women made an informal kickline in front of a shrubbery-adorned tent and started prancing as they sang "Country Roads." The men across the abyss seemed to feel left out, looking over shyly as the women's raucousness continued. In competition, they struck up with marching songs. And then, when they ran out of words, they hit upon animal noises, settling into actual howling and barking. It was an extraordinary combination of sounds; tension and hysteria were there, but swamped by an incoherent, complicated exhilaration they had not anticipated and did not understand. After mail call they settled down on tarpaulins to clean their weapons. Julie Drake's mother had sent at her request a synopsis of what had been happening on *General Hospital* over the last few weeks. Once Julie was known to possess this information, a cry went up across the bivouac site, "Whatever happened to Bobbie Spencer?" As Julie read the news from her letter, even Lynne Hunt's face lightened. She stopped polishing to listen, and said gruffly, "That Heather deserves everything she's got coming to her."

When chow formation was called, the trainees, as a special concession, were allowed to leave their helmets behind. They screeched in delight. After formation, as Sergeant Stokes sauntered toward his car, Baird called after him, "Toodles," and Stokes, turning around, said, "That's 'toodles, Drill Sergeant,'" and waved goodbye.

6

Marching as to War: Early American Partisans and Patriots

Out at Range 17 I had spent a long time talking with the sergeant who had told me about the achievements of the Wacs. He had drawn me aside, and, sitting on a rickety platform, drawing patterns in the earth with a stick, he said, "Finally in this society we're getting away from the old adage that women are mental cases. Look at the stock-market crash, when all those men *jumped out of windows*." He continued, ignoring the amused stares of his colleagues, who seemed to have heard his views before, "See that little girl up there who was crying?" and he pointed to one of the crips sitting disconsolate in her tennis shoes. "She's crying because her foot is hurt and the doctors haven't helped. But it's rage. A male in the same position would be swearing. It's just a difference in style."

Sergeant Rickey paused, stared at me, and said, "If you have the time, I'd like to tell you a few things. There's a whole lot written these days about women in combat, and most of it's junk, because the media always go looking for the male chauvinist—and there are a lot of them. But some think, like me, that women belong everywhere except in the

infantry." Rickey talked for close to an hour, sitting in the
noon sun as the trainees trooped sweatily past us from one
station to another, grinning as they came abreast. He told me
about his sister, a sheriff in Texas, and reminisced about the
old days at Fort McClellan when he was working as a rifle
instructor. "That was when it was voluntary, but I rarely ran
into a female who didn't want to take it. As a group they
were inquisitive, willing, adventurous. I really enjoyed it,
having people so involved and interested in what I was
teaching." Rickey finished reflectively, "Today's women
won't find anything that hard to adjust to in the military.
These women are not tied to their mothers' apron strings.
It's the males—you're talking about reconditioning the
human male to accept a woman as a wife and mother and at
the same time as a fighting partner."

Later I learned that male reluctance to accept women as
soldiers is not new in this country, particularly in this
century, when there has been no threat of invasion to
weaken the power of old prejudices. Just as marked as the
prejudice has been the determination of American women to
participate in the defense of their country and their homes.
In the Revolutionary War women were organized into a
branch of the Continental Army, where they labored in their
traditional support role, their function a logistical one—to
cook and sew and bandage, to bury the dead and repair
weapons, to nurse and help with the baggage train. When
Loyalist or British troops approached their homes, women,
along with anyone else who was there, picked up weapons
and shot them. They worked as spies and harbored fugitives.
In this they followed in the robust tradition of their pioneer
predecessors, who, in the thousands, took up arms to defend
their families in the new country. Nobody thought them
strange for doing so, just as nobody thought them strange for
plowing or drawing water from a well, or tramping through a
blizzard for supplies, or bearing six children and running a
farm.

A number of women served as soldiers, integrated with

males. Margaret Corbin helped her husband at the cannon until he was killed and then took over until she too was felled. She was an invalid for life, and received a disability payment in the form of one outfit of clothing per annum and a monthly liquor ration from the commissary at West Point, where she had been stationed. She is buried in the West Point cemetery.

Mary Hays, otherwise known as Molly Pitcher, also entered the war with her husband. He served for seven years, with his wife at his side, helping with the cannon, or elsewhere with the wounded. On June 28, 1778, wrote one Private Joseph Martin, who was watching, "a cannon shot from the enemy passed directly between her legs without doing any other damage than carrying away all the lower part of her petticoat. Looking at it with apparent unconcern, she observed that it was lucky it did not pass a little higher . . ." and continued to fight, taking her husband's place when he was wounded. She too received a government pension. General Washington was said to feel that the presence of women like her was a nuisance, and unmilitary, but he had to put up with them, fearing that if they were not there the men would desert.

Deborah Sampson Gannett of Massachusetts was the most interesting of all, a Boston girl who had never been demure. She worked on a farm and learned carpentry, and got herself an education while bound out as a servant to a deacon and his family. By the age of twenty she was a free and adventurous woman who used to dress up in men's clothes, bind her breasts, and tie her hair back in order to wander freely in strange towns and rowdy taverns. Dressed in this way, she tried to enlist but was identified. Her second attempt was more successful, and, under the name of Robert Shurtleff, she served as a private for three years in the 4th Massachusetts Regiment. As a beardless, pretty soldier she attracted the attentions of some persistent young women, but she managed to wash and change clothes and endure the marches and campaigns without being unmasked. She was wounded, and wrote in a memoir, "I considered this as a death wound, or as being equivalent to it; as it must, I thought, lead to the discovery of my sex." Covered in blood, she nonetheless managed to fend off all doctors' inquiries, and, once her head had been bandaged, withdrew with some instruments "procured" at the hospital and removed a ball from her thigh, at the third attempt. She returned to a battle in a blizzard, and even took a prisoner. By now it was winter and, weakened by her wound, she succumbed to a severe fever and was taken to the hospital, so debilitated that this time she could not prevent discovery. The good doctor who had discovered her sex nevertheless took her in and kept her secret so that she could rejoin a regiment, this time the 11th Massachusetts, on a land surveyance expedition that tackled the Allegheny Mountains in a train of Conestoga wagons.

Dr. Linda DePauw, Professor of American History at Georgetown University, speaking at a Library of Congress seminar in November 1979, said, "It is important to realize that these women soldiers were not a bunch of eccentrics. These were the sort of good, solid, patriotic American females from whom the members of the DAR are proud to claim descent."

At the end of the war Deborah Sampson Gannett made her identity public, received an honorable discharge, and became something of a celebrity, even though she had a struggle to get the back pay owed her. Financial need and what Elizabeth Evans, one of her biographers, calls "a desire to justify her enlistment" led her to the speaking circuit. Her standard address was rousing and rhetorical. She insisted that she had felt the need to know why a man "should forgo every trait of humanity and assume the character of a brute"—and she had found the reason: that the war was just and defensive. So it was that she "threw off the soft habiliment of my sex, and assumed those of the warrior . . . swerved from the accustomed flowery path of female delicacy to walk upon the heroic precipice of feminine perdition."

She strode the precipice until 1827, when, at the age of

sixty-seven, she died, in part from the effects of her wounds. (She still bore a musket ball in her body.) After she died her husband petitioned for relief for himself and his children, aid normally available only to "widows and orphans"—and it finally came through, eleven months after he died. The *Congressional Report* stated: "The whole history of the American Revolution records no case like this, and furnishes no other similar example of female heroism, fidelity, and courage." That was not, however, because other such women did not exist. They did.

A handful of women were known to be involved in the War of 1812 and the Mexican War, and there are probably many more who remain anonymous. We know the names of some who served in the Civil War: Sarah Taylor and Mary Ellen Wise and Anne Lillybridge and "La Belle" Morgan and Mary Hancock and the notable adventurer Loreta Velasquez, who wrote a lengthy and overvivid narrative of her exploits, called (in part): *The Woman in Battle; A Narrative of the Exploits, Adventures, and Travels of Madame Loreta Janeta Velasquez otherwise known as Lieutenant Harry T. Buford, Confederate States Army in which is given Full Descriptions of the numerous Battles in which she participated as a Confederate Officer; of her Perilous Performances as a Spy, as a Bearer of Despatches . . .* She was one of those, like Deborah Sampson, who used to dress in men's clothes for a little spicy living, but she was probably unique in writing, "I was perfectly wild on the subject of war . . ." and a perfect example of that kind of buccaneering woman who models herself on a swashbuckling male stereotype.

The bulk of the women in the American Civil War performed more traditional chores. As warfare became more specialized, many of these "women's chores" were taken over by men, but in World War I, for the first time in this country, the idea of women's support services as a part of the uniformed military, or as auxiliary, began to develop.

The women were doing the same work as before, but the lines had begun to diverge into nursing (the Nursing Corps had been officially instituted in 1901) and the support services: 12,500 Yeomanettes, properly known as Yeomen (F), joined the Navy, and the Marine Corps took on 300 Marinettes. The great majority served at home, but a few nurses were found in hospital units in France. By this time the Army and Navy had a total of 23,400 nurses serving everywhere, under battle conditions and with extreme heroism.

One hundred and thirty French-speaking civilian telephone operators requested by General Pershing served at the front lines in France as auxiliaries. Eighteen of them are still alive, including Miss Esther Goodall, who is eighty-three years old and lives in Yonkers, New York, in a big stone house on a hill, the house built by her French parents, her father a music publisher, her mother a corsetiere to the wealthy. The house is piled with old copies of *Vogue,* ancient photographs, paintings attacked by creeping fungus stacked against the walls. Lying rakishly on top of a bookcase is Miss Goodall's tin helmet.

She is tiny, no more than five feet, with a narrow, intelligent face, a roguish expression, and large glasses. The first time I met her, on November 15, 1979, she was sitting on a sofa in the officers club at Fort Hamilton, Brooklyn, where she was to be presented with her honorable discharge from the service, sixty years late. The TV and press people were there, and Miss Goodall (her husband's surname) alternated between flirting in French with the commander and his aides and seizing me by the sleeve and muttering fiercely, "I talk too much, don't I? Do I?" For years the survivors had lobbied for their benefits. They had served under contract to the U.S. Army because the law at that time did not permit them to have the status in the Army that they had in the Navy and the Marines. They worked under hazardous conditions, risking their lives daily without any of the protection of medical aid, housing, and all the other benefits the males had. Congress said on this matter: "The enlistment of women in the military forces of the United

States has never been seriously contemplated and such enlistment is considered unwise and highly undesirable." Miss Goodall, looking pensively out into the blinding white lights and the TV cameras, said, "I feel, better late than never. I always recognized *myself*, after all—and I don't want to feel that this official recognition puts me beyond the pale. . . . You see what I mean?"

The next time, we met at her solid, cool house in Yonkers at the height of summer, the trees pressed against the windows cooling the house with their shade. Sitting on the porch in broad-brimmed hat and spectacles and a smart tan pantsuit, she said, "How it started was that my mother saw the advertisement in the New York paper, and she said to me, 'I see something here and I'm going to show it to you and I'll be sorry I did!'" Indeed, Esther Fresnel, twenty-one years old, was only too happy to go to France and have adventures instead of fitting ladies from some of the best families in Delaware.

In a picture of the first six young women to go from the New York area she stands in the front row, with her arms combatively crossed, staring straight at the camera, clearly thrilled with her uniform, the visible parts being a long navy-blue coat, high laced boots, and a natty aviation cap, in Esther's case worn a little to the side and back. On the left side of each cap is a small badge of crossed flags, the insignia of the Signal Corps. The women look very dashing. In *The Telephone Review* for March 1918: "Imagine with what expectancy they are awaiting their first call."

Miss Goodall is hazy on the early days of training, part of which took place in Grand Central Station. They had a salary of $60 a month (more for the supervisors) and a variety of allowances, for travel, lodging, being overseas, and other expenses. They went over on a troopship.

Miss Goodall was one of the very few women who began service at headquarters at Chaumont and then went on to Saint-Mihiel, "where the real battle took place." Working at headquarters was not exciting. She wrote home to her parents: "I lead a pretty normal existence—if it weren't for the innumerable uniforms . . . and the aeroplanes. Why, one wouldn't imagine any struggle was going on at all . . . we don't hear any cannon nor do shells occasionally disturb the general peace and quiet that prevails."

Behind the poetic diction was a pioneer. In another letter, of August 1918, she wrote, "Sue and I had the great fortune to be attached to the Headquarters of the First Army." Sue was another New Yorker and a flirt. They were thrilled to be in a wooden barracks with candles instead of electric light and no running water. Instead of dancing in white gloves in the evenings, they went to bed on flea-ridden pallets to keep warm. There was mud everywhere and constant rain. They had meals with the men of the Signal Corps, sitting at trestles and eating off tin plates. The improvised toilets, consisting of a big table with holes in it, a seat on top of the table and a big barrel under it, caused them some distress, but they kept quiet. Miss Goodall said grimly, "It was better than the hole in the ground they had us using somewhere else."

The women were at Saint-Mihiel, where one of the major pushes of the war took place. Just before the attack the Signal Corps had laid five thousand miles of wire and installed six thousand telephones. Ten thousand men were operating the system, right in the middle of the battlefield. Six young women, one of them Miss Goodall, worked at a switchboard, sitting on high chairs in their "extra-high tan walking shoes" and navy-blue worsted uniforms. In the week preceding the battle they worked six-hour shifts day and night, with only as much rest as they allowed themselves. The work was exhausting mentally as well as physically because of the concentration and ingenuity required when lines just opened would be bombed out of action. Miss Goodall said, "Men would ask for places we had never heard of, and they wanted them immediately. Sometimes it would take us over an hour to complete one call." There was constant noise from shelling and bombs. Miss Goodall said, almost wistfully, "The sky was black with planes." I asked if she had feared that she might collapse, since when the Drive was on they worked at the switchboard for seventy-two hours without stopping, and she said, "Good Lord, no! Morale was always so good. We were excited to be there with the boys."

She pulled out back issues of *The Telephone Review* and thrust them into my hands. There was a picture of her sitting at the switchboard with mask and helmet slung over the back of her chair, an expression of intense absorption on her face. She said, "A few of them got pregnant—so many love affairs you see—and I was told that the one who committed suicide was pregnant. But I was tough—I didn't get sick and I didn't fall in love and I didn't cry. Oh, one time I didn't go to dinner because I had a bad cold."

After Saint-Mihiel, the six and one other were moved with the First Army to take part in the Argonne Drive. They were quartered in an old French camp, with the glare of shelling all around and the ground shaking from the guns. This time they had to wear their helmets, because bombs and shrapnel were dropping around them. There was no rest as the American forces pushed on. A fire consumed eight barracks, and the young women worked steadily on as the news came through that the Germans were weakening, that Austria had fallen, and finally that Germany had surrendered.

Miss Goodall showed me a letter she had written home explaining her attitude toward work in terms that will occasion a nod or sigh in today's Army women. "You see," the letter said, "the men do not want to be bothered by any girls up here, and quite a few honestly think that girls are a bother if not kept in what they believe to be their proper environment, where everything is convenient and at hand. So it's up to us," she continued gravely, "to prove to these people that we're not just ornaments." This attitude did not stop them from running around on jaunts with a box of candy and a bunch of flowers in their helmets. I asked Miss Goodall if she felt they had been defeminized. She looked at me vaguely, hesitated, and said, "I think the boys loved having us there. D'you know, I really felt it was my mission to talk on the telephone. When I was off duty I sometimes spent the whole night talking on the phone to the boys at the front. I kept thinking it might be their last night."

Miss Goodall said, sitting on the porch with her memorabilia all around her, "I belong to the Veterans of Foreign Wars, but I only go there so that I can get out and be with people. The old men love to talk about war, but I don't—it was something I did a long time ago, and any man who has really been through it doesn't like to glorify it."

7

"A Debt to Democracy, a Date with Destiny": The Women's Army Corps, 1942–1945

By the end of World War I, military planners had realized that American women would in due course have to be used in war, as some European women were. Tentative plans were made. As World War II approached, militant volunteer women alarmed the War Department by drilling in bloomers and demanding to be sent overseas. Prominent people lined up on their side, including Mrs. Eleanor Roosevelt.

Members of Congress had predictable views, ranging from "Take the women into the armed service, who then will do the cooking, the washing, the mending, the humble, homey tasks to which every woman has devoted herself?" to "Think of the humiliation! What has become of the manhood of America!" Pearl Harbor speeded up the plans for an elite corps of 10,600 auxiliaries and 340 officers in the first year, women with skills who would replace male soldiers. General Marshall, the Chief of Staff and a loyal advocate of the women, insisted: "I want a women's corps right away, and I don't want any excuses!" The first WAC training center was chosen—Fort Des Moines, Iowa, an old cavalry post that could handle a population of 5000.

This account of the early and wartime days of the Women's Auxiliary Army Corps and its successor, the Women's Army Corps, is based on the official history by Mattie Treadwell, an engrossing 800-page work that only in its definitive nature corresponds to the general idea of an official history. Anyone who studies today's military women must refer to it, and anyone interested in the arrival of females into a previously closed male world will find it illuminating. A few men in the Army recommended the book to me, saying conspiratorially, "It's all happened before. You can read about it in there." Women who have read it feel in some sense vindicated because others before them had the same, or worse, problems.

Mrs. Oveta Culp Hobby had been appointed the director. She and a tiny staff had to create this mysteriously auxiliary body out of thin air. The Navy had managed to get a bill passed to include Waves in the Navy. However, Congress refused to give the women anything other than "auxiliary" status—something nobody understood and the source of major difficulty in the months to come. Mrs. Hobby and her staff were faced with problems of allocation and budgets and housing and duties and regulations and schedules and uniforms, all to be solved without the benefit of any precedent. Some units succumbed to panic about the impending Waacs, and when Mrs. Hobby's people arrived for an initial briefing, they found their hosts "in a state of virtual siege, throwing up barbed-wire entanglements around WAAC areas," says Ms. Treadwell. (Unless specified, the quotations in this chapter are from her text.) The press, meanwhile, was in its element, the thrust of many of its questions at the first press conference mostly in the direction of nail polish, dating, underwear. Mrs. Hobby had the only WAAC shirt in the world. She had to take an electric fan and an electric iron on her travels so that she could wash it every night.

Predictably enough, at the start the public was battering down the barbed wire to get in. In New York City, when potential officer candidates were called, "1,400 women stormed the Whitehall Street office on the first day and stood in line from 8:30 to 5:00 o'clock. In five days, over 5,200 had received application blanks in New York City alone, although only thirty women could be picked from the whole of New York State, New Jersey, and Delaware." The first officer candidates were selected through a long and careful screening process, which had got off to a slightly patchy start when, at some stations that were using the male questions, bewildered applicants were required to answer technical questions about baseball.

Training of the Waacs was designed to be rigorously military, based on the assumption that, as the colonel commanding the center said, "A considerable percentage of the Army was either opposed to the WAAC idea or very doubtful of its potential success. The best way to combat this attitude was to train the new soldiers in those qualities which the Army values most highly: neatness in dress, punctiliousness in military courtesy, smartness and precision in drill and ceremonies, and willingness and ability to do the job."

The planners decided to increase the number of women from 12,000 to at least 63,000 by April 1944. Mrs. Hobby addressed the first officers-to-be at Fort Des Moines: "You have just made the change from peacetime pursuits to wartime tasks—from the individualism of civilian life to the anonymity of mass military life. You have given up comfortable homes, highly paid positions, leisure. You have taken off silk and put on khaki. And all for essentially the same reason—you have a debt and a date. A debt to democracy, a date with destiny."

The Corps had a predictably bumpy start, in part because there never had been women in or attached to the United States Army before and also because the long-term plans for expansion collided with the immediate need for supplies, uniforms, and training centers, creating major shortages and contradictory schedules and requisitions. There was a major uniform crisis that would have resulted in women drilling in the snow in their short-sleeved seersucker exercise dresses and little else, had they not been issued men's coats, which, draped over hands and feet, eliminated the need for gloves or boots.

By the winter of 1942, 406 MOS's had been deemed suitable for women, and 222 unsuitable, the latter category including all supervisory jobs, and all jobs that would bring them to Washington, simply because General Somervell, commander of the supply services, did not want them there, and engineered an appropriate policy. We know this because he announced it off the record at a staff meeting and one of his staff accidentally recorded: "That policy he particularly does not want committed to writing, because the minute that anybody gets a hold of it & puts it in the paper, there will be a mess . . . he does not want any of them here, except in the office of the HQ of the WAAC and certain ones in G-2, whom for some reason they prevailed upon him to have. Do you get it?"

Meanwhile 4000 women were going through Fort Des Moines every month, and in the spring of 1943 three fresh training centers opened up, to make a total of five. Eighteen WAAC officers had arrived at Headquarters, so impeccable and military that they unnerved everyone until they relaxed a little. Morale among trainees and officers at the centers was high. They loved the field training, the marching and drilling, and they would practice enthusiastically in their spare time. Most were very able, with specific skills, and they could not wait to get out into jobs.

At first the women went primarily to aircraft warning service posts, then out into the service companies; and wherever they served, the demand went up for more. The War Department in the spring of 1943 set a new goal of 150,000 troops by June, or 5800 a month. In July the WAC bill was signed, changing the Women's Army Auxiliary Corps to the Women's Army Corps, a change that, though desired by everyone, plunged the administration into chaos. Who was to be responsible for the welfare of the women now that they were part of the Army? Should a woman be treated exactly the same as a man?

The most enthusiastic women were those who went overseas. The start had been inauspicious. In response to an urgent request from the European theater, five WAAC officers were flown to England in December 1943 to be executive secretaries. The theater put them straight onto a ship to North Africa. The ship was sunk; the five Waacs were rescued, and arrived seasick and filthy. At the Daytona Beach training center the two units chosen for Europe had been enduring a long and nerve-racking wait, because information about their delay was classified and so withheld. Mrs. Hobby flew down there as soon as she heard about the accident, to warn them of the risks involved.

In an untidy box in the storage room of the WAC Museum at Fort McClellan I found a letter written by one of the women at Daytona Beach. She wrote of 300 women listening as Colonel Hobby explained that their shipment was to be either canceled or else diverted to "an unnamed but dangerous combat theater." "She said," the correspondent wrote, "it would have to be on a voluntary basis . . . she said it was time for us to go to lunch and for us to think about the decision while we ate . . . we didn't go to dinner, we all got in line to sign up. The whole battalion, one behind the other . "*. .* our dinner was held over for us until we were through. The officers were walking around with tears running down their cheeks, especially Colonel Hobby." Out of 300 women, 298 volunteered; half were chosen, and for some, the worst hardship they faced was not overseas but at Camp Kilmer, New Jersey, the next staging post, where they drilled in the winter weather, outdoors, in short-sleeved uniforms. All became ill. One young woman was left behind with pneumonia.

North Africa pioneered the use of Waacs overseas, but the largest number served in the European theater, about 8000, or 8 percent of the WAC. The second largest total was in the Southwest Pacific, about 5500, and they did not arrive until mid-1944. Others served in Southeast Asia, in the China-Burma-India theater, in the Middle East, in Alaska and Hawaii, Canada, and Puerto Rico. The Army Air Force was their biggest employer, with a total of 40,000 women. This branch was the first to use and integrate them fully, to require WAC inspectors at all levels where Wacs were used, to request WAC officers in "operational" jobs—that is, those that were not primarily concerned with the women—to admit enlisted women to the men's noncombat schools and propose the same for officers, to make sure that information concerning WAC status and jobs was kept up to date in the field, and so on.

Only about 50 percent of the Army Air Force Wacs were working in thl conventional clerical/administrative jobs. The others worked in unconventional jobs, such as ferry pilot, flying radio operator, flight clerk, and photographer. They were weather observers and forecasters, electrical specialists, sheet metal workers, Link trainer instructors, cryptographers, teletype operators, radio mechanics, control tower specialists, parachute riggers, bombsight maintenance specialists, airplane mechanics, interpreters, chaplains' assistants, radar operators, armament specialists, carpenters, librarians, dietitians, occupational therapists, reporters, editors and historians, topographers, cartographers, sanitary inspectors, geodetic computers, chemists, technical-manual illustrators, and classification specialists. There was one dog trainer.

By D day the women had become indispensable as typists and stenographers, freeing the males for combat. The stations in this country grumbled about having to recruit men to release their Wacs for combat. The European theater replied that one WAC typist could replace two men, while eating only half as much. Although the Corps was firmly established, its problems did not disappear but developed into the problems of integration. The Army, then as now, was highly traditional and run by men, most of whom did not want women in the armed forces; and their attitude profoundly affected the women's work and their morale.

The women's success had been spectacular, characterized by three of the most valuable traits a group of soldiers could possess—efficiency, endurance, and esprit. There were certain tasks at which they excelled. A report from the Army ground forces states: "They are superior to men in all functions involving delicacy or manual dexterity, such as operation at the director, height finder, radar, and searchlight control systems. They perform routine repetitious tasks in a manner superior to men," said the report, revealing the women's eagerness to please, to work well.

Overseas the women had their chance to excel, partly because that was where they faced the most male resistance. They were a handpicked elite, the cream of the Corps, and were used only in the jobs for which they were highly skilled—mainly typing, stenography, and telephone work. For most of the men, going overseas was expected, it was inevitable, and it was one step, a large step, closer to combat. For the women, however, it was partly an adventure, since there was no question of closeness to combat, and partly a reward, since only the most excellent women were chosen.

One unit of sixty women was singled out for an experiment in integration in the field. Throughout the Italian campaign they followed the men closely, only twenty to thirty-five miles from the front, living in exactly the same kinds of quarters as the men (whatever was available), taking with them only what they could carry, wearing men's clothing and what came to be their most prized possession, the green scarf of the Fifth Army. The WAC staff director said of these women, "They were Fifth Army first and Wacs second— perhaps the best-integrated unit in the theater."

Male fears about women in the field proved unfounded. They needed no extra guards, the lack of privacy did not send them into a decline, and they remained phenomenally cheerful. It was not easy for them. The heavy artillery could always be heard, they were constantly on the move, and their hours at the switchboard were long and dreary; but they hardly ever complained, because they were secure in the value of their work. General Clark, who commanded the theater, recognized the importance of honors and apprecia- tion to soldiers, and he made a point of awarding Wacs the medals they deserved and including them in parades. As a result the women did not seem to need the things that became so important under other circumstances—grades and ratings, civilized hours, privacy, decent clothing.

Elsewhere the pattern was similar. North Africa Wacs overworked to the point where they had to be sent home at night. General Eisenhower said that many had taken over the tasks of two men, and that their "smartness, neatness, and esprit" were exemplary. The women who landed in Normandy on July 14, 1944, slept in tents in an orchard, washed in cold water, ate C rations, scrounged for clothes against the cold; and the men, far from being deeply worried about their welfare, loved it. The first Wacs in Paris followed right behind the fighting forces, and, despite the absence of heat and hot water and the damp, permanent cold that left them with chilblains, the sick rate was their lowest of the year. The statistics were impressive. After they had become acclimatized, the women's attrition levels, psychological and medical, were the same as those of the men, or lower. And, unlike the men, they did not tend to get drunk, go AWOL, or violate the Articles of War. As the Air Forces said, they had proved to be less of a problem than anticipated. "It was found that Wacs could live under conditions substantially the same as those of male personnel." Not only had they been entirely worthy of any extra time and effort that their presence had required, but "perhaps the greatest achievement of the Wacs was their triumph over the male military mind." To the credit of the male military mind, it must be said that in Europe and North Africa the male commanders were usually welcoming and generous in their desire to adapt to the women where necessary.

In the Southwest Pacific it was possible to see the extent of female endurance, and also how wrongly deployed the women could be. Wacs served in New Guinea and the Philippines, where conditions were cruel, with humidity, mud, malaria, rudimentary facilities, and continual torrents of rain that flooded buildings, soaked clothing, and turned the enclosures into bogs. Most of the 5500 women here worked for the post office, sorting and checking the soldiers' mail. They also had to censor it, and their supervisor said of the Port Moresby Wacs, "I don't know what there is about women that makes them so sharp-eyed in reading letters, but the ones I have here possess an uncanny knack for picking up hidden security breaches, such as tricky codes a soldier may devise to tell his wife where he is."

These women excelled in the sturdy resourcefulness that has always enabled women to be the sex that remembers the salt for a picnic. The documents in the WAC Museum exude the scavenging high spirits of volunteer ladies, the adaptability women traditionally show when they roll up their sleeves with the smile of pleasure that comes from their secret knowledge that they are better at coping than men are. A letter describes a wedding between a Wac and a GI at which the bride wore a dress "fashioned from a parachute given her by a member of the Airborne troop near here . . ." with a veil made from a khaki mosquito net bleached white; and the four bridesmaids had on evening gowns borrowed from the Red Cross. With this knack for improvisation, the women turned their quarters into a home: bare rooms acquired shelves, a graveled walk cut through the mud, washing machines materialized, dirt floors turned slowly into wood, which eager males brought in, one piece at a time.

The women were so enthusiastic that General MacArthur said of them subsequently, "I moved my Wacs forward early after occupation of recaptured territory because they were needed, and they were soldiers in the same manner that my men were soldiers." That is something for a West Point man to say. He continued, "If I had not moved my Wacs forward when I did, I would have had mutiny . . . as they were so eager to carry on where needed."

Southwest Pacific Wacs worked long hours under harsh living conditions, exacerbated by unsuitable uniforms. The Hollandia women had reveille at 5:30 A.M., and walked to and from work three times a day in all weathers. They worked a minimum of ten hours a day for seven days a week, with only Sunday afternoon off. After work there was still the laborious washing and ironing so that the next day's clothes would be ready. It was too hot to sleep and too wet for recreation. Often inferior WAC officers would come out fresh from training, without field experience, and insist on a degree of barracks cleanliness that almost finished the women off.

The shortages and mistakes over uniform supply were crucial. Some of the first Wacs had arrived in arctic clothing from head to foot, with earmuffs. Most, however, wore the standard WAC uniform of herringbone twill, a heavy fabric that, in the jungle heat, gave the women skin rashes. The overalls became soaked with sweat in the course of a working day, but they were too heavy to dry overnight when washed. So the women would put them on wet and contract jungle rot. In desperation they substituted a light cotton shirt for the top of the overalls, so light that it failed to meet the antimalaria requirements, and they succumbed to malaria. The Army Service Forces met such crises with the attitude that led them to deny Colonel Hobby's request for a WAC off-duty dress on the grounds that this was neither desirable nor necessary, since the men were not allowed to buy off-duty dresses.

The censorship work wore the women down. According to Mattie Treadwell, much of what the men wrote was violently obscene. The women reading it day after day became "demoralized," "nervous, temperamental, and complaining." They felt their eyesight was going, their minds were slipping. By the end of the war 20 percent of them were on daily sick call, 50 percent had eye strain, 8 percent had been evacuated, and many of them were markedly neurotic. Here again the clash between males and females was making the women's work harder.

The Army always has difficulty fitting the numbers and types of people it has into the jobs available, and in wartime, when things have to move so much faster, it is even more awkward. The erratic and burgeoning numbers of Wacs coming through bore little relation to the schedules and plans, and so malassignments were inevitable. It was particularly galling for women to find themselves in nonmilitary jobs, working as waitresses or sales clerks in the PXs, or as laundresses. Others were put on permanent kitchen duty. Officers were plucked from their duties; in Europe 15 percent of the female officers were working as personal assistants.

In some jobs the women were at a disadvantage because of their lack of strength. Former textile mill workers, who had been recruited as riggers under a station-and-job scheme, did not prove apt at this job. The average female rigger managed to rig only six chutes a day, whereas the average man rigged ten. (The women did improve.) In the kitchens, the Wacs found it difficult to unload hundred-pound cartons of food or lug around huge vats of grease and containers of garbage. The other chores, such as nonstop meat cutting or baking, were backbreaking for many of them. The women working as medical orderlies or corpsmen could not manage hours at a stretch scrubbing and lifting, and pushing carts loaded with food or linen. Some worked more than twelve hours every day of the week, with night calls and no time off. When queried about this, the Medical Department made it clear that while men were being asked to give their lives in combat, the women should be asked to give up their health if required. Colonel Hobby said in reply that "any sacrifice was justified, either of health or life, if a true emergency required it, but that, since commanders did not deliberately kill men unnecessarily, the WAC should not unnecessarily sacrifice women's health."

As for the "female complaints," the prospect of which causes male employers, civilian or military, to shudder, there were hardly any. Pregnancy and VD rates were negligible, menstrual problems few. The Wacs went on sick call more often than the men, but as a result their illnesses were shorter and less severe. There were vociferous complaints over the routine VD check, a monthly pelvic and pubic examination, made, usually by men, under far from ideal conditions. The women fiercely pointed out that few male soldiers would care to be examined in the nude every month by a female doctor, and they were mollified by a few modifications.

At Fort Des Moines an important study was undertaken into the psychological factors in women's choice of military life. The survey concluded that entering the military meant subordinating their traditional female attitudes and functions, and losing their feminine individuality by putting on uniform. It meant a damaging conflict with public opinion, at a time when the desired model for American female behavior was passive and dependent. The Surgeon General's office expressed the crux of the problem: "They faced a type of combat which men did not, the defense of their character structure." Furthermore, "Women overseas were subjected to more tension than men because of their scarcity, which resulted in more emotional pressure, and because there was a more radical change in the pattern of their lives."

It was felt that the women overseas were particularly vulnerable, and that they should have been warned that the scarcity of women would make them excessively popular, unable to escape from men, that their homesickness might make them too dependent on men, maybe married men, or on other women, or on alcohol, that their lives would be restricted because of the precautions taken to protect them from danger. The presence of males caused the most unnxpected problems, for example, in the integrated messes. Women hated to eat with men. The food was too heavy and fattening and the women felt on show. Many would skip breakfast or supper rather than run the gauntlet of the mess. They preferred to have a slow, quiet meal at which they could linger and relax in private.

Male attitudes, by influencing the women's morale, also dictated their military effectiveness. To this day the effectiveness of soldiers, never mind the hardware and the deployment, is to a great extent determined by the way in which males and females react to each other.

From the beginning, male resistance had been open and emphatic. The War Department had said in a preliminary survey, "The sole purpose of this study is to permit the organization of a women's force along lines which meet the War Department's approval so that when it is forced upon us, as it undoubtedly will be, we shall be able to run it our way." As early as 1928 the Army Chief of Staff had said, "Successful cooperation between men and women during the next war will depend to a great extent on the attitude of the officers of the Regular Army toward the women of the country."

Male anxiety was understandable. The men worried that women were too sensitive to be exposed to the rigors of military life, the deadly routine, and the loss of individuality. They were apprehensive that the women's presence at operations requiring expertise, patience, or sensitivity might tip the scales and endanger success; that abroad the women might be captured and killed or "worse"; and that the men, by worrying about the safety of the women, would be put at risk.

Resentment combined with chivalry to produce confusion. Much of what went wrong was the result of ignorant and good-natured attempts to deal with the women, with male commanders veering wildly between paternalistic overprotection and overmilitary tyranny. It was a question of muddling through, and by the end of the war Army rules had been amended for the women in well over two hundred categories, from Athletic Activities to Use of Weapons or Arms. However, in 1943 the numbers of women enlisting began to drop dramatically. Civilian apathy was partly to blame, but much more important was the hostility of male soldiers, so virulent and widespread that it scared the women away.

A slander campaign was under way, not just in the newspapers, where coverage of the women had always been somewhat trivial, but in private letters and gossip. Resentment was expressed in towns where Wacs were quartered, to the effect that they were spoiling the character of the town. Most seriously, there were organized rumors that swept through the large cities and were picked up and sensationalized in the press: vast numbers of Wacs had been sent

home pregnant from North Africa; 90 percent of all Wacs
were prostitztes and 40 percent were pregnant; the Army
doctors rejecled virgins; the Army tolerated public sexual
displays and soliciting; all Wacs were issued contraceptives;
Wacs were recruited to improve male "morale." One company commander wrote about the effect of one such column:
"It raised hell . . . long-distance calls from parents began to
come in, telling the girls to come home. The girls all came in
crying, asking if this disgrace was what they had been asked
to join the Army for. The older ones were just bitter that
such lies could be printed. It took all the pride and
enthusiasm for the Army right out of them."

There were fears that this might be an Axis plot. An
intelligence investigation revealed, however, that instead of
the Nazis, those who had spread the stories were "Army
personnel, Navy personnel, Coast Guard personnel, business
men, women, factory workers and others." Also wives,
jealous civilian women, gossips and fanatics, disgruntled
former Waacs, but most often male soldiers. A sample study
was made at Daytona Beach, the least well appointed Wac
training station, in a rough town. The rumors had been vile
there too, and odd. Wacs were supposed to be throwing away
food; this was not true. As to their wild, loose ways, of a
population of 10,000 trainees on one Saturday night, the MP
report listed: 2 kissing/embracing in public; 1 no hat; 2
injured in auto accident; 1 AWOL returned; 1 "retrieved
from Halifax River in an intoxicated condition." Total, 11.

The worst hostility came from overseas before the women
arrived. The "thousands of pregnant Wacs evacuated from
North Africa" rumor turned out to have been based on the
evacuation of three Wacs, one of them ill, the other two
married and pregnant. As one WAC leader said in despair,
"Men have for centuries used slander against morals as a
weapon to keep women out of public life." It reminded me
of West Point, particularly since the slander was so sexual,
indicating that the men who achieved their manhood through
being in the Army felt themselves robbed and emasculated
by the arrival of the women.

In North Africa, apparently, almost 100 percent of soldiers' comments on the Wacs were "unfavorable or obscene." The officers were not spared, particularly if they were taking choice assignments from the men. In the Southwest Pacific, where the women labored under a great many problems, feeling against them ran so high that it seriously affected their job promotion. The awarding of even a single stripe to a woman caused such rage that grades were not recommended for future use. Unlike the Wacs in Europe, where the commanders were in favor of the women and never slow to recognize their achievements, the women of the Southwest Pacific did not get their Bronze Stars when they deserved them, because it was felt to be "inappropriate" for women to receive them. With such an attitude at the top of the chain of command, the troops must have realized that they had unofficial permission to resent the women.

Male commanders could make life difficult for their Wacs in another way—by overprotection. Wacs in New Guinea were locked in compounds ringed with barbed-wire fences. Their existence was literally circumscribed. The rationale was that the women might be raped by the "Negro troops." They never left, except to go to work or for group recreation. As for group recreation, the Oro Bay Wacs—those lucky ones who arrived with arctic clothing—were "marched to approved movies in formation under guard." Their only parties were official ones. If they wished to go on dates, they had to submit the names of men twenty-four hours in advance. They were not allowed leave or passes or one-couple dates. Vehicles carrying women were not to stop en route to their approved destinations. Women were not allowed on boats or planes. Predictably enough, they hated all this, feeling, quite justifiably, that they were in a concentration camp. They knew that to be confined to quarters was an Army punishment for misconduct. Some of them were faced with a year or more of this treatment, and they wondered angrily why they were there at all if there was such danger. The result was, according to Treadwell, "resentment, disobedience, and immature conduct."

These delicate women were the ones who in 1945 moved up through the Philippines as they were retaken. Much of the campaign was conducted during the rainy season, and there were constant air raids, during the course of which the women slithered down into the foxholes with the men. When they reached Manila they found a sacked city, daubed with the blood of hacked corpses. Avoiding the booby traps, the blood and filth, they kept working despite the dysentery that became prevalent. One unit was based in a tin barracks, with outside latrines and no shade or trees, where either mud or dust engulfed them, and dead Japanese were buried so close to the surface that the women had to scatter lime around the mess hall every day because of the smell. Morale in this particular unit was good because of a good commanding officer. These were the women needing to be protected.

The Southwest Pacific Wacs, locked in their compounds, did not suffer as much as Wacs elsewhere from one particularly galling form of restriction imposed by their male colleagues. This was the policy on dating, or fraternization. Most of the Wacs overseas were, as I have said, an elite: highly educated middle-class women who would naturally have chosen to associate with male officers. These men were off limits to them. The women did not enjoy being told that they were beneath their male officer friends. As one of them wrote home, "In civilian life we associated with people of our own choice, and that is one of the many reasons why we are serving in the Army, to preserve our rights of equity." The women, in fact, made so much fuss about this that recruiting began to sag. Mrs. Hobby spent much time trying to relax the unwritten rules so that her women could be appeased. She said that in peacetime certain regulations were applicable, but in war allowances should be made, for "this is a people's army," and "there should be no more restrictions on those in uniform than are essential to their military mission." She suggested that the women be allowed to date men from different installations, but her proposal was rejected. In all, she suggested modifications seven times, and each time her request was denied.

Marriage continued to be singled out for special disfavor. If the soldiers managed to persevere through the paper work and achieve this state, official policy was that the couple be parted. Such separations might be announced by the arrival of a letter stating somberly, "It has come to the attention of this headquarters that you are living with your wife. This must cease at once."

The women seemed to be able to endure almost anything if they were properly treated and welcomed. The Southwest Pacific Wacs illustrated what could go wrong, when, toward the end of the war and after the cease-fire, the medical evacuation rate soared inexplicably. These women had functioned very well, even in the most terrible nerve- and health-racking emergencies that typified the recapture of the Philippines. A formal investigation was undertaken, because the authorities were so alarmed at the condition of the returning women. General Marshall asked General MacArthur for a confidential report. The only response was a press release and a copy of the evacuation statistics for the previous year. The War Department, enraged, demanded a second response, which, when it arrived, had been so censored that the only factors quoted were (1) the late arrival of Christmas presents and (2) the accidental death of eight Wacs in a plane crash. The plans to bring the women home were speeded up. A team of soldiers who arrived to assist in the process found a lot of ill women, gaunt and tense. At a welcoming parade, which was held up for an hour, eight women fainted. The war was over, but some of the women were still working every day and evenings, living on poor food, and sleeping in flooded quarters.

The head of Far East Forces, General Baird, said, "I cannot truthfully say that their contribution, great as it was, outweighed their difficulties. . . . The hardships, isolation and privation of jungle theater are jobs for men. Women should be employed there only as a last resort." Colonel Brown, the director of the WAC at that time, said, "Full advantage was not taken of the experience and knowledge of WAC staff officers." The final opinion of senior Wacs was that the Pacific endeavor had been too rushed. They remained convinced that women could serve under jungle conditions, and without significant attrition, if only there was sufficient advance planning, if the women were commanded by women, if they were given adequate supplies, and if attention was given "to their psychological need to be treated as adults."

There were undoubtedly military men who, despite the evidence of the women's courage, endurance, and often superiority in the jobs in which they replaced men, would have been happy if the Women's Army Corps had, like the war, been signed away with the Armistice. Congress took a long time to decide the question of Regular status for the Corps, brooding on the specter of women commanding men, which it felt would be the inevitable, and dreaded, result of keeping women in the Army. Finally, with only two months remaining before June 1948, when the legislation authorizing the wartime WAC was to expire, the heads of the armed services came to testify before the armed services committees on behalf of the women. General Eisenhower said firmly, "When this project was proposed . . . like most old soldiers, I was violently against it. . . . Every phase of the record they compiled during the war convinced me of the error of my first reaction." He continued: "In tasks for which they are particularly suited, Wacs are more valuable than men, and fewer of them are required to perform a given amount of work. . . . In the disciplinary field they were, throughout the war . . . a model for the Army."

On June 2, 1948, a vote placed the women in both the Regular Army and the Reserves, and on June 12 the President signed the measure into law. The Women's Army Corps sank from public view until the end of the draft in 1973 brought about the All-Volunteer Force, which ran into problems of its own, causing the planners in the Pentagon to dust off the idea of women, which had been put away like a little-used croquet set in a garden shed. However, in the years between the end of the war and the big expansions of the early 1970s, the WAC, ignored by everyone but the men who came in occasionally to work with the soldiers, flourished in its own way. The peacetime WAC was dedicated to some military values, and it modified others to suit its own purposes. There can be no doubt: the WAC was military, "twenty-four-hours-a-day military," as the women like to say.

8

Strac City:
The Peacetime Esprit

Fort McClellan was WAC Center, the heart of it all. Wacs would be detailed to units elsewhere, but, as one veteran told me, "It was the place you wanted to come back to. You were always glad to be home." When I first visited, the WAC past could be felt everywhere. People had been told to take down the Pallas Athene plaques and insignia from the walls, much as if there had been a coup and revered images of past heroes would lead you to jail. The complicated and often bitter feelings of the women watching the newly integrated trainees wheel and stamp to attention on the parade ground came out in little ways. A lieutenant said with a bite in her voice, "In the post newspaper some female trainees were interviewed, and when they were asked what they thought about the change to coed basic, they were saying 'I'm glad, and don't call me a Wac, I'm a soldier!'"

Lieutenant Evans was a serious woman with a soft Midwestern accent and thick blond hair in a pageboy. We were sitting in her office, and as she spoke she twirled the WAC ring that she had found in a junk shop. Evans said, "Those young females don't know what they're talking about. Sure, they go to the WAC Museum—it's mandatory—but they never get any lectures on the past, any sense of something they could be proud of or identify with." She added, "In the old days any commandant on any post would take you to see his WAC company, because they were the best. They were more loyal, and proud. They were regarded as fourth-class citizens in the Army, so they had to prove they were superior."

Later, at her spacious modern house a couple of miles from the post, she told me, "The WAC was strac city. You know, don't you, that 'strac' stands for super giant good military bearing with everything right? It's when you're all dressed and covered and polished and spit-shined at all times." This emphasis on neatness seems to have been a cargo cult, a survival from the wartime days, when newly arriving Wacs would have to march into post looking terrific—a preemptive strike that might disarm the men. Lieutenant Evans added, "We didn't particularly like to give grooming and makeup classes, but some of that was really necessary, because a lot of people came from the hills and they often didn't know how to bathe. Also, there was an emphasis on not looking like men, even though at times we performed like them."

The WAC was small and not in need of numbers. In those days it was such a peculiar thing to join the Army, almost like a vaudeville joke, that any woman who had actually reached the point of taking the oath had to be quite certain of her ambitions. It was not something she could do almost without thinking, the way a man could, and still does. Most of the women I have met came into the Army in the spirit that to many people today seems old-fashioned: to do their patriotic duty as citizens.

Lieutenant Evans expressed a typical WAC view of service when she said, "I'm not in the military so that I can kill people. I'm antideath." Sergeant Reilly told me she had fled a dead-end job in a hotel and an unhappy love affair to join up at the age of thirty-two, when she saw and heard Kennedy give his famous "Ask not . . ." speech on television. What they all seemed to have in common was a fiercely traditional view of the way the world should work, and the streak of independence that made them join the Army.

Lieutenant Evans had been a drill sergeant, and she said, "I guess I'm a persuasive type of leader, not an authoritarian one, and I was proud of that." She had every right to be, for she had earned honors throughout her military career. She said earnestly, "I'd let my troops know right away that I was the best drill sergeant, and they were lucky to be in my platoon. I said as long as they did *exactly as they were told* we'd get along fine. I said that in a week they could be standing out in platoon formation with everybody else, and anyone could go down the line, point to them, and say 'That's Sergeant Evans' platoon.' That was true." She lit another cigarette and told me that the troops trusted her because she was honest with them, and they were grateful to have her when they watched the other sergeants, who had modeled themselves on some men, rant and yell and drop the trainees for push-ups.

The strac element went beyond dress, of course. The women's barracks were cleaner and more attractive than those of the men. Their soldiering was what Army people would call "outstanding" in marching and drill, which the Wacs loved—the top of the desk always neat, the assignments carried out promptly. These things are military virtues. Military men are proud of their neat haircuts, of knowing how to cook and clean floors, how to press and starch their clothing till it squeaks. The Wacs excelled at all of it.

The particular combination of traits that made a woman a soldier in those days was very useful in training and in leadership. Lieutenant Myers had told me about the enthusiasm the women put into field training and war games. "When they first got the terrible black boots, they would beat them and soak them and rub them with saddle soap to get them soft." The training was not rigorous by today's standards, although, presumably, it was hard for many of the women who had come from office jobs or were unused to the physical exertion that is usual for today's young women. A good commanding officer would supplement the physical training with extra exercises for all those swaybacked females with the spindly arms who found push-ups impossible. Lieutenant Myers told me, "It's bad for morale to have a female troop sweating and straining and trying to do one push-up one day and two the next. It's much better if you can give them different strengthening exercises, so that when they next come to do push-ups they can do five or six." That seemed to be a small but crucial difference between the Wacs and the rest of the Army, or most of it. They were ingenious and sharp in their methods; they were classy because they had to be. Lieutenant Myers learned to take advantage of her size and sit up a tree that night out on bivouac, evading her captors as they wandered around peering and stumbling in the darkness below her.

The WAC world was a hybrid—for most of its history proud and military, but without weapons and with classes in makeup and map-reading; with WAC detachments the pride of the post, but their peacetime work, apart from training, largely administrative and clerical. Issues of the late *WAC Journal* bulge with articles like "My Career in the Finance Corps," which seems at first glance to evoke a world of stupefying dullness. However, what made this young woman's work different from that of an accountant or bookkeeping clerk in a small town or a large one was that she was a Wac. That became part of her personality in a way that no civilian job can. The sense of mission suffused her work. The Wacs had little in the way of status or recognition to sustain them, which made their sense of mission even stronger.

Lieutenant Evans is a very attractive woman. She said hesitantly, "It was interesting in Vietnam, because nobody could tell whether I was gay or straight, and everybody wanted to know." Military women who are gay, or even suspected of being gay for reasons picked at random, have been the objects of slander, ridicule, punishment, gossip, myth. Because the Army forbids homosexuality, male and female homosexuals must be very discreet. Speculation is used against the women, very effectively, since it can end careers by rumor and witch hunts.

By mentioning this subject at all I may upset gays who feel that I am increasing their vulnerability, or straight women who raised eyebrows just by announcing in their hometowns that they were going to join the Army. Several women have told me with a kind of amused despair of people who tried to warn them away, of school friends who suddenly were no longer allowed to come over and visit, of sudden aloofness in former friends—and this before they had even joined. I must stress that I discuss gays here from a historical perspective, as an aspect of the WAC past. My purpose is to show that "bonding," considered so essential to men in the military, is not confined to men.

Male bonding seems to have been invented as an idea by anthropologists, the most famous being Lionel Tiger, who said, in effect, that women did not bond except under strange and warped circumstances. Tiger cited covens. Like many people who speak so authoritatively about what men or women do or do not do, Tiger pays less attention to context and the flow of history than to what he considers a biological truth.

The reporter James Morris, subsequently Jan Morris, described the 1953 Everest expedition, in which he participated, as an apotheosis of male bonding, saying confidently, "Men more than women respond to the team spirit, and this is partly because, if they are of an age, of a kind, and in a similar condition, they work together far more like a mechanism." The bond between male soldiers is supposedly so close that it is "homoerotic."

In a lyrical, often anguished meditation on soldiers, *The Warriors*, Glenn Gray says that the comradeship of military men is not like friendship, because it is based on mutual identification under the same intense, often horrifying, perhaps as often unbelievably exhilarating, circumstances.

Anything that serves to distinguish one person from another is not welcome. However, Gray describes the link as a transient one, dependent on the fact of war, and he illustrates his point by talking about the embarrassed behavior of veterans at a reunion. They shared possibly the greatest moments of their lives; now they have nothing to say over the grapefruit segments. The buddy relationship, however deep, was entirely based on circumstances, and its members were, of necessity, interchangeable. If your comrade died in combat, you learned to live with it and not to let grief prevent you from fighting. You even learned to leave him, mortally wounded, to die.

Charles Moskos, probably the best known of today's sociologists working on the military, wrote in his influential book *The American Enlisted Man* (a book that, written in 1970, made no mention of the WAC) that "primary groups" (buddies) were based on self-interest, which lasted only as long as the need for them existed. He substituted the idea of "pragmatic and situational responses" for the "semi-mystical bond." He pointed out that once a soldier went home he did not keep in touch with his unit, nor they with him. Even in World War II the dwindling importance of the "semimystical bond" was noticeable, and it became characteristic of the troops fighting the Vietnam war. After all, a buddy has to be replaceable at a moment's notice if he is killed or captured. Moskos pointed out that the self-consciously masculine ethos fades after soldiers taste real combat. The ultimate standard becomes: to stay alive.

Still the mythical appeal of the bond has always been powerful, from the time of the Knights Templars, who were disbanded for realizing its erotic aspect too explicitly, to the present, when the young black man from St. Louis said to the superior young woman from New Jersey, "We all got to be friends. We's cool." The wartime Wacs felt it; their bond was plucky and high-spirited and proud. They were the improvisers who turned a dank, hellish hut into a home and still kept the seams of their Army issue stockings straight. In real adversity their spirit kept them going. However, there was a war on, and they were in the American mainstream, doing their duty.

The peacetime WAC esprit began with the orientation lecture given at the reception station after uniform issue. The little sets of brass with the head of Pallas Athene on them were handed out, and in a pinning-on ceremony each trainee turned to another, who pinned on her brass. It was an emotional and stirring experience, the kind that raised goose bumps, as military ceremonies are intended to do. It made each young woman one of the band of soldiers. At a WAC reunion the first sergeant of Alpha Company looked around her with pleasure and said, "You can see it, can't you, that bond between them all."

I would say, based on what I have been told by people I trust and respect, that this esprit was overwhelmingly gay. A sympathetic, bawdy, overweight woman called Pat talked about those days in the documentary film about homosexuals, *Word Is Out.* She described mass transvestism, women shaving their hair into imitation sideburns, wearing pinstripes and argyle socks and mail-order tuxedos off duty. She said they would wear Old Spice and walk and sit in a certain way—even smoke cigarettes in an exaggeratedly masculine way. Officers and troops, they were like a secret society. She described her arrival at base: "I came staggering into the mess hall with my suitcase and I heard a voice from one of the barracks say, 'Good God, Elizabeth, here comes another one.'"

Filling the TV screen with her body and her personality, Pat said that everybody wanted to play the role of a dyke: "If you were going to be gay, you wanted to be like a guy, because they were the ones who could get things on. The masculine role was the one to play." The structure of the Army lent itself, of course, to authoritarianism in relationships, to dominance and submission. Uniforms, with all their gleaming brass, have always appealed as costume to soldiers, straight and gay, and just as women off duty would rush to don men's clothing, there have been armies of the past in which men have put on drag. In World War I, so a West Point military science instructor told me, the Romanian Army had to make it a policy that nobody below the rank of major was to wear makeup.

A couple of women felt able to tell me what the gay life was like. One began somewhat guardedly by saying, "All the cadre here was a family. We worked together and partied together. We felt this intense sense of belonging, that we were part of the whole." She said that when she was first in the Army, she fell in love with men, and usually they were married men. She said, "I grew up in a part of the country where there were no black people. I seriously thought homosexuality was a fairy tale, like Snow White." Her first gay affair was conducted under very risky circumstances, since the woman who initiated her was the company commander and she was the company clerk. It lasted six months, and they lived together to the extent that it was possible.

She said, "As a baby troop, I noticed there was an in crowd, and all of them, all the important and nice-to-know people, were gay. It was *desirable* to be gay. The straight young enlisted person finds that out, and then she has to decide what to do. The assumption was that we didn't need men, not for our jobs. We could train, we could do anything that an Army post was supposed to do, and we did it very well. That's why the WAC is so closely knit." I thought of Sergeant Rickey telling his grinning colleagues out at the range that there was a lot to be said for those women who had constructed and used everything on post.

Part of the closeness came from the lack of a social caste system. Most of the officers had come up from the ranks, and, however military their conduct, there was not the abyss that often in the male Army separates the officers from the NCOs. I asked one woman about the senior officers. She said, "Oh sure, of course there were gays, but never *publicly*. If they came to our parties we would all chitchat politely and play cards until they left. We had to be careful not to put them in a position where they could be embarrassed or implicated." The gay cadre had a lot of parties; they sat around at the NCO club and drank beer; they were active in sports. On weekends they went fishing or to the dog track. The unique joy of Fort McClellan was that there was no need to be paranoid. As one officer at another post said to me, "We had no need to conform to an artificial standard. Women were entrenched at Fort McClellan, with *real power.*" The WAC had indeed managed, struggling always, to get real power.

For the WAC the chain of command had special significance because it was composed of females. Fort McClellan was a post composed entirely of females. The structure had a unique power, that of a chain of women protecting, encouraging, and looking out for other women in a world of men. A WAC historian to whom I talked in her cramped Washington office said succinctly, "We really did love the women and respect them and take care of them. We wanted them to meet a nice young man and have babies, and those that wanted a career, we were very happy for them." The idea has become trivialized today into the term "petticoat channels," but it's something that serious working women have come to learn that they need. They used the chain of command for promotions; the women's careers were assessed and guided. With the WAC attending to its own promotions list, deserving women were unlikely to be passed over, and of course they could never be passed over in favor of men.

They could use the chain against, for example, sexual harassment. There was no sexual harassment problem, because a case would be reported as soon as it occurred, the information would go up to the appropriate unit in the chain, and, without question, action would be taken. There were powerful women who could be located. Now they are dispersed, and that feeling of solidarity has gone with them, but it had made the women a corps.

It was not an idyll, and nobody claimed that it was. There were the usual Army problems—fist fights, race trouble, drug busts—the only difference being that these took place among women. Because it was such a small and enclosed world, the jealousies and tensions in couples were oppressive. When a "marriage" broke up, it was messy and disruptve, just as it is in a quiet suburb. There were intermittent witch hunts, culminating in courts-martial and mass dishonorable discharges.

Life was also hard for the straight women who wanted to stay in the Army. There was no way they could be a part of the inner cliques of power. I heard about a first sergeant who had waited unfairly eight years for her promotion to E-8. It was just because she was straight; however good she was at her job—and she was good—the influential people were not making a point of looking out for her. A sergeant I met in basic training told me that she too had had problems. The sergeant had a hefty body, a bawdy manner, and a pickup. She fitted a certain butch stereotype but was rampantly heterosexual, providing an instructive example of the importance of not judging people by appearances. The sergeant told me one day as we drove down bumpy roads to an outlying range that when she first arrived at Fort McClellan the gay women did not trust her. "They felt I didn't fit in, and I'm sure I didn't." It took months before she and her gay colleagues felt comfortable with each other. She said, "I did not feel much camaraderie from them. I felt that if I made a mistake they would run down to the commander and tell tales. With the males, though, we could argue and call each other names but still we'd help each other out."

As the numbers of the WAC crept up during the expansions of the 1970s—to 20,000 in 1973 and 42,000 in 1975— the first men began arriving at Fort McClellan, where signs went up saying OFF LIMITS TO MALE PERSONNEL. "None of them would ask me out," said the sergeant, "because they all thought I was gay."

Some of those pioneering men did not have an easy time of it. Predictably, they were harassed. Women even made a few attempts to set them up in compromising situations, so that they would have to leave. A captain said, "It was very difficult indeed for the men to encounter, and live with, and accept, and conquer the prejudice they met in this women's army; it was more difficult than the other way round. We're used to it, and they aren't." She spoke ironically, and then laughed.

Most serious Wacs knew that the changes were right in theory, but in practice they found them hard to accept. There were bright official trumpetings in *The WAC Journal*, which was to cease publication because, as the women began to be assimilated into their new branches, the need for it diminished. "Some of us who have spent the majority of our Army careers as members of the WAC may be saddened at the course of events which will ultimately lead to the dissolution of the Corps," wrote a colonel from WAC Center. "However, looking into the future, we realize that women in the Army today have many more advantages than was ever possible before." I met a sergeant who had been in Hawaii when it all began. She told me, "The males carried a very deep resentment about it. They had the women lifting huge, full garbage containers onto trucks, just out of spite."

It was a classic case of having the rules changed under your feet. In competing directly against men now, the women were at a distinct disadvantage—even if it was only temporary—because they did not have the years of experience in whatever field they had chosen, and they had to train swiftly in an unfamiliar and perhaps unwished-for new skill. Veterans thought their years of specialized experience counted for nothing. They were not only stuck in the middle, they were without value.

The gays felt particular dread. Their society had been comfortable and sheltered. One woman told me, "The first of the big-time annual witch hunts was in 1972, when a corporal deserted, and she named thirty-two people. I was one of the people told to take a lie detector test to prove I was not gay. I was very hurt; I said, tell the *girl* to take one. . . . Later I needed to get a security clearance for flight school, and the CID said, 'You refused to take a lie detector test and so we assume you're guilty.'" She said wanly, "I didn't know how to complain. I was just a baby troop. What could I have done?"

The more integrated the Army became, the more trouble there was. Gay women saw the bad days ahead, and they began to withdraw, to live discreetly, as they had never had to before. There was a new caution in their lives, personal and professional, for in the Army they are intertwined.

In November 1978 Mary Clarke became the first woman major general. On March 21, 1979, the Women's Army Corps was ritually disestablished, and, in an emotional ceremony at Fort McClellan, the flag was retired and carted away to the museum, where it remains on display. It was a traumatic experience. There was no focus left for the women, who felt it impossible to identify with the Army. "You couldn't," a former Wac said to me, "it was too large."

I discussed the disestablishment with a colonel at the Pentagon, who had been deputy director of the WAC at the crucial time. A shy, slow-speaking Southerner, she spoke so diplomatically that I had to listen between the lines. The passage had not been uneventful, that at least was clear. Leaning back in her large chair in a small office in one of the recesses of the Pentagon's ground floor, the colonel told me all about the concern they had with opening new MOS's for women, about the hours they labored in opposition to plans for separate housing for women, and separate basic training. They worked for better uniforms for the women, they tried to think of all the problems that would arise: how a man would react if a woman burst into tears in front of him, whether a man would know a female uniform if he saw one. They consulted with the policy makers about the formulation of the crucial policy on women in combat, a policy that still operates today. The work was endless, but the only part of it that was both endless and a failure was the attempt to set up some kind of a Pentagon advisory office for women's matters after the disestablishment.

They asked to keep the director's office. This request was

refused. Then they asked for a "senior adviser, women in the Army," with a small office of no more than six to advise the Secretary of the Army and the Chief of Staff. This plan was rejected because it smacked of separate—that is, special—treatment, when the whole point of disestablishment was to integrate. As the colonel talked about this and subsequent plans for the women's welfare, all of them rejected, her voice was calm, her drift chronological. The gist, however, reminded me of two other circumstances: the integration of West Point, where the attitude had been so confrontational, as in "We'll give you equality and we'll start with PT," and the requests Colonel Hobby had made so repeatedly for better policies and better uniforms, requests that were always turned down as if they were unreasonable demands for privileged treatment. The colonel said blandly, "The men seemed to think integration was going better than it was."

The women wanted someone to look out for their interests in Washington. They kept the gentle pressure on, asking instead for a Deputy Director of Personnel and Management for women, who would attend to clothing, maternity, promotions, and other special matters peculiar to women. This plan was turned down because it would have kept a woman general on the staff. Eventually agreement was reached: a senior female officer in personnel would have the role of senior adviser on women *as an additional duty.* Colonel Lorraine Rossi, a woman of talent and wide experience and the Director of Equal Opportunity Programs—a post that is, in this egalitarian all-volunteer Army, not an inconsiderable job—was given this "additional duty." She became the only person at the Pentagon who could be said to have any special responsibilities for the 56,840 Wacs to be integrated. Rossi had no backup staff. An announcement was to be made, so that the women and their new commanders would be aware of her existence and know whom to approach for information if necessary, but this did not happen. The colonel in the Pentagon said, "Nobody knew of her existence, not even staff." Colonel Rossi said to me subsequently, "We were reluctant to treat women as a separate minority, and so we tried to channel all matters pertaining to them into the appropriate action agencies."

Lieutenant Evans told me about her first glimpse of the integrated world outside Fort McClellan. She was sent to drill sergeant school, one out of four females and fifty-two males in her class. "In the class before us," Lieutenant Evans said, "a female had been DMG [Distinguished Military Graduate]. This meant she was Number One." She paused. "Our instructors told us that would not be happening again. However, it did, with our class." I asked, "Who got it?" She said, "I did. We were one, three, and five, and we got a lot of harassment. The men in competition with us were having special study halls and tutoring, and we'd go to our dayroom in the female quarters to study by ourselves." She told me that the men were given mock exams in preparation, and, smiling, gave me a sidelong glance and said, "If we'd complained, it would probably have been worse than not saying anything." Then she added, "But they didn't realize what they were doing—they were making us *try harder.*"

Lieutenant Evans loves the Army—they all do—but she and the others felt, in their different degrees of irritation or despair, that the price of integration was unnecessarily high. I discussed the changes with a stalwart of the old WAC Band, a first sergeant who was known for her dedication and pride. She told me that the band used to go all over the country, to the Rose Bowl and the New York World's Fair, to parades in small towns, high schools, civic auditoriums. They would give concerts twice a day when they were touring, and stay in shabby hotels where they had to look out for the younger women in case men tried to get into their rooms. They spent hours washing and ironing. The sergeant said wistfully, "A good troop would put in the practice on her own time. We all put in extra hours because we wanted the unit to do well. There were no discipline problems."

This sergeant is a conscientious soldier. She said, "Although I hated to see our band go, the women's liberation changes were great." During a long silence she seemed to be trying to think of examples. Then she said, hesitantly, "But this Army is very different. There was more discipline in our Army. When I was growing up, ministers, doctors, firemen, policemen used to be looked up to. You could count on them. Then people cursed and spat on them, shot them. Our society learned to be suspicious. The same happened in the Army. It used to be difficult to live off post. We were all together, we shared the problems and the good things. Now everybody drives a car, and they can go farther and get away."

Other women I met were more upset about the loss of power. A WAC historian in Washington told me, "With integration we lost the ability to produce young leaders, because when men are left to themselves they put their own kind into positions of leadership." They felt cheated, and in a way they had been. A captain at Fort McClellan said to me in despair, "All they talk about these days is being equal. They're not interested in the good things different people may have to offer." And that is the way many Wacs feel about the dissolution of the WAC esprit.

The band sergeant escorted me out through the deserted rehearsal hall, and she said, "Now we can't fill the band from the training units here because the women go off to the school of music and then to any band they choose." We were becoming morose. She said, "The band has become nice, like a regular office. We're like every unit now. It's just the numbers, though—we can't get a good sound without the numbers."

One of the most extraordinary events I attended at Fort McClellan during that basic training cycle was the second biennial WAC reunion, when seven or eight hundred former Wacs and Wacs on active duty from all over the country rolled up in buses and cars for two days of singing, reminiscing, tours of the post, dances and dinners and toasts and speeches. The event began, as do all the best military events, with a parade, held just outside Alpha Company's buildings—one of the original WAC training buildings from the days when Fort McClellan was WAC Center. A lieutenant sitting next to me in the stands said, "They're coming in from the roads, the way we used to do it in the old days." All the available companies on post were marching to the parade ground in an elaborate pattern from all directions—a defunct practice, revived for this occasion as homage to the Wacs. They noticed; a little sigh and murmur of pleasure went up from the crowd of women in pastel pantsuits, and hats worn in preparation for the threatening rain. General Clarke climbed into a jeep with a tiny white-haired pretty lady in a powder-blue suit, who looked like an idealized grandmother. This was Colonel Mary Hallaren, a previous director of the Corps, and during World War II the director of all the 8000 Wacs in Europe.

The jeep drove slowly along the lines and back, and General Clarke saluted as one company after another presented arms. The colors were paraded by four women, two colonels and two lieutenants, marching with stiff precision and elegance, one with a gleaming blond bob of hair visible under her helmet. People were clapping and looking sentimental. A young Specialist-4 said cheerfully to me as the parade broke up, "Oh, General Clarke probably cried. She always cries."

That night there was a ceremonial dinner. The women sat at long tables, eating roast beef and gossiping while the 14th Army Band played. The diners looked upon the band with mild disfavor because it was no longer the WAC Band, even though the first sergeant was a WAC stalwart from the old days, and a loud cheer went up when she shyly introduced herself. As the wine and the conversation flowed, people became rowdier, and the WAC songs began. A printed sheet of the songs with the official lyrics was handed out, but there was a near riot when the band played a familiar WAC song, announced as "The Wacs Are in Back of You."

The composer of the song, an indignant, elderly woman, stood up, literally shaking with rage, to complain. She said, leaning against a chair back, "It should be 'The Wacs Are

Soldiers Too,'" and a roar of support went up from all the women there while the coeducational band of the new Army stood embarrassed and waited for the cheering to stop so that they could continue with the program.

General Clarke said, "We had that little bit of rain out there at the review because it was so hot out there, and we *decided* to have rain." General Hoisington, who had so terrorized the West Point cadets, said, "On the program it says 'Mistress of Ceremonies.'" She paused, and with the timing of a pro, said carefully, "I'm no mistress of ceremonies, I'm master of ceremonies." General Bailey, a pretty woman with her white hair in a pageboy, said, with a slight smile, "I was sitting next to General Hoisington on the stand, and when it started to rain she told it to stop, and it did." It was the first time I had seen powerful women joke so openly about their power.

General Clarke was the main speaker at lunch the next day. She looked as poised and gracious as always—nobody can reach the rank of general without learning to mask her or his feelings—but her speech was nervous and peppered with such unduly down-home terms as "gals," "guys," "y'know," and "folks." My neighbor leaned over to me and whispered, "You know why she's this way? Listen to her speech. You'll hear that it's an apology—she was so involved in the disestablishment of the WAC."

Clarke spoke to a respectful but not a particularly affectionate silence. She said, "These young women today have a difficult time, more difficult than we had, because of the all-male environment. The Army is saying to them you're equal—but you can't change the attitude of the males overnight. We've been trying to do that since 1972 . . ." She faltered a little, perhaps aware that this was not exactly the upbeat hymn to integration that she wanted to deliver, and then said firmly, "Let me tell you, the young women coming in today are of a caliber that can compete, and in lots of cases they're not just as good as the men, they're better." There was polite applause. She said, looking around the tables at the women who had finished lunch and were having cigarettes with their coffee, "I know you worry about the esprit." She looked almost apologetic, just as my neighbor had anticipated, and said, "I know how nostalgic this reunion is for you, and how you worry that the Corps is gone—but don't worry. The Corps is living in the hearts of everyone who ever served. It will never die." More restrained applause, and a four-piece female combo began to play music for dancing, songs like "Feelings" and "The Way We Were," and a few couples moved to the dance floor. There was high emotion in the air, a mixture of intense delight, nostalgia, and some real bitterness.

9

Passing Muster:
The Days Before Graduation

The reunion took place on the last morning of bivouac, and small parties of former Wacs visited the range where Alpha Company, Second Battalion, was sweating it out on Fire and Maneuver. In teams of two they had to storm a foxhole and finish off its phantom occupants with a hand grenade. They had practiced earlier on impressively rugged terrain, hurling themselves behind shrubs and hillocks with determined gusto. The qualifying range was much less adventurous, its imitation hillocks made of neat woodpiles resembling jumps at a gymkhana. The trainees had live ammunition, and Joan Clark stepped up for her turn.

The instructors and their assistants wore yellow hard hats and bulletproof vests. Clark crouched, took aim shakily, fired, and rolled over in a spasm of agony. The instructor's arm went up; all shooting stopped. Clark was moaning and cupping her eye with her hands. "Oh, God," she whimpered, "don't let me go blind, oh, help me." People were very cowed by this. A couple of men carried her to an ambulance, which raced to the hospital. Clark returned late that night with a black eye patch; a fragment of hot casing had ricocheted into the eye, but there was no damage.

The instructor who walked with me between the lanes said city kids could not think on their feet. When he told one of the more anxious women that she had passed the first time, she lost her composure, blurting, "Oh, thankyouthankyou, I'm so happy, thank you, what do I do now?" Two women forgot all they had been told, one firing without pause into nowhere, while the other, who was supposed to shout "Ready" and be still while her partner shouted "Moving" and moved, took off like a hare, jamming her weapon so that it would not fire at all. When told of her no-go, one of the pair lowered her head and set her lip. She looked up at the sergeant sideways with a mutinous gaze, while tears trickled down one cheek. The sergeant regarded her for a moment and then said slowly, "Now, don't you be like that with me, young lady. I'm not being *mean* to you; I'm trying to help you, and I *will* help you get through this test, believe me." She trailed off. He gave me a look and said, "I have three kids of my own, you see."

Julie Drake and Ann Schulman had been chosen to do their qualifying test in front of three busloads of Wacs, who arrived at the range late, after the trainees had become irritable from standing in the sweltering heat, waiting. Julie said excitedly, "We did it right, first time, and they all clapped us." These Wacs had mixed feelings about the changes at Fort McClellan. On the one hand, they sighed and laughed in a superior way when they were shown movies of the post's new amenities—the sauna, the large, modern PX, the all-wood squash and real tennis courts. We didn't need any of these embellishments, they thought. On the other hand, they watched young women like Julie and Schulman with some awe. "We never did that," they murmured, looking at them lying in the dirt with their fatigues rumpled and dusty and their wobbly helmets askew. "Remember the seersucker dresses we wore for PT?"

The trainees raced through weapons cleaning. By now it

seemed quite normal for the men to help the women who had small hands with the handguards on their rifles. Upstairs in the bays, amid disco music from duelling radios, women were writing letters, curling their hair, ironing, or just sitting on the floor against the lockers with a cigarette in hand, enjoying the luxury of a mind cast adrift into utter vacancy. As the women unpacked their filthy things from bivouac, staring at muddy ponchos and canteens and tent pegs and wondering what to do about them, they talked about men. Baird's sensible friend from Virginia said, "This place has really changed my attitude to men." Jarrell said quickly, "Mine too, because I'm not so concerned with finding someone now. I know I can make it on my own." One woman tidying her locker turned around to say, "The guys take care of us." She explained: "Just now when we were running, I made it all the way until the last round, when my breathing went, and MacLoughlin came up and kept on at me, saying, 'Come *on,* come *on,* you can do it.' It makes them feel more masculine to help us, and we feel more feminine." Her face bright, she said, "It's great all round."

Simmons the crip, who was lounging nearby, added, "It gives us a better way to gauge competition. Most of us aren't used to competing, but the men teach us." They all agreed emphatically, saying that they felt they had the best of both worlds, because they could be all sweaty and athletic, and then come in and take a shower and put on a dress and be girls again. Of course none of them had seen a dress since the reception station, but they clearly meant what they were saying. Jarrell said, grinning broadly, "The men just *eat it up,* being with us. They love to get us to keep up with them."

A message to assemble downstairs broke up the little group. They all filed into the dayroom and waited. The dayroom was cool and fragrant. Sergeant Bell called the troops to attention, and then Lieutenant Myers appeared, gingerly preceding Nancy Miller, the young woman who had broken her neck. Nancy wore a neck brace and lots of steel and rubber that gave the effect of scaffolding around her head and shoulders; at two points the steel frame was screwed into her skull.

After a collective gasp of shock, they all broke into applause. Nancy stood like the Tin Woodman, smiling uncertainly, and then, starting to cry, she turned to Lieutenant Myers and buried her face in her shoulder, mumbling through sobs, "You did it to me, you creep." Lieutenant Myers patted her scaffolding and said proudly, "Nancy was out of bed two weeks earlier than she should have been!" "AW RIGHT!" they chorused. Lieutenant Myers continued, "That shows the power of Alpha Company!" One of the black caucus shook her head in pleasure and said softly to herself, "We rough!" Nancy hugged her drill sergeant, Stokes, who clutched at his chest in a mock heart attack of ecstasy.

The drill sergeants had warned me that the trainees would lose their interest after bivouac. One said, "If you don't watch 'em, in a week they just slide, and it gets faster. They don't want to work anymore, they just want to graduate." Or, as Sergeant Reilly put it, pausing in one of her interminable phone calls, elbows propped on the desk, a cloud of smoke from her cigarette wreathing her head, glasses down on her nose, "This week is a nightmare. It's all hugs and kisses and taking photographs, and everything they've ever learned goes right out of the window." The sergeant was right.

End-of-cycle testing went badly. PT was tested every week, and all the weapons qualifications had taken place out on the ranges, so on this particular Thursday morning, under the pine trees at the bottom of the hill, they were being tested on the assembly and disassembly of weapons, on guard duty, military customs and courtesies (saluting and address), first aid, drill and ceremonies, and nuclear-biological proficiency (how to check and don the protective mask). The drill sergeants sat in the bleachers, swinging their legs and joshing as they waited for the people who were no-go's to come back and tell them where and how they had gone wrong. A trainee with one no-go would compose himself or herself and return for a second try, but anyone with a double no-go would have to retake the test on another day and risk missing graduation.

Lieutenant Myers was visibly nervous. She paced up and down, pushing at the dirt with her foot and talking compulsively to the young lieutenant from West Point and to Sergeant Bell. Trainees began trailing over to the bleachers with hangdog faces. After an hour Sergeant Stokes said angrily, "I've had eight men and seven females in my platoon. I didn't expect to see this many in the whole goddam day." Lieutenant Myers said, scowling, "I *hate* this." The air was full of anger and unvoiced blame. A female drill said, "They're messing up things we can do nothing about." The West Point lieutenant said, "There's been too much shucking and jiving." Lieutenant Myers, walking off, said that she had tried to direct the emphasis toward tactical training, not saluting. She was working herself up to make a case against this man's Army, where drill and courtesy and ceremony were so prized, but the lieutenant from West Point stopped her before she could begin by smiling ironically down into her furious face and saying, "You couldn't run an army without all that."

Lieutenant Myers and I walked around the various points at which the tests were in progress. At weapons assembly and disassembly, supervised by a small fat sergeant with a heavy German accent and a sardonic manner, the wretched crip was fumbling in a sweat of fright, but she managed to finish in the time. Most of the women were harangued on their slowness, which they could not do anything about, since it was caused by their small hands on the handguards. A big, emotional black woman came stumbling out of the tent with a large, dark stain spreading down the insides of the legs of her fatigue pants and an expression of embarrassment and fear. Lieutenant Myers led her swiftly away to the car and back up to the barracks to change.

In a lull, a clutch of testers surrounded me and complained about the decline in standards. One said that when he was at jump school in '67, out of 1180 who started, only 700 graduated. He said belligerently, "Now the physical requirement is *nothing*. It doesn't mean a thing to have those wings on you—you're not an elite the way you used to be."

When Lieutenant Myers returned, I asked her what could be said to men like these. Lieutenant Myers said, peering severely around at her dejected trainees, "The only way to deal with an argument like that is to break the guy's neck or challenge one of the more rotund ones to a one-mile run. We would both finish, but he would die of a heart attack." Clearly, she had thought about these things many times. She continued, poking vigorously in the dirt with her confidence stick, "Remember, it's the *men* who provide the buses to take us to the ranges. If the women aren't pushed, how can they succeed? Standards in basic may have declined, but it's not because of the women. It's not because they can't do it."

The West Point lieutenant said quietly that it was a mistake to listen to people who ranted about the decline in standards. Usually they were romanticizing their own pasts, or remembering basic training as it was conducted in wartime or on infantry posts. He said, "Most of these people are going to be medics and paper pushers, just like most people in the Army are." He added, "We just can't train on the basis of exceptions, those times when people who aren't trained for combat find themselves on the front line. All we can really hope for is that they know how to defend themselves with the M-16." While the cadre continued to stand in its tight group discussing military policy under the pine trees, trainees shuffled from test point to test point.

The unpopular captain from Battalion HQ had said one day as we watched Alpha Company assemble in mild confusion, "Of course Bravo Company is much more military." When I had told Lieutenant Myers that somebody had made this comment, she chuckled and said, "I expect it was a man, and he said that because Bravo is run by men." Captain Dixon had also said, as we stood watching the trainees clumsily receive their initiation into drill, "Today's Army isn't so good. These women should have stuck to their

traditional place." Gazing out over the lush green parade
ground, he added, "Women aren't mentally prepared to pilot
a helicopter under fire; they're not even prepared for life in
Germany, where you might be one of a hundred and fifty
people living miles from anywhere in huts made by Hitler."
The other men were either more flexible in their attitudes or
else more discreet.

Back at the building after testing, I asked two of the male
drill sergeants what they thought of the way in which training
was conducted. Sergeant Stokes, grinning out sardonically
from behind his thick glasses and neat mustache, said,
"Okay, women in the military serve a purpose." He truly
enjoyed training women; Lieutenant Myers called him a total
chauvinist, and she was right. He teased, flattered, and
yelled in ways that kept his females docile and adoring. Still,
he did not like the changes in training that accompanied their
arrival. He said, "I keep having to hold myself back, slow
down on the marches. There are songs that are 'too provocative' for me to sing in front of the women. And if I tell a man
to do twenty push-ups, I know I have to tell a woman to do
that—and I know she can't." He said, and he is a gentle
man, "They baby them *too much;* you can't run them more
than a quarter mile the first week, or on hard pavement for
the next two weeks, or 'get carried away with physical
force.'" Nevertheless he resented the curbs on his freedom.
"It really wouldn't hurt to shake the shit out of some of them
or curse them out."

Sergeant Lester was spending a lot of time in his cramped
and airless office, its walls covered with family photos and
pictures of his platoons. Dragging on a cigarette, his eyes
circled with fatigue, and a litter of reports to be filled out
splashed across his desk, he told me that he was depressed
with this cycle. Trainees, fretting about one thing or another,
knocked timidly on the door every few minutes and were
dispatched with a thunderous "GO AWAY." Lester said,
"The troops should really be pushed. I worked at Fort Dix
and the troops there outshone these one hundred to one,
easily," he said. "There they *molded* people."

He said, "If you have to get someone into physical shape, for instance, how can you do it except physically? But there are these restrictions. We can't even stop people piling their plates." He grew melancholy and said, "Lieutenant Myers is a wonderful commander and she would be a great combat soldier, but, you know, the prejudice against women doesn't diminish. I have always had female bosses, so I'm used to them, but, mostly, men just give the women a little chance to mess up. They are thinking; I hope you blow it."

After testing, the whole cadre was depressed. Senior Drill Sergeant Bell told me, "I'm absolutely crushed. They tell me they have a case of the nerves at testing, and I don't want to hear it. We have given them too much of a break and they have screwed up." At the graduation service rehearsal in the tiny white WAC chapel, Lieutenant Myers looked at her charges and said in measured tones, "I usually don't say anything apart from goodbye at this point, but I just want to talk to you about what you accomplished or did not accomplish." She paused and began, "I'm not quite so proud of you as I'd like to be." The troops stared back fractiously. When they left the chapel they sang their new cadence with extreme lustiness, "YOUR LEFT RIGHT, SENIOR TROOPS."

The mood of the last few days was bumpy with high spirits but low morale. When the women first tried on their dress uniforms, it was very reluctantly. The Class A uniform, or "greens," for the female soldier is dark green and bulky. The black beret perched awkwardly, as if deposited by a gust of wind. The uniforms had been measured and altered all that time ago—it seemed like months—when many of the trainees had had quite different shapes. As they struggled in and out of the clothes they complained noisily. Simmons, the crip, told me she had lost fifteen pounds; Patty Sharp had still not gained enough weight to satisfy the physical requirements, so they had taken to weighing her in boots and a box. Elizabeth said, smoothing the jacket down over her hips, "I've gained eleven pounds, and all on my butt," and she slapped herself in mock horror. In reality she looked like a recruiting poster, her hat correctly positioned. One of the women, in a skirt for the first time ever, flexed her thick muscular legs and said, smiling slowly, "Air!"

They lined up and Lieutenant Myers came to inspect them, bringing with her a tremor of WAC esprit, a ghost from the days when people really knew how to starch and polish. All the drawers were open, all the clothes hanging to face the right direction in the locker. Lieutenant Myers, resplendent in dress uniform and the regulation amount of discreet lipstick, walked slowly, attentively around each trainee, looking for pieces of thread or shadows on the brass that would indicate insufficient polishing, a crooked alignment of brass and badge. The trainees stood stiffly, facing straight ahead, eyes level and chins tucked in, while Sergeant Pace grimaced anxiously.

Lieutenant Myers is so small that in order to inspect the top shelf of the lockers she had to climb up onto the beds and peer in. It did not occur to anyone to find this funny. At each locker she would murmur, "Towels incorrectly displayed" or "Photographs untidily affixed" before continuing.

The most eagerly awaited visitor, without question, was Clark's Jimmy, for the wedding to be held on post on graduation day. Jimmy and his best friend stayed at the guesthouse. Both were fair and pale, and very quiet. There was little opportunity for Jimmy and Clark to be together, but he would appear at the company or stand at the back of formation like an anxious ghost. His short hair, growing in after the Navy haircut, gave him the look of a slum child who had been treated for ringworm. In fact he was only a few years older than a child. Clark crashed about in a dither of delight, all her illnesses and accidents banished.

Sergeant Stokes taught the trainees new words to the maddeningly catchy tune of "Sha Na Na Na/Hey Hey Hey," a famous sixties song. "No more chow line/no more weapons/ hey hey hey, goodbye . . . ," they sang as they regarded, with the superiority caused by six weeks of training, the chaotic, scuttling crowd that was Delta Company in its first week of training. Delta troops did not know how to march, how to sing, even how to stand. One of the women, swinging along at the back of formation next to me, whispered out of the side of her mouth, "I know it's mean to laugh at them, but I *just love* it."

The atmosphere up in the bays grew rancid. People began to exchange casual blows in the laundry room ("Why you hit me, Linda?" "Because you were mentioning my name. Don't you mention my name."). The Californian, sitting with a red bandana tied around her head and the tranquil gaze of a stoned person, said, "The first two weeks here were so neat, such fun, I even thought of going Regular Army, but now there's so much bullshit and trauma and so much wasting time. Look at us now—we could be doing something."

The whining complaints and the slowly increasing sense of disillusion were not inevitable. It was not that the women particularly minded having to clean the bay and being yelled at by drill sergeants. Sergeant Pace, who had replaced Sergeant Lester when he was detailed to another company, would scream so savagely that trainees dozing on their beds would leap up frantically, eyes wide in shock. Still, when she had finished, they would cluster around her to ask about PT scores or make conversation, simply because they thought she was neat, just as the men did. The problem was that since bivouac they had begun to feel that their achievements were not so terrific.

Just in the nick of time Simmons the crip managed to run a mile. Most trainees had reached level 13 in PT, the top score. This meant running two miles in under twenty minutes and doing a certain number of push-ups and sit-ups. Level 6 was a passing grade; it required a one-mile run and fewer push-ups and sit-ups. Simmons had missed everything, forever watching dolefully from the sidelines and dragging her lumpish cast to some new "guard duty." Out on the range one day I had watched her plodding after the company up a steep, slippery hill. When she stopped to light a cigarette, Lieutenant Myers' quiet voice came from behind

her: "Trainees are not allowed to smoke while walking."
Simmons gasped. "Let's forget it," Myers said. "It's between you and me, Simmons." Later Lieutenant Myers had
said that she would do anything possible to help Simmons
through because she was so strongly motivated.

Once the cast came off, the drills and her friends spent
time in the evenings coaching her. She was savagely impatient with her slow progress. One night just before dinner,
Elizabeth and Sergeant Pace took her out to the parade
ground and forced her through the mile. They ran alongside,
clutching fiercely at her T-shirt and picking her up every
time she buckled; they bullied her and they encouraged her.
At the finish she stood livid and panting, with large patches
of sweat on her T-shirt, while Elizabeth and Pace patted her
on the back, saying proudly, "See? You did it!" As soon as
she got her breath she looked at them and at me and shook
her head. She said evenly, "No, I didn't—you helped me—I
didn't do the mile run."

Patty Sharp still did not know how to make her bed, clean,
assemble or fire a weapon, or perform *any* of her military
duties without help from her fellow trainees or the sergeants.
Her drill sergeant, Lester, told me his operating principle:
"The Army needs numbers, and we're in the business of
giving them numbers. You have to remember that Patty will
always be a garrison troop, and she might be perfectly
capable at her job. In all conscience, she shouldn't graduate." He pulled a list toward him and began figuring. He
dragged on his cigarette and said, "But if I was going to kick
her out, I'd have to kick out all these people too."

Whatever his reasons, the trainees were enraged about
Patty. As they mopped and bickered, she walked around
flipping people's key chains out from the necks of their T-
shirts and saying with an odd little grin, "Sergeant Lester
won't do anything to me." The men ignored her for the most
part, but the women took her inadequacies personally, as a
reflection on their own performances or a threat to their
success. Her very presence made theirs insecure; Patty was a
living example of the argument that women were too small,

frail, emotional, unreliable, and that they were allowed to
"get over." The growing cynicism of the trainees and the
gloom of the cadre prompted me to ask how the Wacs would
have done things differently.

The most pro-Wac woman in the company was also the
most anti-integration. Cooper was in her late twenties, a
sergeant, boyish and slight, with a mischievous look and a
short mop of black hair. She said bitterly, "The Wacs always
set an example, and they kept the adrenaline pumping.
Those women were tough," she added, "they set high
standards, and if you didn't meet them, you were gone."

Cooper had no time for the male complaint that they did
not have the freedom to push trainees to their limits. "You
can *always* find ways," she said. "You can keep them so busy
that you zap them. Most of the men are too soft with the
women—they won't push them at PT, do exercises that
strengthen their swaybacks to help with the push-ups. Why
don't they build in stages and continue at AIT?" Cooper
talked with the assurance of someone very young, but she
had known Fort McClellan under very different circumstances. She said, "Not all the females were perfect, and
some ranted and raved, but the standards were higher, and
they took a nose dive when the first male drills arrived.
There was suddenly all this *macho mystique.* Suddenly nothing
was *explained* to the trainees anymore. Now they tear up the
beds and scream and yell. They never write things down
about the trainees, and the trainees never know from one
moment to the next what's happening, so how *can* they be
responsible?" This seemed a reasonably accurate description
of the chaos in the bays, where the drill sergeants' conflicting
instructions were as open to interpretation as a chicken's
entrails.

Cooper said, her monologue warmed by anger, "The
males came in outranking the females and just threw out all
the old things because they wanted the control. Our trainees
were better than Fort Jackson trainees—you would have
been able to *see* the difference. The men could have sat down
and pooled ideas, but they weren't interested." Cooper

maintained that she could have adapted to the men but she could not adapt to the declining standards and the lack of esprit that they had brought. She said, "That Sergeant Butler with his poem about Private Littlebit is rare now. Now you'll hear officers and NCOs making sick jokes about how 'the Army'll screw you every time' in front of the trainees." Cooper ended: "I'm tired of this; I'm getting out and going to school instead."

On the last night the women seemed determined to prove their irresponsibility. At bed-check time the Californian realized that her prized new twenty-five-dollar running shoes were lost and presumed stolen. Abandoning her customary reticence, she began to yell and slam locker doors. "My running shoes to me are like a dress to someone else." Another young woman, who found that her steam iron had been used and left plugged in with water in it, stormed around slamming all the doors that were left to slam and screaming violent threats. It was 10:15; Schulman fled to the latrines to play her guitar, and the voice of a trainee droned from a corner, ". . . and polish my pumps and polish my low-quarters."

Downstairs, Lieutenant Myers toiled at the paper work that ushers a cycle of trainees in and out. Her face was pale, and with a philosophical expression, she said, "This bunch was good in the field and terrible in the building, and there was a definite decline in esprit." She said she felt that this had less to do with the falling off from WAC standards than with uncertain policies. "They're always changing the rules on us," she said. She agreed with Cooper that one aspect of WAC training should have been held over, namely, the special PT to strengthen the muscles of the young women who had never done any serious athletics before joining the Army. She said, "I'm coming to think that success in PT is the clue to it all."

Lieutenant Myers was careful not to criticize her NCOs. She said sometimes their actions were dictated by jealousy and infighting, but that happened in any unit, whatever the balance of males or females. "But," she said, "the crucial thing is numbers—there have to be enough women wherever there are women. That's the problem with sending them to combat. I couldn't let them go unless they were virtually equal in numbers."

Eyeing the wreckage upstairs, Lieutenant Myers said, "I'm not at all pleased. Last cycle they got *so much* sleep; the dayroom was always gorgeous." The trainees were given twenty minutes to find the shoes; the crip noticed Patty Sharp carefully tidying her locker and said explosively, *"Are you graduating?"* Patty slammed the door shut and said, "Yes. I'm sorry. I'm graduating if it means sitting up all night." She came over to me to show me that on the back of her Platoon photograph Sergeant Lester had written, "Young lady, you have help draw America closer by your wonderful efforts." Joan Clark was also tidying her locker, in a tired and methodical way, as if she were hypnotized. It occurred to me that the contents were her trousseau, and this was the night before her wedding to someone she had known for a day. At 1:00 A.M. the MPs were called to investigate the matter of the running shoes, which were never found.

Graduation day itself was blustery and rainy, so the parade was canceled. The entire company was in a terrible mood. Sergeant Pace and Senior Drill Sergeant Bell were engaged in a close conversation just short of a major quarrel about Patty Sharp and whether or not she should graduate, with Sergeant Pace seething and red-faced, Sergeant Bell a study in cold composure. Sergeant Pace said Patty Sharp had never done a detail and could not make her bed. "I have been hearing this for weeks," said Sergeant Bell calmly, "but nobody has brought me anything in writing."

Upstairs, the bays looked terrible, with long scrapes and scuff marks across the floors, tumbleweeds of fluff around the beds. As usual, three furious people were making Patty's bed for her. Somehow they stumbled out to formation in a semblance of order, but some had hair sticking out oddly from under their hats, and creases accidentally pressed into their sleeves. Colonel Burke, the Director of Initial Entry Training at Fort McClellan, was the honored guest. Lieutenant Myers clearly was very fond of Colonel Burke. For weeks she had been congratulating herself on her courage in asking him. Lieutenant Myers had told me he was a brilliant man, but, she said hesitantly, "in many respects you would have to say that he's a chauvinist. He'd probably like to keep women out and be their protector although he knows they have the ability. He's the type who calls you a dumb broad so that you get mad and prove yourself."

Colonel Burke, a handsome man, had a wide, flat face and sensual lips. He inspected the young women with a flirtatious and debonair charm. To Julie Drake he said, gently smiling, "Next time we have an inspection, fix your hair so that I can see your pretty green eyes." Lieutenant Myers looked into the distance; Julie blushed and her expression turned gauzy. Small clusters of parents began to appear, and their children were summoned on the squawk box to be clasped in long, silent, tearful embraces, just as if they were back from the war.

Most of Alpha Company's women were too exhausted to concentrate on their graduation. The halting service began late because the band did not arrive on time, and when it finally did arrive, it set up and began a dirge of tuning. A baby at the back embarked upon its own dirge, but when the band swung heartily into the theme from *Rocky*, the trainees seemed to rouse themselves, and some gasped and smiled.

Lieutenant Myers introduced members of the cadre and then Colonel Burke, who beamed roguishly and made a few remarks about Lieutenant Myers' climbing the tree in the night problem. He said he had threatened to put her in his vest pocket if she did not behave. The trainees gazed ahead dully as Colonel Burke moved into his climactic peroration, a welcome and a call to service. He cited heroes of the past and referred consistently to "the young men of this country," building to a crescendo with lists of famous battles and references to amber waves of grain, against a duet of two babies.

As parents and friends lined the roadway, grinning and taking pictures, the new soldiers marched from the chapel back up the hill. The sun had come out; the company looked impressive, with Jarrell, stiff and military, carrying the guidon in front, the men seemingly tougher and more robust, the women more feminine, with their discreet makeup and panty hose. Fisher's family were standing next to me. Her father said, "I hardly recognized her when I saw her first. She has contact lenses now, she's lost a few pounds, she's had her hair cut off, and—do you know something?—when I squeezed her arm, it was *hard*." He said this with a touching mixture of bewilderment and pride, and glanced sideways at his son standing next to him, as gawky and freckled as Jeannie but with shoulder-length red hair and a "Kiss" T-shirt.

A little later Clark's wedding was held on the other side of post. The rain had ceased, but the afternoon was gray. Lieutenant Myers had bought a bunch of pink, red, and white carnations for Clark's bouquet. At the tinny old piano sat Claire Hayes, from Vermont, and Clark was followed up the aisle by an honor guard of seven, one of them Elizabeth, her face split by a wide grin. She had every reason to be happy, for her entire family and two boyfriends had made the drive from Dalton, Georgia, to be there for the graduation, and she had decided to try for Officer Candidate School. The ceremony was short and simple. "Do you, Jimmy, pledge your love and life to Joan?" asked the ginger-haired young assistant chaplain as the congregation consisting of cadre tried to think positively about this marriage. Later Clark and Jimmy sat in state at the graduation dinner, eating the special graduation food—shrimp, banana custard—with grave dignity. They cut the cake, then hugged, canoodled, and posed for photographs.

The bus for Fort Sam was waiting at the front door. All the medical specialists (including most of the women) would be leaving on it. Trainees ran upstairs and finished packing, throwing out hair spray and talcum powder because the cans were too bulky to fit into their duffel bags.

I went over to the Public Affairs Office to do my own outprocessing, and was talking about the happy atmosphere for most of the past six weeks at Alpha when the captain in charge, a sympathetic figure, said, "I have to tell you, confidentially, that out there at places like Fort Polk, Louisiana, they don't like women and they don't treat them well." He said Fort Polk was deep in the bayou, eight miles from the nearest McDonald's, and then he dialed his opposite number at Fort Polk to ask how many women were serving there. "Too damn many," came the reply. At that time there were about 7400 white males and 500 white women, 4000 black males and 200 black women. I heard an echo of Sergeant Lester's voice saying, "Mostly, men just give the women a little chance to mess up. They are thinking: I hope you blow it."

Back at the building I watched the trainees in turmoil and talked to a rambunctious friend of Lieutenant Myers', a captain from the other side of the post, who said, "Of course they'll encounter prejudice. I've been picked on and burst into tears. But you have to fight it. I sit there with tears in my eyes and think: I'm not going to cry—I refuse to do this, you son of a bitch, you're not going to make me cry. You just have to change your habits," she said; "fight instead of crying to Daddy. The system is set up to fight prejudice—if only people will make it work."

The trainees began to come down. Sergeant Stokes stood watching them get on the buses, speculating as to who would cry the most. Jarrell hugged everyone, her eyes streaming tears, and ran back inside. Stokes said wonderingly to another of his trainees, "You've been crying nonstop for days." The bridal pair, who had spent three hours together, kissed and hugged, and Clark, smiling and crying, climbed unsteadily up the steps of the bus and found herself a window seat. She stared down at Jimmy through the shaded glass, and he up at her; all around people waved and sobbed and yelled their farewells. Elizabeth boarded, crying, and said she would write. Sergeant Stokes muttered, "They all say they'll write, but they never do." I glanced up and saw a few people hanging from the windows and waving, the only ones who were left behind. I ran upstairs to say goodbye and found them ramming their final possessions into their bags and talking about the party they were going to have at one minute past midnight at the Gamecock Hotel, just a few miles from the post. It was going to be a wild night.

Jarrell ran a hand through her short hair and said irritably, "It's a shame that here are these people that have knocked themselves out to do well, and then you look at *Patty* graduating, and you know that you could have got by with what she did, but you wouldn't have." They moaned agreement, Walters from California saying how much she had wanted to be pushed to do her best.

I asked what they thought about the men. A quiet black woman who had been a capable and unobtrusive squad leader looked up from her packing and said, suddenly seeming much older than her eighteen years, "Oh, men are okay. Men are men. They still think they have the power and you have to follow them. It doesn't make any sense to me to argue."

10

Obstacle Course:
West Point

"This is not at all like McClellan," Major Nederlander told me in the pastel grandeur of the West Point Officers Club, its long windows hung with heavy curtains, the Muzak barely audible. Major Nederlander, who had spent twenty years in the Army, much of it at Fort McClellan, was one of about twenty-five women, mostly officers, who had met for a rare lunch in one of the private rooms. I was introduced to Colonel Collins, the highest ranking woman at West Point, and to a clutch of captains and lieutenants, who were standing in their dark-green uniforms and talking, with glasses of rosé or club soda in their hands. The lunch was an informal affair that had been arranged so that the handful of women scattered throughout the Academy's faculty and administration would have the opportunity to meet. It was January 1980, and most had been at the Academy for close to four years.

Major Nederlander is a small woman with short gray hair and a straightforward manner. She said conversationally, "I've worked all over the place, with men and with women, and this has been the most difficult year of my career." We arranged to talk another time, at her office. "You will see," she said, "that they have put my desk behind a pillar." She continued, her alert, intelligent face creased into a smile, "They have put me there to remind me of my situation. It doesn't move. If it did, it would at least give me more incentive to push."

We sat down to eat at round tables. I was placed between Colonel Collins and Lieutenant Parrish, a perky blond woman in her late twenties who was a Tac, or tactical officer, West Point's equivalent of a drill sergeant. As we ate chef salad and rolls the conversation turned to combat and how the idea of it was sensationalized. One of the captains said earnestly, leaning across the table, "All those things that men say about women and combat are myths. All that business about what happens to you if you're captured, about how men and women couldn't fight in the same foxhole, and about women not having the stamina for battle." Colonel Collins grinned and said, "Women have already been prisoners of war. Look at what the nurses did in World Wars One and Two. Women can hold up under terrible conditions just as well as men." A tall young woman with a Scandinavian accent blushed and said, "This place bears no relation to the real world or to life in the Army. They don't seem to understand that equality does not mean we all have to be the same."

The conversation branched into a discussion of the more extreme limitations on the cadets. "A twenty-four-year-old had to write me a note asking permission to go into town to go to the bank," said Lieutenant Parrish with amused incredulity in her voice. Colonel Collins murmured, "Did you know that they classified the results of some of the astronauts' tests because the women did better than the men?" (I later learned the basis for this story. When the first men were tested for the Mercury program in 1959–1960, twelve women were also tested, secretly. Three of them performed exceptionally well but were not allowed into the program. Today women are in training, but as "mission specialists" for the space shuttle, which means that they will be crew members, able to do anything except pilot the craft.)

Voices in a chorus told me that nothing out there in the Army was as hard as it was meant to be. Laughter began to rise. One woman said, *"Any* of us can lead a basic training company." Another one said scornfully, "Women can easily do Ranger school." As the wintry lunchtime sun gleamed on the silverware and the brass at the women's collars, they began to talk about violence against women: wife-beating and rape and murder were mentioned. "We are all vulnerable, and we all need to know how to fight," said a captain. One of the officers said, folding her napkin, "As for that business about men and women sharing foxholes, if you are next to a male in a foxhole in a combat situation and you need to urinate or change your Tampax, you'll just *go ahead and do it!*" Another interrupted: "Why, I'd just bleed right through!" They laughed, as much at her ironic tone as at her words, and agreed. I left for a class on the psychology of war, thinking, No wonder the men suspect sabotage when the women get together in the private room upstairs.

Major Nederlander, walking back with me, said, "McClellan was unique in that there was a support system. When I was there in '78, it had the lowest incidence of trainee abuse of any training center in the Army. The men in my office thought we were doing a big cover-up because they weren't getting any reports of harassment. But women take better care of their troops. I think they have a better concept of leadership than men, countrywide as well as Army-wide. There's a care and concern about your people and about getting the job done properly. The best male leaders have that, but most of them are too lenient. They just issue orders, and don't bother to follow up to see if action has been taken. Here, for example, they say there will be no more harassment, and leave it at that."

West Point is an influential part of the Army. A great ballyhoo accompanied the first female cadets to arrive there in July 1976. The women of the class of 1980 suffered and toiled for four years in a miasma of male resentment, and always in the public eye. The stories of their initiation may be familiar. I review them briefly here because they are illuminating, especially as seen through the eyes of the women officers, who also were new to West Point, also had a difficult time, but were in a much better position either to resist or, at the least, to judge what was happening with the seasoned attitude of professional soldiers. Nobody asked for their opinions; frequently, when they offered opinions they were ignored. However, these women, about fifty of them, out of a faculty and administration of more than a thousand men, were in a unique position to give an opinion, as career soldiers and outsiders. I shall present their views later.

Fort McClellan had been primarily a female post until the WAC was disbanded and brought into the mainstream of the Army. West Point was an all-male institution that, following a decision of Congress in 1975 to integrate the service academies, reluctantly opened its doors to women. The parallels between Fort McClellan and West Point do not extend a great deal further. At Fort McClellan, even though General Mary Clarke remained as post commander (now she is at the Pentagon), within months of disestablishment, men predominated at all levels, as they do in the Army. At West Point the new policy meant a major symbolic change, but because there were so few women, the composition and the nature of the place remained defiantly unchanged. While Fort McClellan was powerless to resist the influx of men, at West Point men had the power to begin with and did not have to relinquish any of it when the women arrived.

At Fort McClellan there was little evidence of status. It was not just the faulty targets and the shortage of drill sergeants; there did not seem to be enough paper clips. People were always improvising. West Point, however, had impressive stationery. The Academy, with its slablike granite buildings, its wood-paneled offices and looming statues of famous graduates—Bradley, Patton, MacArthur—exuded wealth, privilege, poise. Watching the St. Patrick's Day parade down Fifth Avenue in New York from the window of the Army Public Affairs Office, I asked a group of people around me what they thought of West Point. A ruddy-faced colonel from New England said candidly, "I hate the way those West Pointers talk about their mission. They talk so self-righteously, so moralistically; as if *nobody else* has any morality." He said, "As a graduate of ROTC, I resent that."

West Point has always provoked extreme reactions. To some extent the Academy invites this, with its self-assured hauteur that can give a third-generation West Pointer the air of an English aristocrat with a few thousand acres tucked away on the Scottish borders. On my first visit to the Academy, sitting in the thickly carpeted offices and gazing into the courtyard through mullioned windows, I asked whether I might meet a female cadet. They said cheerfully, "No problem," and dispatched a messenger. Within minutes a pink and smiling young woman was sitting next to me, as if deposited by a genie. She wore layers of the heavy gray uniform, culminating in a cape, and the shiny peaked cap, which she took off to reveal a gleaming crop of hair. She ran a hand through her hair and then listened politely. All she needed was the impetus. Clearing her throat, she began to tell me in a clear voice, her eyes a little abstracted, about all the ways in which West Point had enabled her to become realized as a person, to feel confident and self-reliant. I wanted to believe her, but she seemed to be talking to me over a public address system.

This cadet was one of 119 admitted alongside 900 males in July 1976. The faculty and alumni had bitterly opposed the idea. Once the decision was reached, General Knowlton, who had said he would resign as Superintendent if women were admitted, did so and was replaced by General Berry, who prepared to carry out the mission. "We have our orders," he wrote stoically in the alumni magazine, "and it is our responsibility to implement them to the best of our ability."

Under such circumstances the military mind often comes up with a survey. West Point is particularly susceptible to surveys because, in its fascination with the superrational approach, the Academy has built a whole department around sociology—the Behavioral Sciences and Leadership Department. BS&L became notorious with Project Athena, a three-volume study of the women and the Academy: the preparations for them, the attitudes of all concerned before and after their arrival and at various points of their progression through the four-year curriculum.

In two initial surveys, conducted in the summer of 1975 and the spring of 1976, the attitudes of cadets, staff, and faculty were explored. The findings were, in essence, that although these men were full of conventional pieties and hearty good wishes for the advancement of women, in practice they wished the women would do it somewhere else. "When it comes to women in the Army, cadets were quite negative," said one report. "Cadets had strong fears of 'reverse discrimination,'" they "were very pessimistic about the impact of women cadets on pride and discipline," and so on. An instructor in BS&L told me that his colleagues had been shocked and surprised when many of the cadets admitted that they would be happy to see the women cry.

The preparations for these unwelcome women included modifications of the uniforms and also of the barracks. The women were to live in little pockets of eight to twelve, distributed among eight of the thirty-six companies. They would share rooms in twos and threes, and of course the latrines would be modified. One of the first things a visitor notices at West Point is the apparent ubiquitousness of female latrines, marked with enormous signs. Clearly the authorities had realized that a shortage of latrines would be an obvious and direct form of sexism. They were slower to stock the latrines with sanitary napkins, but those too arrived, evidences of femininity that looked as incongruous in the barracks surroundings as the copies of *Mademoiselle* in the library. Consciousness-raising was informally exercised on the barbers and tailors. I was told, "We couldn't let those old Italians near the female cadets without explaining things to them." As for the uniform, as Project Athena reports it: "Hart Schaffner and Marx designed new women's uniforms. Care was taken to insure that women cadets would 'blend.'

One exception to this was to design the women's full dress coat—the coat worn during the most formal parades—without tails. This was done to make the coat more stylish when worn to social affairs, and to facilitate the fit of the coat to the women's anatomy." As a jovial colonel at the Public Affairs Office told me, laughing, "This bunch of men decided that since the female bottom had a tendency to stick out more than a man's, it would look stupid and demean the uniform if it had a tailcoat over it." In the long line of cadets standing rigidly erect or marching like clockwork soldiers, each one in an immaculate gray coat with white trousers and the crossed white straps of the pistol belt—there, gleaming and round, and disrupting the harmony of the line in a not unpleasant manner, would be isolated female bottoms. That design decision was reversed.

There were conferences, briefings, and discussions. Seminars were held on such subjects as human relations and women's role in the Army. Female-related visitors from Wacs to hair-style consultants appeared at the Academy, and West Point faculty and staff members made fact-finding trips to other posts and to Washington. Most cadet briefings were directed at the class of '77, who would be the upperclassmen, or "firsties," in authority over the women through their first year, and who had to log many hours with the experts. Reading about this, I remembered what Alpha Company had done in the way of preparations: "Oh, we wandered over to the MP school and asked them what they did."

Most attention was given to determining what, if any, changes should be made in the strenuously physical curriculum of the Academy to accommodate women. Little was known about the average healthy young woman's strength, endurance, or potential for development. So the physical education department employed Dr. James and Dr. Sue Peterson, who did most of the pioneering work. Dr. James Peterson, a kindly, rumpled man in his forties, is ex-Army and a firm advocate of the women. His wife, a civilian, had taught aikido and self-defense to males and females at the University of Illinois. She was given the task of running the combat courses for males and females and devising the appropriate way to train women in close-combat techniques, concentrating on their strengths, whatever they might be, rather than on the adoption of traditional male fighting maneuvers. Various tests were conducted, and local students actually went through some of the exercises of Cadet Basic Training, which is the initial two-month period of training known as Beast Barracks. The tests showed that women had less leg strength, less over-all power, less endurance, and less grip strength. Six pull-ups are required on the physical aptitude test taken by all entering cadets, and most women tested could not manage one.

The physical training was modified for women and so were the ways of testing, so that women could be tested fairly. All this was done with care and deliberateness. However, the authors of Project Athena, Volume I, noted with rare canniness: "Perhaps the biggest gap in planning for the integration of women was the emphasis in preparations on the physiological aspects of integrating women into a pre-viously all-male environment, almost to the exclusion of preparing cadets, and officers, for the emotional and attitudi-nal factors which would later take on such significance."

Most of the cadets who arrived in July 1976 had visited the Academy only once or twice before. West Point at first glimpse is awesome, even frightening—a pile of granite buildings on high bluffs overlooking a bend in the Hudson River, two hours' drive north from New York City. It is a fortress, not a college. The ethos is rugged, based on a Spartan life of intense competition—particularly in athlet-ics—arduous, continuous study, both academic and military, and, pervading everything, strict adherence to discipline and tradition as exemplified in the motto Duty, Honor, Country. The idea is to elicit real leadership from a well-rounded individual. West Pointers proudly think of the Academy as a combat school, even though about 15 percent of the gradu-ates in any given year do not enter the combat arms. Typical graduates are not intellectuals—they are practical, dogged, and competent, and often very successful, as they move surely up the ladder to the top positions at the Pentagon, in the field, and in business.

There were cracks in the structure. In 1976 the Academy had weathered a rough period when its cherished ideals were publicly and loudly held up to question. Some attributed the worst mismanagement and excesses of the Vietnam war to the rigidly deterministic approach to warfare taught at West Point. A large cheating scandal had violated the Honor Code, one of the Academy's most valued traditions.

General Goodpaster became the new Superintendent in the spring of 1977. A four-star general with a Ph.D., he had been persuaded to come out of retirement and accept a demotion in rank in order to help the Academy through its morale crisis. Some of the changes he began to make in the system coincided with the arrival of the women. Sounding a little like a modern Polonius, General Goodpaster told me that his policy was to supplement the existing "four main lines of cadet development—academic, military, physical, and moral/ethical—with social development in which the cadet develops his or her personality or individuality." The style was to be "supportive rather than adversarial," to lead by example, not by bullying, to stimulate inner more than externally imposed discipline. He did not, for example, favor brutal hazing. Supposedly it turned boys into men, but General Douglas MacArthur, who had been forced to do deep knee bends over broken glass until he fainted, was never in favor of it either.

The women cadets coming into Beast Barracks were immediate beneficiaries of Goodpaster's changes. Beast is that two months in which a civilian is rendered, first, a worthless dung fly in uniform, and then, after weeks of yelling and scrambling and 5:00 A.M. inspections and mind-less learning by rote, together with all the classroom and field instruction on the first principles of soldiering, a real plebe. Plebes used to have to stand at attention all the time, and at meals they sat and ate in silence, at attention. This kind of needless debasement was eliminated, over the fierce protests of alumni who went through the rigors of the old Beast and believed it made them the men they are today.

Of the hundred and nineteen women who entered the Academy on July 7, 1976, hardly any were pioneers. (Those who were found themselves poorly equipped for the long, slow struggle ahead, and had vanished by Christmas.) They hesitated to call themselves "feminists," partly because the word would have been inflammatory under the circumstances, but they were women who wanted their equal opportunity and were not ready to settle for anything less. However, in outlook they greatly resembled the men: they were conservative, serious, patriotic, and many came from military families. They had performed better in high school than many of the men, and had participated in more extramural activities. They tended to be less athletic, both in strength and in inclination, and, on average, smaller, lighter, and weaker.

Amy Branch is typical. An Army brat from a suburb of Dayton, she is tall and pretty and black; also patriotic and religious—a good citizen in the making. Sitting in the cafeteria one freezing morning, she told me what it was like to be a celebrity in her hometown. "As soon as I got the nomination, the newspapers and radio station came to my house. The newspapers built it up so big I couldn't have backed out if I'd wanted to. A radio station called me at home, but I'd gone to school, so they interviewed my mom instead. Another picked me as their Citizen of the Day. They called it Amy Branch Day, and all day long they had sixty-second blurbs about me. It was a real thrill." She laughed, poking at the ice in her cup of soda with a straw. "My father was in the Army for thirty years," she said, "but that didn't really have anything to do with my decision. I just heard about it one day, how they were opening the Academy up to women, and I decided I didn't have anything to lose. So I thought I'd sign up and see what happened. Why not give it a try?" Most of the cadets I met had approached West Point with the same mixture of wariness and nonchalance. A female officer said to me later, "You couldn't do it any other

way. At eighteen you're too young to think seriously about
signing away nine years of your life, and nine years is a *long
time*."

The male cadets of the class of '80 were confronted with
some surprises. When required to deal with women as
colleagues and fellow students in the art of war, they
experienced a jolt of disorientation not unlike that experienced by the Japanese soldiers emerging from the Philippine
jungles to find that not only was the war over but that now
Japan was providing most of the rest of the world with
electrical appliances. The shock was accompanied by bitterness, rage, and bewilderment, and the result was—as I heard
from the class of '80, their teachers, and tactical officers—a
collision between the young males and females and a
sustained and violent outburst of hostility from the men.

The stories came out in the cafeteria over paper cups of
coffee at 8:15 A.M.—which for a cadet is the middle of the
morning—and they came out in halting, polite voices as
people sat carefully on their narrow iron beds. Alice Sullivan,
an articulate twenty-three-year-old who had been studying
for a degree in marine biology at the University of Colorado
when she decided to try for West Point, was, of all the
candidates I met, most detached from what had happened,
presumably because she is a little older and has a skeptical
streak that developed into a tendency at the Academy. She is
slight and pale, no athlete, and she smokes a pack a day. She
calls herself a wimp.

Alice told me that the problems began with the uniform. It
had no pockets, which made life impossible for plebes, who
are constantly required to scribble down notes. All the
buttons and zippers were on the wrong side, and the plastic
zippers on the trousers would break. (A few of the women
ventured out to formation in a skirt once, but only once.)
Because the design and fabric of the bulky uniform did not
flatter the female figure, and because the jackets fastened on
the wrong side, in inspections the women never had a trim
"gig line"—the line made by jacket edges and trouser seams
when everything is correct. Irate upperclassmen, sniffing for

perfume, would poke and peer at the quaking women, and, unable to find a violation, conclude that what was wrong was what they had suspected all along. The cadets were girls!

Every cadet makes war stories out of the rigors of Beast. Amy Branch sat with me one morning in Grant Hall, with gossip and laughter all around, and she began to tell me her war stories. Grant Hall is probably the only place at the Academy that bears any resemblance to a campus building. It is a long lamplit hall with soft sofas and a fireplace, the walls hung with portraits of distinguished graduates. This is the only place civilian visitors may enter unescorted, a staging post for dates. The cafeteria at one end, wood-paneled and comfortable, with light pouring in, is where cadets can relax in mixed company while eating candy bars and doughnuts and cracking a book for the next class. What distinguishes it from a cafeteria on a real campus, however, is that no one in there is cutting class.

Branch said, "I remember the first time I really cried," and she told me about it. "One guy said to me, 'I can see by your rosy glow you must have been——,' and I said, 'Now, you wouldn't have said that to your mother, your sister, or your girlfriend or my roommate, so *don't say it to me.*' He said, 'Can't you see I'm joking?' I got so mad."

Most of the abuse of the women was expressed in these sexual terms. A quiet, graceful cadet called Joan Reeve said to me, "When we were in formation we had to stand at attention in silence. The guys would gather around and say sexual things about us that we couldn't respond to. They would surmise about our weekends and they'd talk about how many women they had gotten to bed. It was embarrassing." She looked for more effective words and said, "Just to be talked about as if you're not entirely human is a kind of terror." Alice Sullivan, sitting cross-legged on her bed, told me, "They would warn our classmates not to go out with us because we carried a lot of diseases." She laughed thinly at my horrified expression and said, "Of course it was just quite standard to be walking out to formation or class all neat and

straight and say to an upperclassman, 'Good morning, sir' and
have him say, 'Hi, whore.'"

Upperclassmen expressed their rage through enforced
haircuts. One of the Petersons in the physical education
department told me, "They would be sent to have their hair
cut, sometimes daily, and it would be savagely chopped off
in tiers, so that it looked quite terrible." Some cadets
managed to ignore it or rise above it, some seemed to invite
more. They told me about finding condoms overflowing with
shaving cream stuffed into their beds, obscene slogans
written all over their walls; they received vibrators in the
mail; they were called terrible names.

Reeve told me, "A sexual double standard was operating.
In the beginning it was the ones who were prettiest or the
most feminine, who wore perfume and makeup in formation.
The guys didn't like that at all; they felt that if the women
had time to do that, they should have been polishing shoes.
They turned on the pretty women because they felt they
didn't belong at West Point. They wanted to drive them
out."

Another cadet said, "A lot depended on the company. The
ones without women were the worst, and so they moved
some in." Sullivan said, "In my company six out of the
eleven women would collapse on the floor and hyperventil-
ate." She lit a cigarette and added, "This stuff was not
supposed to be going on. And you wouldn't believe how
terrified most of the women were. One was literally too
scared to leave her room—as soon as they see you, you're a
target—and so she would urinate in the sink at night rather
than risk going out to the bathroom." Sullivan said wanly,
"We could not let the authorities know what was happening,
because if we did we would be harassed further. We were
victims, and there was nothing we could do."

There were visits from upperclassmen in the night. One
sober young woman said, "It never happened to me, so I feel
nervous about telling you, but I *know* it happened a lot
between one and four A.M. when everyone was asleep.
There are no guards, no locks on the doors, so you can just

wander wherever you want." She said firmly, "I know of some plebe women who had this happen, and they couldn't tell."

Ellen Davis did tell. She was pretty and feminine-looking, with a high, girlish voice. A basketball star, very competent and keen, she was one of several women moved into a previously all-male company in order to improve antifemale attitudes. Ellen proved to be a catalyst for the hostility. She weathered several incidents of minor harassment before the night when an upperclassman came into her room at 2:30 A.M., and she awoke to the feel of his fingers between her legs. A friend of hers told me, "She just froze. She went downstairs and spent the rest of the night on the floor of another girl's room, who, when she woke up in the morning, found Ellen just sitting there in shock. They took her to the hospital, and the regimental commander took care of it. He was well known for his attitude; he'd brag about how many women he'd lost from his regiment. He's still there," she added.

The proceedings that followed were like an old-fashioned rape trial before a board. Ellen was put through a lie detector test and asked about her previous boyfriends and whether she was a virgin. The assailant was allowed to graduate but not commissioned, which made the rest of the women furious. They felt he had received the honor of graduation without the obligation of service—almost a reward. Ellen did not come back from vacation. Alice Sullivan told me, "One of the most interesting things about that was the reaction of the guys. They kept saying, 'Why are you all so upset, why's she so upset? She was just finger-fucked.'" There was a long pause, and Alice said, "I look at them, and I don't believe they said it, that they don't understand what it means to have your body violated." As a result of the incident the women, who share rooms, were not allowed to spend the night alone. If their roommates were away, they had to move in with other women for the night. They bitterly resented this, and moaned, "Why should *we* have to move?"

The other side of the sexual double standard was also in

operation. It was not only the very pretty women who were picked on. Many of the others were powerfully built and muscular, a tendency that the rigorous training increased. Professional athletes are probably the only women who are more fit than West Point cadets. The men like to date lissome, elegant types, and they judged the women as potential dates. So they sneered at the heftier women, saying they had Hudson hips, and indeed some of them did. There were serious weight problems among the women, and among the men too. Amy Branch told me, "The food is very good, and when the tension is great, which it was for at least the first year, we all tended to compulsively eat, for comfort." In addition, the daily menu, relentlessly adjusted to the needs of hulking male youth, the prospective infantrymen, consisted of 5000 calories a day, itemized on the printed menu.

The men did not understand the workings of female physiology. There were a few attempts to educate them, but they probably had as much effect as other "leader-prep" lectures with subjects such as "Women as Leaders in American Society." The scorn and the cruel jokes with which they tormented the women cannot, however, be attributed simply to ignorance. Their behavior was not comparable to that of construction workers whistling at girls on their lunch hour or callow fraternity boys slopping their grain alcohol down the front of a dowdy girl. Something more than casual cruelty was involved, because West Point's ethos was and still is, however much the benign General Goodpaster and his aides may have attempted to change it, centered on athletic prowess.

"The training on the athletic fields which produces in a superlative degree the attributes of fortitude, self-control, resolution, courage, mental agility and, of course, physical development, is one completely fundamental to an efficient soldier." This was the view of General MacArthur, who created the intensive program of athletics. As far as the men were concerned, nobody could be a good officer without being a good athlete, or, at the very least, a good runner. The fear of "wimping out" would cause the less brawny men to throw up in secret terror before a PT test. The program had been modified for the women—something that the men could not forgive. The rationale was that the women should try almost everything, and that the requirements would be adjusted to meet their level of potential achievement. This was the only way for the women to reach their capacity.

The exceptions and modifications were crucial. Rough sports—football, hockey, lacrosse, rugby—would not be integrated; the women were to wear chest protectors during pugil stick training and fight only other women; the flexed-arm hang replaced the pull-up. On the reveille rifle run, all cadets were to carry an M-16 instead of an M-14 (an M-16 weighs 6.5 pounds empty—2.5 pounds less than an M-14). To accommodate the smaller reach of the women, the M-14, used in drill, had its operating rod spring shortened.

The separate grading scale on the obstacle course and the three-mile run meant that a female could get a low score and pass, while a male who got the same score had to go to summer school to make up—and this in an institution that was making so much triumphant noise about equality.

Furthermore, since the women learned neither to box nor to wrestle, and their close-quarters training emphasized self-defense, they never had bloody noses. The men were outraged, since deep down they knew that war is about bloody noses. They felt that the women's presence at West Point was a total cheat and public relations exercise if they were not to be put on the line physically. In hand-to-hand sports the men were graded, but the women did not have to compete in their simulated combat lessons in self-defense. As the men saw it, they did not have to try so hard. West Point teaches competition, but it lets the women escape when they cannot cope. It lets them get over. This was a visceral feeling so strong that nobody could miss it. Not all the men felt it, but the few who did not kept silent, because it was unwise to speak out in favor of the women.

Jim Peterson had told me one day in his dank office at the gym, "To be accepted you have to run well. If you can just manage to keep up, there's a chance that you will be left

alone," which was, exactly and simply, what the women
wanted. Worst was the daily enduro run in summer field
training. One serious cadet, not known for exaggeration, told
me, "Oh, yes, it was the worst summer of my life, definitely.
You'd kill yourself trying on the runs, and you'd still drop
out, and the guys would curse and jeer and say terrible
things. It was so degrading."

So the women hyperventilated and stopped menstruating
for months at a stretch, they ate compulsively, and tried not
to tell their parents on the phone how hateful it all was.
Every few days there seemed to be a new questionnaire from
BS&L, stirring up the tensions. In the lull between questionnaires there was the press. Out at field training that first year
some of the female cadets literally hid in their tents to
escape. Without warning they would be pulled from formation and into the Public Affairs Office to meet a member of
the press who had driven up from New York for an in-depth
interview and had forty-five minutes. The articulate and
attractive women were particularly in demand. I saw the
same three or four in magazines or newspapers, on TV many
times—whenever there was a landmark in their collective
career—reflecting gravely on the answers, being serious,
personable, and a credit to the Academy.

General Goodpaster did not understand how much the
men hated to see the women singled out, with reporters
hanging on their every word. They felt like phantoms. "But
we're the class of '80," they would mutter fiercely, and take it
out on the women later. General Goodpaster's female
advisers had told him of this, but up until the week before
graduation he was saying kindly how nice it was to see the
women get their due. Of course the women, however much
they complained, were flattered. Sullivan, whose name was
the first word in a major magazine article, told me, "Our real
rewards happen with the reporters, and the world outside
here. We go out there, women cadets, and people say 'Oh,
how fascinating, tell us what it's like.' That's when we get
our strokes." Still, they felt the price was too high. Lurid
stories appeared about the women being forced to bite

chicken necks (a survival technique learned at summer camp), and there were always misquotes to bring them trouble. Then *The New York Times* ran a press release on October 10, 1979, which had been put out by BS&L after a survey. The first two sentences ran: "Female cadets here adopt traditional masculine personality traits to be accepted as leaders. They also want both marriage and a full-time military career." This did very little for the women's sense of self-worth, already confused by the contradictory demands the Academy made on them. Furthermore, they felt used: by the authorities, who would present them as an experiment that had triumphantly justified itself, by the Petersons, and by the BS&L people, who were using them as objects of research, furthering their careers through the obstacle course the women faced every day.

The women had one obvious recourse: group solidarity. A framework was provided for them to "share their experiences," in the phrase of the time. The Corbin seminar, established when the women arrived, was intended to provide a support group for them. Colonel Prince, from BS&L, told me lugubriously, "The administration sanctioned and funded it for two years, but they *just wouldn't* come in. Just like the blacks before them, they adopted a strategy of merging, blending in." Alice Sullivan was the cadet most firmly behind the club, and she was not happy with its accomplishments. She told me with a weary, exasperated tone, as if she had been through it many times, "There's this peer pressure to conform, and the women pick it up. They came to meetings only if they had boyfriends, since it was one of the few places where they could be together." When I asked another cadet about Corbin she said defensively, "That seminar has bad overtones. It's revolutionary. The women want to unite and be better than the men!" She admitted that change itself might not be so terrible, but said firmly, "I'm working on change *on my own*. Their approach is wrong—getting a bunch of people together to say how we should resolve this, diminish that tension. . . . It's all just talk." This feeling was inevitable. Whatever the theory behind Corbin, in practice the women were discouraged from making themselves separate or conspicuous. There was not even one class or lecture on WAC history to enable the women to discover their own, separate traditions. Equal meant similar. They were to merge with the men, and hence, always, to fail.

Other cadets would have liked things to be different, and spoke wistfully of closer links with the female officers. However, the officers were few and elusive. Some were regarded as unsatisfactory. Others were deliberately harder on female cadets so that they would not seem to be giving them privileged treatment. One officer told me wryly, "I would call them in and say, 'Please understand—I may seem to be ignoring you, but I'll be looking out of the corner of my eye.'"

All-women meetings were doomed, because they made the men suspicious. "Just by having a meeting we might miss some company detail. The guys would look around, see we weren't there, and assume we were getting some kind of special attention." The final word on female bonding came from the defensive cadet who shunned Corbin. She said, "We can talk to some of the officers anytime, or go to the counseling center—but I would want to do things myself. I want to keep it under my hat, not let my male classmates know that behind their backs I was getting the poop from the women officers. I take care of my own needs, and they can take care of theirs."

So, understandably, the women tried to be invisible, and they avoided making waves. They could never succeed as men. That is, however, what they attempted. They *never* wore skirts, they lowered their voices to avoid attention, and they always looked as military as they could. For some, these efforts to merge took an extreme form. One young woman had a breast reduction. Her big breasts were not simply uncomfortable through all the physical exercises, they caused her to be tormented as well. Many of the really pretty young women left West Point. The rest learned to adapt. Some of them became religious. As one said to me, "Nobody's told

West Point men it's okay to express your feelings. There's such a lack of love here, even between your friends, and so people turn to God." A slew of cadets rushed into marriage, and by the day of graduation thirty out of the sixty-two remaining women were engaged. West Point men often marry after graduation, and the sociologists say it is because they are apprehensive of leaving the structured security of Academy life. As for the women, they wanted to withdraw. Being engaged to cadets made them at once attractive and protected.

A few women did not need to withdraw. Amy Branch told me, "Because I'm black I know how to deal with the pressure right from the start. I know what it is like to be a minority. I was talking about this the other day with my black classmate and she said, 'I'm sick of these white girls talking about pressure. They don't know what real pressure is.'"

After four years of stress and adjustment the Academy and its inmates grew more tolerant. Fennessy, sitting in a cloud of cigarette smoke in her shared bedroom, said, "It's not cool to display the hostility anymore. Those who feel it keep their negative feelings under cover." The word from BS&L was: "Flagrant, odious abuses are gone, and if they recur the administration will deal with them." As a result, male officers and cadets now complain in private about being silenced. One young male captain, asking to remain anonymous, told me, "It's galling, because if you express any negative opinions about the women, your career is ruined. But the women are out there complaining to the press about every tiny thing." We were sitting in the basement of a classroom building, in a library, and talking in low voices. He cleared his throat and said, "I must say that when I came here I had strong opinions about the women, and as I worked with cadets my opinion changed. And all credit goes to the cadets. I had felt that the women would be unable to command the respect of the typical soldier or have a command presence, or stand the job emotionally and physically." He continued, choosing his words very carefully, "Some of the women who are here are unable to fit these categories." This was not a ringing endorsement, but it was not at all bad for a West Point graduate.

Nowadays women are not an aberration. If one drops out, there is not a crisis, and fewer women are dropping out. They come in better prepared mentally, and they have had sports programs in school. The new women are cheerful, irrepressible. One evening I watched the Academy in a swim meet against Wellesley. It was the first time the Wellesley students had competed against West Point, and nobody was surprised when they lost. Afterward, when the teams were eating dinner, the male cadets still in the vast and shadowy mess hall whistled and grinned, eyeing the Wellesley students, who looked incongruous, almost startling. With their long, damp hair and the Fair Isle sweaters and plaid skirts they looked so unmilitary alongside the West Point women with their heavy gray uniforms and neat, dry, short hair. The Wellesley students were dumbfounded by the unfamiliarity of their surroundings and by the cadets.

They asked awkwardly about rules and uniforms, saying, "When do you have to *salute*?" I asked one young woman sitting next to me if she would ever enroll in a place like this. She looked at me strangely and said with an abrupt little laugh, "Heavens, no!"

The three West Point swimmers at our table were round, smallish plebes and extremely cheerful. I asked about the horrors of Beast, and whether they found harassment or strict regulations unbearable, and the answer was a steady, jolly saga of contentment. "There's nothing to it!" they chorused. "The men? They're too frightened to say anything bad," they said airily, and as they mopped up the cake and looked around for more, I thought for the only time during my stay at West Point that this bore some relation to college life elsewhere. They got up hurriedly, so as not to be late for a movie, and I overheard one cadet say softly to another on the way out, "How could anyone ever think of going anywhere else if you could choose to come here? Where else would you get such a good education?"

These younger cadets found the class of '80 irritating, ghostly reminders of trouble in the distant past. One of the ghosts said, "If a woman stood up in a lecture, we'd all sit in agony, thinking, don't ask anything stupid. The men would boo. But now the yearlings act so girlish. They say things we'd never say, and they wear skirts!" She admitted that the battle-scarred women of '80 affect a weary superiority, a heavy-lidded look that says, "You think *you* have it rough, but let me tell you. . . ."

The four years, bad and good, have produced sixty-two exceptional junior officers who have gone into MOS's from field artillery to signals. One of them, Andrea Hollen, was awarded a Rhodes scholarship. As the first woman to graduate, she gave her uniform to the Metropolitan Museum, in New York. The administration, with the Army behind it, has tried hard to get joint assignments for the married cadets. For as long as they remain in the Army, these particular women will be the center of attention, as the first ones to have made it through.

They are impressive, so graceful and poised, with an air of real authority. Amy Branch said, "I feel proud that I can do so many things. When I came here I'd never run a mile. Now I'm so amazed at what my body can do, I want to brag about it." She continued, her face glowing, "All this physical stuff tones up the body, and my legs look *great* now." She was a public information officer's dream, rhapsodizing, "I haven't lost my femininity. I don't mind the uniform—it's just one less worry. And sometimes when the guys look at you, you know it's not to find fault, but they're thinking maybe, Wow she has a cute walk!" I plaintively said, "You sound very upbeat." She became serious and leaned closer, "Sometimes I get *mad* when people complain about this place. You should know before you come that you're going to have to suffer and give up some real world pleasures, so don't complain. Either get out or shut up. That's the way I feel."

Others agreed with Amy, saying, "You have to handle all the punches they throw at you. Your coping mechanisms have to be okay." This jargon is thrown around at West Point as cavalierly as rolls in student cafeterias. The women's coping mechanisms were indeed OK, but there was something else going on underneath. The night we talked, this same cadet brought with her to Grant Hall fourteen pages of legal pad covered in scrawly handwriting and three scrapbooks of journal entries, press clippings, photographs, programs. The fourteen handwritten pages were the beginning of an autobiographical work she was planning. Called "Point Blank," it would describe her West Point experiences. I read what she had written as we sat in front of a blazing fire in the Hall, with Steve Forbert on the radio, while male cadets and their dates whispered and held hands in corners as they pretended to play backgammon. The writing was heartfelt and clumsy, with much foreshadowing along the lines of "little did I know then." As we carefully sifted through the clippings, she explained, a serious look on her face, "People just don't know the truth of what happens here. The press misquotes you all the time. But it's *important* to get it right."

There is an interesting Ancient Mariner quality to these women, who, although so wary of reporters, are still trying to explain, to themselves as much as to anyone else, what happened. Despite all the changes for the better, and those composed voices telling of self-realization, I felt a disturbing fog of worry all around. It is too easy to dismiss what happened as growing pains—the same kind of story we hear from Dartmouth and the coal mines and other all-male enclaves that have had equal opportunity legislated onto them, the same male revolt against a loss of their power and exclusivity. Harassment in the military means more than it does in an office or a factory. The Army in general, and West Point to a marked degree, are based on idealism. To attract young people and turn them into career soldiers, the military does more than offer job training, food, and shelter. It appeals to their idealistic patriotism. The best soldiers are those who are prepared to forgo the conveniences of civilian life because they believe in serving their country. If they do have this ideal of service, they will stay in the military even if they are stationed in a dusty desert fifteen miles from town, even if they have a CO who cannot bear the sight of them and there is a shortage of spare parts for their machines.

At Fort McClellan the ideal of service meant feeling tearful and ennobled when Sergeant Butler read his poem about Private Littlebit; at West Point it is expressed as Duty-Honor-Country. Even the most antimilitary would agree that in an army those impulses are healthy and can be transcendent. The West Point women, traditional, serious, and interested in service, spent twenty-four hours of every day in an environment that was not like college or an office. Their uniforms, their Spartan barracks and the lack of freedom, their haircuts—all these things were acceptable if the system not only functioned but also provided support and encouragement. The rigors of the training are imbued with an ancient idea of comradeship—as Henry called it in *The Red Badge of Courage,* "a mysterious fraternity born of the smoke and danger of death"—and the assumption of a shared purpose that unites ranks, classes, people of all kinds. Believing this, only to be ridiculed and loathed at every turn, being taught to respect your superiors, only to hear your instructor say furiously as he stands by an elevator, "Personally, I don't believe women belong here"; living in an atmosphere where all are primed, coaxed, and pushed to succeed, only to have everyone watching you for failure—these things vex the spirit, creating a true nightmare. Cadets could neither flounce in to the boss and say "I quit," nor trail home at night and moan to their families. Occasionally people would say scornfully to them, "If you can't stand up to this, what will you do in combat?" The difference was that in combat they would not have expected to be tortured *by their own side.*

The women had been changed by this atmosphere. They often mentioned their intolerance. One said, "I'm far more intolerant and cynical about people. I notice it when I go to New York and arrive at the Port Authority Bus Terminal, and I look at all the heavy people and wonder how they could have let themselves go like that." She said, "They make you a tabula rasa here so that they can turn you into a new person, but the problem is that you take on the bad attitudes as well as the good." Others, who hesitated to call themselves feminists, agreed about their anger and bitterness. They told me how they overreacted with raw anger to casual remarks; only a few, however, would say they disliked the male cadets.

They also became emotionally withdrawn. Some cadets believed that was part of becoming a professional—holding yourself in, practicing self-discipline. In this way the women *were* actually becoming more like the men, more self-protective and intellectual about themselves. This was not "defeminizing," this was part of becoming an officer, for males and females.

However, there was also a pathological aspect. I saw it when about fifty of the graduating class assembled at the Officers Club on a frigid, starlit night to celebrate Andrea Hollen's Rhodes scholarship. It was a big occasion; the Officers Club looked gloomy and grand. The women arrived in twos and threes, mostly wearing jumpers and turtlenecks or slacks, with some discreet costume jewelry and a touch of makeup. They sat at round tables and ate adult food—filet mignon, beef Wellington. For a moment the young women behaved engagingly like coeds, asking for piña coladas and daiquiris, neither of which could be obtained. They stocked their plates with enormous salads and began to reminisce.

Initially they were shy because of my presence; they kept saying with a sweet pleasure and surprise how rare an event like this was. They could not remember the last time a group of comparable size had assembled for fun. As time passed and the Chablis flowed, they started to laugh about the upperclassmen, and they imitated the instructors, saying, "Now, you men first and then the girls." Gradually my table, which sat six, became encrusted with more and more chairs, because my tablemates were the raconteurs of the group, and the famous story of how they almost stole the Navy goat was imminent, to be told with all the flourishes and embellishments it had picked up along the way from its first telling.

Everyone laughed wildly and gasped in delicious anticipation before all the punch lines, but it was a slim story, with more pathos than belly laughs. Nobody, then or later in the evening, became raucous or risqué. A herd of young women with a little wine in them can be hilarious, but the cadets did not even raise their voices. It reminded me of the poignant story one had told me about the graduation day parade. She said, "It's a riot. One year all the guys had alarm clocks inside their jackets, and all the alarms went off at the same moment, but the people in the stands were too far away to hear."

Sue Peterson had told me that the ubiquitous calm and politeness were just a social front, that, underneath, the males and females were similarly hesitant, fearful of what would happen to them outside, where the unwashed hippies live, and the stoned troops—and the pregnant troops. I discussed this with a very young instructor, a civilian, pretty and soft-spoken and popular with the cadets. She said, "When they come over to my house they are *so quiet*. They never talk about how it really is until two or three in the morning, when they're tired and full of drink. Then they begin and they won't stop. I just love them," she said, "but it took some of them three years to tell me what happened to them as plebes." It was as if the hostility had created a climate of rape, and the women—guilty, withdrawn, eager to please—were its victims.

These women are loyal to West Point, although not in the traditional way. Their loyalty is a judicious respect tinged with cynicism. One young woman stood up in the dual-career class and said haltingly, "At home the men don't understand what I'm doing or why I'm doing it. They don't feel happy around me anymore. Whereas the males here know, and they have seen me through everything. We've become close." At this wan testimonial a small glow lit the features of her male classmates, indicating a moment of true fraternity. However, not one of those I met seems sure she will stay in the Army after the initial five-year commitment is up. A professor in BS&L said to me in a rare jargon-free moment, "Why would

they want to stay, after all?" Most have avoided the male-
dominated specialties. Supposedly this is because a career
soldier can get stuck in a field in which all the advancement
is achieved through combat positions. However, Alice Sullivan expressed a common view when she said, "I don't want
to fight all over again. I don't want to be encumbered by
men. I'm tired of breaking down attitudes."

I interviewed General Goodpaster in his spacious paneled
office with heavy, masculine furniture and the portraits of his
predecessors around the walls, staring out as keenly as Peter
O'Toole in *Lord Jim*. The general was courteous and soft-
spoken. After each question he leaned forward seriously in
his armchair and spoke gracefully, sonorously. I felt hypnotized, my questions slipping away on the steady flow of his
talk. Everyone liked General Goodpaster, and he was very
committed to his female cadets as well as the males. He said
with reassuring firmness, "Women are participating in the
Army in large numbers and making a fine contribution. With
women in the Army, you must have women officers. If you're
going to have women officers, they're entitled to be trained
at as good an institution as there is. The notion that you
could have a mini-West Point for women is nonsense. And so
you come to say that they should be here."

When I asked him about all the bad things that had
happened, he replied patiently that they were aware of
problems in the past and were doing their best to remove
them, although he had yet to find anyone who would come
up with a constructive definition of femininity so that he
could establish what precisely the women at West Point
should or should not have to sacrifice.

The cadets knew why West Point had taken integration so
hard. One summed it up accurately when she said, "I was
watching a talk show with my dad, and the woman who had
climbed Everest was on. She said people were saying Mount
Everest isn't that hard to climb. If a woman can do it, it can't
be that tough." West Point was a dream for the male cadets,
a vision, a rite of passage from which they would emerge as

men. One of the male instructors told me, "The place has a mystique. Most of the men depend on external recognition for their feelings of self-worth, i.e., on doing better than somebody else. They feel, My God, if a woman can make it, what does it mean *I* am?"

The female cadets could understand the young men's feelings, but they could not accept the protracted and vicious ways in which they were expressed. "I don't think it's the male cadets' fault," said one of the female officers; "they're very impressionable. But there's a silent sanction of the system here." This officer was Captain Acker, one of the handful of women on the teaching staff. She and her colleagues provided insights into the trouble which the cadets, for all their urge to explain and record, did not have.

The Academy had conducted a long search for suitable female officers to add to the faculty and administration. Because the WAC had been so small until the expansions of the late 1960s, high ranking and available female officers were not easy to find. Few of the younger officers, although older and often better educated than men of equivalent rank, had the experience or training that was required, since there is nowhere else like West Point. Some of the female officers they found had served as career Wacs for ten or fifteen years until, with the disestablishment of the WAC in 1978, the rules had changed under their feet. Some had been de-tailed—the first women—to a previously all-male branch, or unit, or company, and so they were familiar with not simply the Army but also with the specific problems of women in the Army. However, in all the coverage of West Point, in the surveys and interviews, the female officers—women who have proven themselves—are virtually ignored. This reveals more about attitudes toward the women in the Army than the attention received by the cadets. While they were not hounded by the press or BS&L for their views, the officers had to live with the results of this exposure, and as professionals they deplored the way things were handled.

Captain Acker teaches in the humanities. An intense

woman, and one of the few to wear the skirt uniform in an environment of trouser-clad legs, she looked vulnerable in her carefully unremarkable panty hose and shiny patent leather shoes. She told me that since she had never really been a Wac, her uniform was considered sloppy by the other women. She always ironed creases into her sleeves, which was not proper, but she compensated for such infringements (arcane to non-Wacs) by appearing immaculate, gleaming as if sprayed with Pledge, from her glossy tight black chignon to the heavy makeup on her angular face. She wore as much gold jewelry as she could get away with and still look military—rings and three gold-and-diamond bracelets. Nowhere at West Point did I find a relaxed woman officer, and Captain Acker, sitting in her office at the end of a working afternoon with knees and ankles neatly together, was less relaxed than most.

It was Captain Acker who, in her third week at the Academy, was waiting for the elevator next to an instructor who began "a tirade about how women didn't belong here." "I hadn't been here long," she told me, "and I didn't know what to do about it. But when cadets vocalize attitudes like that in class *they go unchecked*. It's a professional responsibility, male or female, to point out that the attitude is incompatible with the goals of the Academy. If a cadet is not told that, then he gets the feeling that it's okay. It becomes reinforced a few times, and that gives him carte blanche to take more aggressive action."

Acker laughed softly when I mentioned that sexism had in theory been abolished, and she said, "I have no composure when they talk about doing away with sexist attitudes. I just giggle and see people marching out the front gate with all their household goods in rickshaws. It sounds as if they're going for an operation."

The clearest example of poor management, in Acker's view, is the Project Athena study as a whole, and in particular that portion dealing with the so-called "masculinization" of cadets. The press release quoted in *The New York Times* enraged everybody. Captain Acker said, fury barely con-

cealed behind her pedagogical demeanor, "I have gone over
the Athena report, and I still don't know what constitutes
these masculine and feminine attitudes. They said females'
not wearing skirts is a masculine attribute. No one," she said
emphatically, "looked at the *occasions,* at the torment they
received if they wore skirts, at the emphasis on uniformity."
Indeed, the report made it sound as if the females had grown
chest hair and thrown away their deodorants just because, for
example, they said that they valued work as highly as
marriage. One of the first cadets I met said to me in dismay,
"Last time *The New York Times* said we were humorless. Now
they say we're masculine. I think they hate us."

The people who put out the misleading release do not hate
cadets, but there was general agreement that, as Major
Nederlander told me, "These people are using the women to
further their own careers." Certainly when I talked with one
of the authors most involved, he spoke with the drugged
excitement typical of sociologists in the grip of their subject,
but seemingly without any real sense of responsibility for
what he was doing. He said with a quick smile, "What
surprised me about our research was that the cadets weren't
aware of what the Academy was doing. They were apparently
operating in an information void. It was very revealing," he
said with a peculiar gleam in his eye. Captain Acker gave me
a speech about this man, his colleagues, and his work.
Clearly this was a favorite subject of hers.

She began: "All these statistics and interpretations have
done the cadets a great disservice. For one thing, the
numbers of women are so small that to base generalizations
on them is probably of little value. And the questionnaires
simply inflame prejudices all over again. They pass a survey
around this office, and suddenly I hear things from the men
that I've not heard in years." The cadets would tell me this
too, that every time a female was pulled from formation to
talk to a reporter, every time a man was asked how he felt
about having a woman in a "leadership position" over him,
his wounds magically turned raw again. Captain Acker
continued, "General Goodpaster has great confidence in

these people, but I don't think they operate in a professional manner. Very rarely did I know where these questionnaires were going or what they would be used for." She said, "I feel that if someone's prying into my life, it's a professional responsibility to use the data, to be *careful* whom it's released to, be careful how it's analyzed." In the thick of all this I remembered Fort McClellan, where the only firm conclusion that they had all been able to reach after the arrival of the first males was that many men had a tendency to overload washing machines.

The word that surfaced over and over again in conversations with these women was "professionalism." They took great pride in their own, and, understandably, had arrived at West Point expecting to find it reciprocated and enhanced. It could be said that the changes made at the Academy, the seminars and workshops about the role of women, were welcome and indeed called for, and in a sense they are. The male cadets sitting there in their marriage class and in the dual-career classes that I attended would blush and furrow their brows mightily and say, for example, "A lot of the guys here are threatened by you women. You aren't just some nobody. You're a cut above. Most of the guys in the Corps like to have a relationship where they know they are superior, and how can you feel that about a girl when she beats you?" The arguments made sense, but there was something wrong with all this.

One of the instructors said that the problem was caused by overzealous adherence to "the MacNamara syndrome," which, simply expressed, has brought management techniques borrowed from the corporate world into leadership, and is greatly resented throughout the Army. The instructor said impatiently, "We're trying to be too much like business—but I raised my right hand as I came in, and I said, 'till death do us part.'" She said West Point had been unmilitary with regard to the integration of women. In the third volume of Project Athena it was stated that the confused, crucial question of the importance of running in relation to leadership would be dealt with in a one-hour leader-prep session.

Male cadets, and female, think it wimpy to discuss problems in seminars, and in this case they are probably right.

Captain Acker said of the cadets, "Their sense of military responsibility is supposed to be all-encompassing, but they aren't *getting* that." She said, "We should not be talking about sex discrimination in terms of equal opportunity and affirmative action. We should see it as an ethical, professional issue—that we have a mission and we utilize our personnel. The cadets know that this place is built on the cornerstone of duty, honor, country, but they should be told what duty means."

Margaret Mead wrote: "To the woman who makes a success in a man's field, good behavior is almost impossible, because her whole society has defined it so. . . . A woman who succeeds better than a man . . . has done something hostile and destructive." Nobody expected the men to be consistently and wholeheartedly on the side of the women. The female officers realized that change would be slow, but they, like the cadets, could not forgive or accept the blatant prejudice that they encountered. At this level there are no foaming condoms, but the talk is as slanderous and the double standard as marked. The very attractive women were always under suspicion; at least one had her career ruined when some foolish horseplay in which she and a male colleague indulged after a drinking spree became inflated into a scandal of major proportions.

West Point is even more of a rumor mill than most posts. It is small, with a stable population dominated by cadets and families, and without the large numbers of enlisted troops and varied battalions that typify the more sprawling installations. The sudden arrival of a handful of women, most of them single, plunged the place into a tizzy of malicious whispering. Captain Acker, a most discreet and punctilious person, said with a bitter catch in her voice, "Men have a difficult time looking at women in an asexual manner, especially a powerful woman. They figure that getting her in bed will take care of everything. But the women won't go to bed with married men here, and so if men see them acting in a friendly way with other women, they just assume homosexuality." Just as with the WAC, gossip about homosexuality was used as a slanderous weapon that turned what might in civilian life be standard harassment (harassment should not be standard, but it is) into a war.

Several West Point women told me that they had at one time or another been under suspicion or the subject of an investigation. One said, "It really bothers me. If I as a ranking woman can be that vulnerable to attack, what are the other women going through?" There is no question of female solidarity under these circumstances; the women are so few and so scattered. At intervals one or another of the more activist women has tried to get regular lunches going—nothing strategic about them, just a chance to meet and exchange news and tell war stories. Every time that happens, the men are liable to say, in the words of one male instructor I talked to, "So what's going on? You plotting the revolution?" Captain Acker told me that not long ago a man had walked up to her and said, "Hey, I've heard the rumors. I'm going to offer you the opportunity of a lifetime to prove they're not true." This was the West Point faculty in its fourth year of integration.

Some of the worst rumormongers are women. A highly placed female officer who had worked with men as equals, subordinates, or superiors during her Army career said to me one day, "These women who participate in rumors are unaware that they're being manipulated. And of course when the men hear the rumor, they take it as a credible statement of fact, because, after all, a woman must be brave to take the risk of telling. They are very slow to question motivation." The motivation is familiar to women who have found themselves in a highly competitive and hierarchical environment, whether it's a college or an advertising agency. In school it's known as "sucking up." In business and the military it could be called the "subject-nation syndrome," in which the women who inform on other women have submitted to the organization and its rules so totally that they will do anything to be accepted, even if it means disassociating themselves entirely from other women to prove how much like men they are. Since integration at West Point was conducted on the basis of making the women merge with the men, the temptation was an obvious one.

Most of the women find it hard not to be suspicious of or competitive with one another. Captain Acker told me that it is not easy even to pick up the phone and ask another woman for advice, whereas in the WAC, whatever their personal feelings, the women had a strong sense of themselves as a team, and would feel obliged to act professionally. She said that out in the Army, the women support each other more. At West Point, it was generally agreed, the women could not work as a team. Female bonding did not exist, at any level, as I saw in the course of one pleasant but not very relaxed evening I spent with some of the women. Seven of us sat in the bachelor officers' quarters, in a paneled, high-ceilinged apartment, with a log fire burning. We ate popcorn and potato chips and sipped beer and wine.

The women were a cross section of women on post: the head nurse from the hospital, instructors, someone from the personnel office (where much of the interesting business on any post happens), a lieutenant, sprawling in cowboy boots and cord slacks, who shot significant glances or uttered a short cynical laugh from time to time. The others glanced sideways at me and complained routinely about their terrible quarters and the difficulty of getting an appointment at the hospital.

Nobody seemed to want to mention the larger problems of life at West Point. Indeed, they carefully avoided them, and I did not press them. There was paranoia in the air, in the nervous smiles as I was handed the popcorn, in the sharp jocularity. On subsequent occasions when I saw the women around the post they would smile and move away. I later asked one of them if I was right in sensing anxiety. She said cautiously, "They're not necessarily paranoid, but several did come up to me afterward and ask whose side you were on."

Edgy and isolated, these women have the time, and the

incentive, to think about the Academy—what is wrong with
it and what is right. For some it has been an educational
exercise in watching the hierarchy at work. Major Nederlander was in a particularly useful position for this, since she
had sat in on hours of meetings, drafted and redrafted
endless policies affecting the women, and had at every turn
tried to explain to the Superintendent what was wrong with
their situation. She described vividly the collision of methods
and views that she saw. "The men are out of touch and
elitist, and of course they mistrust the women. The women
have total ignorance of male games." She described meetings
as "a ritual dance, where the women do not realize how the
men use the rituals to protect themselves." With the men in
the outer office visible through the glass, busily pushing
paper to further their careers, she leaned forward with a glint
of amusement in her eyes and said confidentially, "There's
this very bright, very influential woman on the Board of
Visitors here." She mentioned a woman whose name is on
the letterheads of serious charitable organizations. "She
looks at the men, sometimes talking, sometimes saying
nothing, and she can't comprehend. She tries to figure out
what they're saying; she feels she should understand, and
she blames herself. Rather than looking and saying what's
wrong with him, she says what's wrong with *me*, and while
she's doing all this self-evaluation she's lost her opportunity
to contribute."

Major Nederlander said smoothly, as if she had said it to
herself many times, "Men say we're too task-oriented,
because we want to do the task and get it right. But men like
to give it the broad brush. They say, 'What do you mean, the
problem with the integration of women? We addressed that
last April.'" In my mind were those unreconstructed officers
trundling their attitudes off in rickshaws and down the street
to the Highland Falls bus station. Major Nederlander is bitter
after four years of hard negotiation. She said, "Do you know,
the top academic officials discuss who had it worse, the
blacks twenty years ago or the women!" She added vehemently, "It's great to be a successful white man and sit there

and say women don't have it as bad as blacks. *How in hell do they know what either went through?* "

Captain Kathy Whitcraft is tall, with thick blond hair and bangs and makeup, a sensible, determined woman who had come from the Engineering Corps, where she had been the first female engineer, via the command of an all-male engineering company, to be the first female Tac at the Academy. She had always been a woman in a man's world, and had acquired that manner, talking with brisk impatience about the other women, saying they had not learned about the rules of teamwork, the tradeoffs and favors. Captain Whitcraft talked inexorably over the Muzak in the dining room at the Officers Club, and she spoke like a true West Pointer, in crisp, logical sentences.

"Oh sure, sexual tension is everywhere," she said with a faint smile. "When a man gets to work with you as a professional, and he finds it enjoyable, he gets a crush on you. That's the only response he knows. But after a while that wears off. He realizes that just because it feels good it doesn't have to be love. That's why the argument about 'put two people in a foxhole and one ends up pregnant' only goes so far. When people are used to working together, the social relations calm down. It's cooling here now; there were real passions, but now we're more like brothers and sisters. You can feel good about somebody and have it be friends." She told me wryly, however, that still she could never be accepted. "I'm called a *nongraduate,* even though I've graduated from a bunch of places."

There is the mystique of West Point in microcosm. If you did not graduate from West Point, you did not graduate, in the same way that if you are a woman you are a nonman, and if you do not run well you are not a good leader. Whitcraft, because of her position as a Tac, had had to confront the question of physical leadership head on. Looking levelly out from under her bangs, Whitcraft said, "This is the most macho place I have ever seen. I am thirty, my cadets are seventeen, eighteen, nineteen, and I have to run with them every morning. To build up my strength I go to the gym three times a week and run mile after mile after mile. It reduces me to tears." Her face was composed, but the words came out in a flood. It was Captain Whitcraft who had told me, with anger and regret in her voice, that she had to be visibly hard on her female cadets so that they would not be accused of getting over. She went on, as the dining room slowly emptied, "Some of my guys are terrified of failing at PT too, and their way of handling their insecurity is to be *very cruel*. The attitude is so pervasive that every officer would be mortified to go running with the troops and fall behind."

Whitcraft told me about the life of a Tac at summer field training, when she got up at four every morning to go running with her company. She said, "I would go back to my room and cry because it was so stressful, it was so terrible to think of failing. I had never failed at anything before PT."

One of the officers said one day, "Did you hear the story about Kim Huffman, the one who left last spring? They said she had a fear of success, but probably she just couldn't tolerate the two-facedness we see here every day." I heard the full story from Huffman's closest friend, the cadet whose name was always mentioned whenever I asked which member of the class of '80 was the most likely to become a general.

Leslie Carr has red hair, an intelligent face, and a serious, uncompromising manner. One of the few female company commanders, she told me she had learned swiftly that becoming a good leader meant a drop in popularity and a steady erosion of her friendships. She was a credit to West Point; she loved all the physical challenges and had excelled in the tough air-assault course at Fort Campbell, while the handful of other women who took it with her kept falling out or dropping behind. Leslie told me that she, unlike her friend Huffman, had quickly become realistic about West Point's shortcomings.

As we sat in Grant Hall surrounded by the cheerful hubbub of the early-morning break, she gravely told me,

"People perceive me as being cold and distant; my Tac the other day asked me if I felt emotions. And I told him, 'Sir, in plebe year if you show any emotion you're weak and you don't belong and you're a prime example of why women don't belong here. . . . So that's all fine and good, sir—you don't show any emotion. Then you work your way up, and all of a sudden you're accused of not showing any emotion and being a cold, insensitive person.'" She said, "Huffman could never understand why I would just cry in my room and not let anybody know. She finally came to understand."

Huffman was the ideal cadet. She had been Regular Army and had attended the West Point Preparatory School at Fort Monmouth, New Jersey. Leslie Carr said that the administration had been anxiously looking for a woman to groom for a powerful position. Huffman was good-natured and uncontroversial, Leslie said, "naïve, innocent, and relatively neutral, involved in a lot of activities. She was the prime candidate; they pushed her to the top to show that integration had worked." They appointed her the Regimental Executive Officer of Beast Barracks, which was the Number Two position and very important. She attended endless meetings, and gradually began to feel she was a token presence. Leslie said, "It was the patronizing attitudes, and then she realized that the policies were already formulated and typed up before the meetings." Huffman was optimistic at the start, but, said Carr, she was unprepared for the conflict between her expectations and the reality, which was to have a token say but really to carry out orders. "I'll work within my chain of command and go as high as I can and bend people's ears, but when the ultimate decision comes down I'll accept it, as my duty. But she'd never been in that kind of conflict; she could not accept being used like that."

So Kim Huffman resigned. The authorities were dumbfounded. They offered her anything she wanted to get her to stay. "They had so much invested in her," said Carr, "but she refused." Huffman left the Academy abruptly, but came back to talk with the Superintendent and the Commandant of Cadets. She could not be persuaded to rescind, and they could not understand her reasons. The Commandant of Cadets addressed the entire class of '80. Leslie said, "For twenty-five minutes he tore her apart. She was wimping out, they had been wrong about her—and after he had finished he refused to take questions and ran off to watch a game on TV." Carr said, "It was such a traumatic experience for the administration. They put all their faith in that one person, who then said you can shove it."

The female trainees who left Fort McClellan were already feeling the first twinges of doubt—they had begun to suspect that the Army would not present them with the promised challenge and thereby justify the bold decision they had made. The female cadets who left West Point were exhilarated and proud that they had weathered the four years, but they had deep doubts about the way their colleagues and superiors had behaved, and the system to which they were so loyal. The female officers were bitter; they could not feel a bond, because they were not part of the class of anything. Major Nederlander said, "West Point is twenty-five years behind the Army. I have a love/hate relationship with it, and I hope it will change. But the way it is here now, everything reinforces the male ego. Women are not welcome; they are tolerated. *At every turn* they have to justify not only their existence but their birthright." She added bitterly, "I thought I could handle everything, but I have learned otherwise here."

The men were bitter too, the ambitious young teachers and the older men, set in their ways and dusting off the same set of lecture notes year after year. They hated the changes that had undermined the fine old structure of the Academy like termites. They were furious that consciousness-raising had come to the Academy, but they did not blame the Academy. Their loyalty overcame their logical thinking, and, secretly, they blamed the women.

Males and females alike, they had all wanted military professionalism. They defined it differently, but they felt the same frustration at its disappearance. Just as at Fort Mc-Clellan, the men brooded about declining standards, and so did the women. West Point in its obsession with tangible data heaped up mounds of documentation on things that could be measured, such as skinfolds, and on things they thought should be capable of being measured, such as the attitudinal component. At the other extreme, they fell prey to workshops and role classes. The women were supposed to look and behave like men, but the differences were monitored and spotlighted to such an extent that the mission of preparing all cadets to join an officer corps of shared talents and equivalent ideals was quite obscured.

Clifford Alexander, the Secretary of the Army during the four years concerned, was known to have a low opinion of the way West Point conducted integration. He told me, impatiently drumming his fingers on the table as he leaned forward in his cavernous Pentagon office, "West Point, just like Harvard, is less important than it thinks it is. If it was in North Dakota, you wouldn't know it was there." This was the voice of a man who had found himself having to intervene in such important questions as selecting a new football coach for the Academy.

Alexander was right only up to a point. Attitudes that prevail at the Academy are found at all levels of Army life, however inappropriately. A disdain for women as physically inadequate and therefore unmilitary is the least well founded and the most pervasive.

11

Small-Unit Tactics: Women in the Integrated Army

An army has to be effective in its peacetime mission if it is to function well in an emergency. Later on I shall discuss the combat effectiveness of the integrated Army. The mission of the Army in peacetime is readiness. All the training, the waiting, the field problems, going to classes at night, visiting the motor pool and lounging around—all that is about waiting for war. This small nucleus of 770,000 men and women would in a war be the core. The people who are good at their jobs and comfortable in the workings of the machine are the crucial ones. We need to know how well the 65,000 soldiers who are women are doing at their jobs, and how valuable they are to the Army. One way of finding out, traditionally popular in the Army as at West Point, is to conduct a survey.

A WAC historian told me with a dry smile, "You can understand that we women who have served for twenty years or so don't respond very enthusiastically to a survey about whether or not women are capable of doing the things they did in World War Two." Most of the surveys about capability are highly ambiguous, just as they were at West Point, but

224

other aspects of military success can be measured more successfully: the cost of training and recruiting women, for example, or the most effective use for them, the length of time they can be expected to stay in. Are they a bargain or an expensive luxury purchased to keep the All-Volunteer Force on its feet and please the politicians, who, as a current military speculation has it, are foisting their social experiment onto the Army?

There appear to be two sets of data. The good data, about all the advantages women offer, tend to be older. For example, the women coming into the Army have traditionally been older and better educated than their male counterparts. Before 1978 only 10 percent of female enlistees came in without a high school diploma, and they had to have the GED. The attrition rate among that 10 percent of women was nearly 59 percent. So in 1978 the Army restricted recruiting to high school graduates who scored 50 or over on the entrance test. Because few women were needed, the Army could afford to take only the best of those available. These women, according to statistics, have been losing much less time at work than men do, even if time off for pregnancy is counted in. Furthermore, they have been staying longer. Of the men recruited in 1973–76, 64 percent were on active duty in June 1978, while 70 percent of the women were.

Martin Binkin and Shirley Bach carried out a study for the Brookings Institution, *Women and the Military,* published in 1977, in which they estimated that the women were not simply cheaper in terms of recruitment, training, behavior, and retention, they were also cheaper in annual per capita costs of medical care, housing, and transportation. After all, most Wacs did not marry, and they had no dependents. There were other savings. In World War II, Army experts had calculated that 100,000 Wacs could be fed more cheaply than the equivalent number of men: the difference would be $2,099,115.

The operating assumption in the Pentagon was that if the shortfall in males became too acute, young women could

easily be brought in to replace them; they counted on an
ample supply of "high quality" young women. After all, as
the familiar line goes, civilian women earn, on average, fifty-
nine cents for every dollar a man earns, whereas military
women would take home the same dollar as the men.
However, when the military opened itself up and equalized
the standards of entry, it became clear that the women were
not flocking in, and those who came in were not, perhaps,
such a bargain.

The less good statistics date from the beginnings of the
integrated Army in 1978. It appears likely that over 40
percent of the enlisted women recruited in 1979 will leave in
the course of their first (three-year) term, whereas the
comparable rate for men is likely to be 32 percent.

Recent Army policy has been to put the women where the
skills are in shortest supply, rather than concentrating them
in their previous terrain. That alternative would probably not
be upheld in the courts if the Army wished to return to it. So
the question is whether enough qualified women will come
forward to fill those jobs, and whether they will justify their
training by staying in the jobs. There are signs that the
women who charged so enthusiastically into the "nontraditional" MOS's opened to them—mechanics, electronics,
helicopter repair, and the like—are slipping back into the
more familiar female occupations. Some 1978 figures showed
that 51.7 percent of all women in the so-called less traditional
skills (such as data processing, military intelligence, law
enforcement) were reclassifying too, back into the old
reliable jobs. Approximately 8 percent of Army women get
pregnant each year, and at any given time 13 percent of the
women in Europe are pregnant. Taken together, these
figures are bad news for the Army; the trends are expected to
continue.

Officials at the Pentagon now say that the "high quality"
women they were hoping to attract seem to be staying away,
and the "low quality" women are less deployable than "low
quality" men because they cannot be put to so many uses.

Females, they have found, are less flexible than men. Even the women with high school diplomas (normally an indicator of staying power) are leaving at a rate not very different from that of men who did not graduate. Clearly it is difficult for women of high quality as well as low to stay in the Army. The question is why—and there are two sets of answers. The first, and more obvious, has to do with low standards of admission and performance and the problems of a newly integrated Army.

A year after the trainees of Alpha Company had graduated and dispersed, I revisited Fort McClellan and found that, even in such a short time, the women had lost command. Almost all the cadre I had known, from Alpha Company and the battalion, had gone. The colonel in charge of Second Battalion was a man. So was the captain who had replaced Lieutenant Myers in command of Alpha, and the first sergeant, and the senior drill.

I visited Lieutenant Evans, the former Wac who had told me what it meant to be strac. Her home, like those of most career soldiers, was full of souvenirs from abroad and framed photographs. In this case they were supplemented by plaques and trophies, Lieutenant Evans being very highly decorated and also an athlete. She proudly pointed out a large circular hooked rug on the wall, worked in tones of russet and orange, which bore the profile of Pallas Athene. Again I thought of the banned images, lying stacked in cartons in the WAC Museum or removed to people's homes, there to sit like household gods above the hearth or at the threshold. We spent a long afternoon together, and she told me, "I think that it's getting to be just like any other post with all these men around. And when General Clarke leaves she'll be replaced by a man."

Lieutenant Evans told me about the sharp drop in standards, saying that Fort McClellan had been sheltered from the deterioration that was taking place in the rest of the Army, until integration. She said, "I think it's been happening for years, maybe since World War Two. You know, you hear stories of the old Army, and it's just like your parents saying, 'When I was your age I had to ski four miles to school every day.' You don't know if it's true. But I tend to believe them."

Lieutenant Evans has a low opinion of integration. She said, "Sure, we had bad soldiers in the old days, but now things can be so much worse. I went through MP school with a couple of bad types. We came in from three-four days bivouac in the field, and it was late, and we had to clean all the weapons we'd used. I was on my second weapon when I noticed a female across the table position herself between two guys and say, 'Gee, what do I do with this *spring* thing?' She knew how to clean a weapon as well as anyone else there."

Evans grimly told me that sex between troops and drill sergeants was becoming common. "We divide the drills into the good and the bad," she said, "and the bad sleep with their trainees. In one company the female drill was told she couldn't sleep out on bivouac because the men wanted to be able to sleep with the female trainees." She added, "I don't know what's happened to the standards. We say the new motto is Screw Up, Move Up." She added, "I guess a lot of us are bitter in a way, but it's just a waste of energy. We have to live with the situation as it is. From what I've seen, I don't especially care for it. I just wish people wouldn't blame us for all the things that are wrong with the Army today. But they have to blame someone. So why not women? We're used to it."

Lieutenant Evans was earning a good salary, a clear total of about $1300 a month, and she will retire on over $1000 a month. In order to do that she will be marking time, waiting for the years to pass. She said, "I'll just go to work like everyone else. Now I'm not a Wac, I'm an MP, because I have something on my collar that replaced the Pallas Athene brass we had to take off. But I'm not loyal to the military police," she said, smiling. "MPs tell MP jokes and it doesn't affect me. I don't feel a thing."

Not all former Wacs feel so cheated. Sergeant Reilly, after eighteen years of service, had her niche in the new, integrated force. She was working for the wimpy Captain Dixon, he who loved to quote Kipling, but, like a seasoned professional, she had adapted to the change. She announced that she was happy. "Oh, Captain Dixon has learned a lot," she said, "and he's prepared to listen to me." Lieutenant Myers once told me that the key link in the Army is the senior NCO, for he, or she, is the person from whom the junior officers with little or no command experience learn all the important things. Sometimes the junior officer may be too proud or insecure to ask for advice, or take it when offered—especially if the veteran is a woman and the greenhorn is a man.

"I have no problems with the men," Sergeant Reilly said. "I'm too damn old and I'm very efficient, but what I don't understand is the change in training." She went on to tell me that standards had dropped so drastically that she was quite at a loss. "I don't think more than six of ours have a high school diploma. Mind you, we're at the low point of the year, but we have *trash*. We'll be lucky to graduate a hundred and five out of a hundred and fifty-five!" She told me about disciplinary offenses and AWOLs, and people having sex in the showers. I visited several officers and NCOs in their homes off post, and I heard from all of them, ardent WAC advocates or not, that they were disappointed in the new Army.

In the autumn of 1980 General Meyer, the Army Chief of Staff, addressed the deep morale problems among his soldiers, male and female, which had been highly publicized in the wake of the debate over registration. Congress, horrified that so many soldiers were moonlighting and living on food stamps, opened its purse. Money flowed into pay raises, enlistment and reenlistment bonuses, educational, medical, travel, housing, and subsistence benefits. General Meyer was aware that the failing optimism of his troops required more than money and he announced a large package of proposals intended to "increase stability and enhance cohesion"—that is, to make soldiers feel that they belonged, and enable them to develop unit pride.

The scope of the measures showed that he knew that military effectiveness had a great deal to do with whether or not soldiers found their lives in the Army rewarding, an idea that had been overlooked in all the bickering about high and low quality and mental categories. Stability was to be achieved by having the officers in command of companies remain for eighteen months and by developing a way to keep groups of soldiers together if they were deployed to different places. There was talk of a more "regimental" system to replace the frequent and alienating rotations of individual soldiers, introduced in the era of Vietnam and continued thereafter.

The uniform was to be modified. The airborne units that had spent two years bemoaning the loss of their maroon berets were to get them back. Young recruits in basic training were to be given insignia identifying them by the branch they had chosen. The Army has set about learning how to accommodate its women soldiers by removing clothing or equipment that has, through its inadequacy, made them unable to function at full capacity. These are the things that *can* be changed. The research work is done at the Human Engineering Laboratory at Aberdeen, Maryland, and the Natick Research and Development Command at Natick, Massachusetts. In 1981 two kinds of fatigues were being tested: a unisex version of the male fatigues, and a special female design, with shirts that are narrow at the shoulder and wide at the hip, trousers that are shorter in the leg and wider at the hips. As for the notorious boots, the Army stopped using them in May 1979, even though about $680,000 worth of stock remained. Women were issued male boots, which, although far from ideal, are an improvement. The old spit-shined boot was to be replaced by rough brown boots requiring no polishing. This time the Army announced that it would be doing very careful tests on the women to see if the unisex principle could be applied to the boots. A total of 1800 female recruits at Fort Jackson were monitored during their training.

Women have also been testing replacements for the wobbly steel pots, the new helmets made of Kevlar, a strong synthetic material resembling plastic. These helmets are made in four sizes, designed to fit everybody. There is a new bulletproof vest, which is proportionately larger in the chest in the smaller sizes, on the assumption that the smaller military personnel are, for the most part, the ones with the bigger bosoms. The field-pack harness has also been re-designed so that the straps that used to cross over the chest now curve out on a frame. The women tested long under-wear and sports bras, and the modified protective mask that fits women's narrower faces in its smaller sizes.

These and other changes represent a large expenditure of money. When the Army spends a lot of money, it is serious about the matter at hand. Research is under way into the modifications necessary on the interior of Army aircraft to accommodate the lower eye level of a seated woman, and to make it easy for her to operate the controls and gunsights. In an equally adventurous but more outré experiment, the Army is also testing a "disposable cardboard tube designed to enable women soldiers in the field to urinate without undressing." It may be hard not to smile at such an idea, but if the invention were truly efficient, it would remove one of the obstacles to women's full acceptance in the field, for their modesty and that of the men would be protected.

General Meyer also announced in 1980 that standards of performance were to be raised in various ways at all levels, from the entrance tests to those that determine which specialty a recruit will undertake, and to the SQTs (Skill Qualification Tests), which determine how well a soldier performs at his or her job. All these changes were both desirable and necessary. New PT tests were devised, to be taken twice a year by all soldiers forty years old and under.

The three-event test was intended to toughen soldiers by requiring a minimum number of push-ups and sit-ups and a run. It sounds admirable. The actual requirement for a man under twenty-five is a minimum score of 40 push-ups, 40 sit-ups, and a two-mile run in 17.55 minutes. However, a woman of the same age is required to do a minimum of 16 push-ups, 27 sit-ups, and a two-mile run in 22.14 minutes.

Clifford Alexander, former Secretary of the Army, told me, with the weary emphasis of a man who had spoken too often to too many deaf ears, "It's very important to this institution that it utilize the people who are in it properly. It's very important to the 62,000 enlisted women in the Army that they will get the respect of those around and over them, men or women." Large numbers of Army men and women chortle at the very idea of women's getting respect if strong and healthy young female soldiers are required to do fewer than half the number of push-ups asked of the average male, and substantially less on the other two exercises.

No initiatives were to be aimed specifically at the women, even though so many women were leaving. There is throughout the Army, just as at West Point, and just as there was during the early days of the WAC, a feeling that to single out the women is favoritism, and that it is most sensible to treat males and females alike. In some ways that is an admirable policy, but so long as the PT requirements are permitted to be so different for men and women, it is not being carried through. The policy is, anyway, an unrealistic one. Women, for all their tradition of service, are only three years old in this man's Army, and, as anyone can see, that has not been a long enough time for mutual adjustment.

The deeper reason for women's unsatisfactory record in the statistics and in their job performance is male resistance to them, expressed in a variety of ways.

It comes out in the studies. The classic studies of actual female performance are so few that too much is made of them, like blue jeans in Russia. Two of them took place in the field: Maxwac in 1976 and Refwac in 1977. Both were designed to monitor female performance in the field and to assess the effectiveness of various ratios of men to women. To generalize, both studies showed that most women who had been adequately trained and issued the appropriate clothing did quite well. In cases where they did not, it was readily agreed that with adequate training or leadership they could have performed adequately. There was great resistance to the women, however, from all ranks, most visibly from their peers, the enlisted males, whose prejudices triumphed over the evidence. Only when there were a number of women around and the men were working closely with them did the prejudice grow fainter.

Prejudice was expressed differently by the women's superiors. Often women trained in physically demanding or nontraditional jobs were simply not allowed to do them. The men would leave them behind on guard duty, complaining that women were no good in the field because they did not like to get dirty. At basic training I had watched the women carefully to see how obsessed they would become with personal cleanliness and how they would cope with the Spartan facilities while out on bivouac. Jarrell expressed a fairly typical view when she shrugged her shoulders and said, "Lots of us come from the rural South, and we get used to that sort of thing, think nothing of it. People are very poor down there and a lot of them have outhouses." As for sharing showers, "That's fun" they chorused in their new Southern accents.

The fewer the women, the less responsibility they were given, and that, as one report said, was because of "the attitudinal component." The attitudinal component meant that "although NCOs generally admitted that women can perform well in their tasks, most NCOs just do not want them around." Another survey demonstrates that male soldiers can become overly concerned with women using their femininity to "get over." An "evaluation of attitudes" survey offers the unsurprising information that naïve female trainees too often give in to sexual intimidation from superiors.

So many factors are involved in the idea of effectiveness. Military urgency is one. What if Refwac had been conducted in wartime? What if the sample had been composed of different people? Ten years from now? The results of the notorious Project Athena surveys from West Point varied greatly in the course of just three years. Any sociologist will say that the most important aspect of a survey is the operating premise. Surveys like these were not only dealing with a very small number of women at one particular time, they were devised to explore the problems arising from the simple presence of women. This thinking is deeply at odds with the military mission, which is to work with the soldiers available, on the assumption that they will become an effective team.

A drill sergeant looking at a female trainee on Day 1 of basic training does not think, This woman is weaker than a man in the following respects. . . . The sergeant's job requires that he or she think, How strong can we make this woman; how best can we use her? The deterministic bias of most of these surveys obscures the facts of women's capability and reinforces prejudice, just as it did at West Point. Thus everybody is rendered less effective.

Male resentment is expressed most overtly and comfortably against women who are suspected of being gay. Many times during basic, one male drill or another would confide that he was amazed by the lesbianism. Sergeant Stokes said he did not mind the unfortunate ones who were "like men"; the genial black MP said, in tones of horror, "Do you know some of these women *shack up* together?" A couple told me of bad times in the old days—gay female drill sergeants "having relations with their troops" and the terrible tensions and fights between them and the first male drills to arrive. Some of the women they identified as gay were heterosexual.

The men's resentment and unease might take the form of sexual bravado. One woman kept a butter knife in her office drawer so that if a particular drill sergeant whom she had asked not to bother her continued to bother her, she could rap his knuckles. He did and she did, but only once; then there was a truce.

I asked a captain at Fort McClellan if the gay women felt more vulnerable than before with all the men around. She said, "It's still very overt. There are still people in men's shoes and trousers with back pockets. But they have to be more careful with the men around." She added, with a wild laugh, "Think what it does to these macho Army men, wondering if they're competing with women in bed as well." This woman had taken me to visit a couple of her gay friends, a black sergeant who had a pornographic painting of a plump, naked, white female bottom on the wall of her dimly lit living room, and, sitting huddled on the sofa in the corner, a skinny young white girl, also a sergeant, who had just arrived from Germany. There was much banter and rowdy laughter when I was introduced as writing a book about "the ladies in the Army," and the black sergeant, wearing only a bathrobe, flounced, laughing, into the kitchen to get an ashtray, looking and sounding exactly like a man in drag.

For the most part, gay life on post was still stable and domesticated. "There could never be a gay rights movement here," the captain said, "because people are too afraid. But there should be. These gay people are the type who are nice to their nephews and nieces, and look good, and do a good job," she said deliberately, as if she had thought this over many times. "We make *excellent* soldiers. You don't have to worry about pregnancy and day-care facilities for us." A captain at West Point had told me something similar about the gay women who had worked for her. She said that they were her best troops, because they were so serious about their Army careers and were not using their military service as a way to find a husband. My Fort McClellan source continued, "As for combat, I found a passage in a book that says a homosexual army could defeat any foe, 'for who would throw down his weapon and desert any friend of his beloved?' Now," she said, "we have to pretend. We have to show up at the officers club with a man once a month; we have to drive all the way to Chattanooga to the gay bars so we won't get spied on. If we have a party for our friends, or a cookout, people driving by will see a whole bunch of women, and so we have to be ready to lie, to say we were organizing the softball match."

The witch hunts have continued. They follow a standard procedure. A list is drawn up, and its existence becomes known. The list originates with a jealous male or, in the classic and more common situation, a disgruntled female attempting to enhance her career by informing on other women. There is always someone to leak the contents of the list; then anyone whose name is on it suddenly becomes solitary, because her friends do not want to be seen in her company in case they too are drawn into the net of suspicion. Names are named, suspects are watched and called to testify on each other; the whole process is long, cruel, and bitterly divisive. A lawyer who had represented military women in discharge proceedings showed me the transcript of a court-martial in which a naval intelligence agent who had interrogated Navy and Air Force women and allegedly denied them the right to counsel, a telephone call, or access to a female officer, was quoted as having said to one young woman that he wanted to talk to her about politics, government, and cannibals. When the woman asked him what cannibals were, he said that cannibals were people who ate other people.

Gays are not the only women to be resented. Those who embark on a nontraditional MOS are equally vulnerable. Of the women who graduated from basic, none was more vulnerable than Sue Jarrell, the nineteen-year-old guidon carrier from Asheboro, North Carolina, who was going into helicopter repair. It was Jarrell who had told me at a picnic that she wanted to learn survival skills, while another trainee, watching her in amusement, remarked mildly, "Jarrell is gung-ho Army." I remembered Sergeant Stokes saying after graduation, "Jarrell is the one I'm most pleased with. When I first saw her she was so skinny and shy and she just hung back, but then she really blossomed."

Jarrell is stationed in Kitzingen, a pretty little town in southern Germany, not far from Würzburg. The country is peacefully rural, its hillsides terraced with vineyards, and in the fields old women in print dresses stoop down, picking cabbages. In among the low hills and rolling plains are small medieval towns, many of them walled, with round towers, red-tiled roofs, and winding, cobbled streets. This is where some of the largest numbers of American troops in Germany are concentrated.

Jarrell appeared at my hotel at 6:30 one evening, in tight jeans with a billowing print top, and just enough makeup to give her color. She looked very young, fresh, rosy, and divinely happy, since at her side stood her beaming husband of two weeks, a German Air Force pilot, tall and blond, whose name is Egon Traber. We strolled around in the sunlit evening looking for a place to eat; the streets were almost empty of people and cars. There was only one soldier in the *Gasthof* where we sat down to veal cordon bleu and lager.

"Basic was a big sham," Jarrell said bitterly. "It set you up for something that never happened. Sergeant Stokes seemed to love the Army, *dearly*, and be U.S. Army twenty-four hours a day, three hundred sixty-five days a year. Lieutenant Myers was so professional; in the mornings I used to go down and take the guidon out at four-thirty or five, and sometimes she'd be there and I'd be terrified she'd ask me something I couldn't answer." She told me she had left for her AIT at Fort Rucker, with jump school to follow, feeling thrilled about the Army.

She had met Egon at Fort Rucker, and they grew fond and animated, reminiscing about the good times when they had worked hard all day in school, cleaned their barracks and done laundry and shoeshining in the evening, and then gone out to party. Then there was jump school at Fort Benning, where she said she began to feel disillusion. Jarrell did not complete jump school. She said, "I'm getting out of the Army. Don't give me a hard time about it."

The next morning at 6:30 A.M. I was standing outside the hotel, shivering a little in the early mist, when Jarrell drove up in her yellow Saab and leaned over to open the door. In fatigues, with boots gleaming and her short hair clean and brushed, she looked like a model soldier, like a boy, but a pretty one. The barracks was just three-quarters of a mile out of town, hidden in some trees. As we drove across the broad river Main she told me that the entire post contained about 1200 people, and maybe 3 to 6 percent of them were female. She said that at Fort Rucker, a school of four or five hundred, there were never more than a handful of women.

The figures are commonplace, but what they actually mean is one pair of bare legs in a West Point formation, the voice on the other end of an Army telephone that says automatically, "Can I help you, *sir*," and, in Jarrell's case, a high, drafty hangar just after sunrise, dotted with Hueys and Chinooks in various stages of disassembly, and with men, their voices booming off the walls into the space, and then, oddly, the high sound of one woman's laugh.

Jarrell had originally worked on the helicopters, as she was trained to do. Some women who chose MOS's such as helicopter or missile repair had, with the best intentions, found themselves in difficulties at school because, unlike men, they had not spent their teenage lives messing around with machinery in the garage or even learning electronics in shop. Jarrell had no such problems. Her father is an expert mechanic, and he had a workroom down in the basement of their house where she, always a tomboy, had spent a lot of time watching him and helping. She made a high score in her exam; she loved the work, and had no problems with the weight of the toolbox. But after three months she was taken off the floor for "disrupting the work flow." She said, without any false modesty, "I guess they were right. I was mad at the time, but then I realized that I'd been working all the time and not paying much attention, and there *had* always been four or five men standing around. But I was used to it, you see. I always hung around with the boys at school."

We were standing in the cramped operations room on one side of the hangar, glassed off so that the supervisory officers and NCOs in there could see what was going on. This was where Jarrell worked. She put down her knapsack and started fishing around in it. She found what she was after and showed me proudly the color photographs of her wedding. Egon was dressed in his black and white dress uniform, with his face ruddy and the sunlight glancing off his blond hair. Jarrell wore a floating white gown, with flowers in her hair and in her arms. She glanced up from the photos as another female walked by the glass, and shouted, "Hey Brophy, is it shirts-in this week?" The answer came back yes, and she made a face and tucked the shirt of her fatigues inside her pants, saying, "They're always changing the rules. One week we have to leave 'em out so as not to incite the males, next week we have to tuck 'em in so we don't look different from the males."

The room filled up with men, captains and warrant officers, drinking coffee in the raw chill. There were, I was told, close to one hundred people working in the hangar, three of whom were women, with a fourth woman on supply and another on emergency leave. Matter-of-factly Jarrell told me, "The one on emergency leave is supposed to be pregnant. She's always pregnant. Most of the pregnant women are single, you know, but they don't want to get out. It's just something that happens."

Somebody came in with a plastic bag he had found full of essential tools. The captain pushed his cap back on his head in pleasure and, rummaging through, he pulled out a small bottle of Revlon Natural Wonder nail polish. I watched him closely, waiting for an expostulation or a cynical smile, but he said agreeably, "Oh, good," and explained, "We use this; it makes an excellent substitute for a certain kind of paint that we find hard to get."

While Jarrell tunneled around in paper work I glanced at

PS, the preventive maintenance magazine, notorious for its visual aids, which mostly consist of busty blondes in pink sweaters. Congress has instructed the Army to doctor *PS* in an attempt to reduce the sexism. Jarrell said, "The men are real mad that they're taking the sexism out. They say that we hinder their lives by being here. I think that's absurd!" she said, vigorously erasing illegible handwriting, "but I still don't think they should change the comics. That's how the men think; they think dirty and talk dirty. That's what the Army is like. You have to learn to live with it, because you certainly can't change it. That kind of thing is not meant personally and you shouldn't take it that way." She went back to her work.

The warrant officer, a veteran of helicopter maintenance, stood listening with a gentle smile. He said, "Of the eleven women in this company, about three or four are terrific, and that includes Jarrell here. Three or four are terrible, just like some of the men, but after a while you don't notice them as women." I had heard this before, and I wondered whether he meant it. He continued, "Three are supposed to be mechanics. One is Jarrell, another is working by her own choice as company clerk, and the other one is pregnant. None of them has a problem with the fifty-pound toolbox, but over there with the trucks and their tires it's a different matter." He talked about the need for a physical test that could adequately measure the amount and kind of strength needed by a person, male or female, for any particular job. This reminded me that although there is supposed to be relative freedom of choice in the Army, anyone who flunks out of the training he or she has chosen can be reassigned to any specialty in which there is a shortage—which accounts for male would-be musicians becoming cooks and, nowadays, female would-be medics toiling in the motor pool.

Comparable problems arise with the women working on missile repair. Jarrell told me of one who sat in Frankfurt for two weeks without an assignment; I heard of another in Texas who was transferred to the motor pool. There are so few missiles to be repaired, and opportunities to work on them—in short, to practice one's skill—are so rare that when they do come along, they have to go to the men; if they did not, morale would plummet. This kind of reality explains the dry statistic of women "leaving the nontraditional skills."

That evening Jarrell told me bleakly that the hangar was inefficiently run. She confirmed the reports, widely discussed in the papers, of unhealthy working conditions, a shortage of equipment and personnel, and delays and backlogs in work. She minded the long hours and the inefficiency less than the men's attitude, she said, the constant assumption that because she had been moved to a desk job, the code word for cushy, she was somehow "getting over." She told me, almost in tears, "The guys take *everything* out on me. They complain that if women are equal, they should have short haircuts like the men. But I know the regulations say women should keep a feminine appearance. It's not my fault, *any* of this," she said. "I didn't write the regulations."

Jarrell said, "Nobody seems to want you to succeed. If you're a woman and you're good, you don't get praise. All you get is more work. And then the men—they always make everything come down to women in the Army, why *are* there women in the Army. Sometimes I wish they'd kept the WAC, and we could have had our separate repair units and everything. I mean, *why not?*"

Lieutenant Myers had told me once: "Women are so few and so visible that any one woman represents all of them. Men already have their place in the military. If you have some schmuck and they discharge him, nobody pays any attention. If one woman has problems, suddenly all the men start saying women don't belong in the Army. We haven't established ourselves, and that makes it a nonstop struggle."

Jarrell said that when she arrived in Germany she had to participate in the Headstart program, in which troops are told about the country, its customs and currency, its laws and language, and are given a few essential phrases to learn. The first class was a question-and-answer session with the post commander, who was cautioning the young males about sexual harassment when a male soldier stood up and said, "I guess it happens because there are so few young women, not enough of 'em to go round." Jarrell said, "The commander was flabbergasted—and I was so mad, I stood up and said, 'Excuse the hell out of *me*, sir, but I'd like to correct the impression that we're here to cater to any Tom, Dick, or Harry on post. I'm here to do a job.'"

The resentment many Army males feel toward women is just one end of a spectrum of confusion expressed as catcalls, favoritism, slander, a quick hug instead of praise, or rape. In the days of the first female expansion, many women moving into previously all-male fields faced a kind of problem described to me by a young captain in the Signal Corps who had been sent to Fort Carson. She said, "There were four females and one hundred and fifty men. They didn't know what to do with us. Some of the gals used their femininity to get out of certain jobs in the motor pool, because they didn't want to be greasy and dirty. And permissive NCOs let them, so the guys were furious. As more women arrived, the men learned how to deal with it. They had to teach us things, because we'd never done them before, and we all had to learn to work as a team." That is a classic example. The trouble starts with the first women, and unless the unit is properly run, it escalates instead of disappearing, and it affects everyone's work. Major Nederlander had told me that the problem was worst in the nontraditional MOS's. She said bitterly, "Those jobs with the greatest numbers of men have the lowest-grade men, the ones who ventilate the greatest hostility toward women. So the women experience a great deal of hardship to add to the dirty job. Of course they'll leave if they're not welcomed."

Since full integration, however, the problem of harassment has become widespread, and also more widely noticed as women learn to be bolder in reporting it. The chorus of protest represents a traditional female weapon against abuse—veto power, the cry of "no," and it is in that spirit that we have to study the statistics of women leaving. They are saying "no," and also "goodbye." The first reports in the media were triggered by a series that ran in *The Baltimore Sun* in December 1979, about alleged harassment at Fort Meade. The articles were sober and the information chilling. The women of the lowest rank seemed to be subjected to the worst of it. A young PFC reported that men would stare and comment on her body as she walked by. "A lieutenant would send me notes, asking me to go out with him," she said. "If I didn't go out with him, he said I wouldn't get my leave passes." An MP was victimized by her partner on night duty; she had to physically remove his hands from her body every night. Out in the field she was picked on and made to do things over and over again. Another woman said, "I don't want to be in the Army. I don't believe the Army is any place for a woman until they have as many women as they do men. There's nothing you can do to be equal. You always have to defend yourself, physically and emotionally." She said the company commander told her she had asked for trouble because of the clothes she wore.

Fort Meade was not the only place. In the wake of these stories, investigations were reported from forts Benning, Bragg, and Dix, and at the Presidio in San Francisco, where a colonel in the criminal investigation branch was found guilty of eight specifications of sex-related offenses. Facing a possible sentence of twenty-one years at hard labor, he was let off with a fine of $15,000.

General Mary Clarke was quoted as saying that sexual harassment was going on "at some places," but, she added, "I personally do not consider it a great problem." Many women still hold this remark against her, since they know that for every case reported, many are not, and that of those reported, a large number are ignored, or else the unfortunate victims are so intimidated for speaking out that they withdraw the complaint, or leave the service, or both.

In June 1980, soldiers were called to testify before the

House Armed Services Committee on the state of the AVF, and a PFC, male, when asked by Congresswoman Holt how he would assess the performance of the women (none of the soldiers called was female) said, "I think they make the morning formations look better," and thereby caused, according to *Army Times*, "the biggest laugh of the day." Female soldiers do not find this funny. It is a reflexive way of thinking that they cannot ignore. The PFC might equally well have said of women soldiers who were not pretty that "They make the morning formations look terrible."

Hearings were also held into the harassment problems, but the women who were called to testify came from extremely mixed backgrounds, and included a "former nude dancer," who, simply by being a former nude dancer, must have aroused many slumbering preconceptions. General Clarke said at this hearing that one case of sexual harassment was a serious matter, thereby performing a tardy about-face. A former deputy director of the WAC, a colonel now working at the Pentagon, said, "You shouldn't just talk to people at training posts and at the aggressively male posts. You should talk to someone at Fort Lee, somewhere quiet, in a quiet job." The only soldier I know who spent any time at Fort Lee is a parachute rigger, who went to rigging school there, and hated it because of the prejudice. She told me that at Fort Bragg, home of the crack 82d Airborne, where she is now, the men are easier to deal with.

The first of the former trainees to mention sexual harassment to me was Julie Drake, who had been so willing and cheerful once she lost her whispery shyness. She is a medical specialist, and therefore working in a field traditionally dominated by females. Julie had gone from Fort Sam to Fort Ord in California, about which she wrote, "It was an infantry post, so the guys were very rude if you walked down the street. Worst was my company commander! I couldn't believe him. In basic I was taught to respect officers, but him, it was just impossible. He said vulgar things about my body to other men."

Julie shared a room with two other women, who "were dirty and slept around like a lot of girls do in the Army out of loneliness. So of course they got preg. and V.D. One had a miscarriage in the room." She said she liked the Army, even though it had taken her some time to get used to it. "I had a choice to either live forever in the bay or else deal with the men, who were very obnoxious. So I learned to be assertive and bold."

Julie's friend, Cindy Hopkins, was also working as a medical specialist, in a clinic at Fort Hood, out in the middle of the Texas desert, near El Paso. In basic, Cindy was a serious, rather shy young woman, staring intently at her Miami Shores Police Department album, getting tearful when tempers crackled and flared around her. Cindy was buxom, no athlete, but she sweated and strained, and conscientiously got herself into shape. Right at the start of our renewed conversations she said, "I have been *really* down. I felt so bad, I even went and talked to the chaplain, and he said, straight off, the only way to get out is to get pregnant! The chaplain! It made me so mad I just decided I had to get what I want." Cindy has a new edge in her voice; she is learning to make waves even though she knows that nobody in the Army likes you to. She said furiously, "Fort Sam and Fort Carson were great, but Fort Hood is my permanent post. This is the headquarters of air defense, the Cav. The only females working here are medics and in supply and the mess hall. There are five females in my company, combat support."

"The first week," Cindy said, "I had guys, mostly black guys, knocking on my door or just pushing it open and saying, 'Hi, you wanna go to bed?'" I asked how she coped. She said, resignedly, "What could I do? I closed the door. But there are so few guys here you could have a relationship with. Even the nice ones." Cindy said that she had a boyfriend, and he walked her to work every morning to protect her from the whistles and insults. They found it hard to have time alone together, because she shared a room with an older woman, a Filipino, who became upset if she found them even hugging and kissing. Cindy said, "Even my friend is prejudiced. He went in front of an E-5 board and said, 'Women are okay as long as I don't have to work with them.' And they didn't scold him or anything!"

When I asked Cindy about the chain of command, she said hesitantly, "My sergeant is against us. He wants to get rid of us. He wouldn't let me go to work in the clinic even though that's what I'm trained for. So he put me in an aid station, where we don't have anything to do. So I end up spending a lot of time in the motor pool, because we have three vehicles there that we use when we go out on field trips. The field trip was great," she added wistfully. "We went to New Mexico and it snowed."

A few months later I spoke to Cindy again. She said, "Well, I went to my company commander, and he made the sergeant let me go on a ninety-day TDY. He sent the sergeant up before the battalion commander for saying all those bad things about women." I asked what had happened. Cindy laughed and said, "They told him to straighten out and look after his troops, but he doesn't. He's an E-7, twenty-seven years old, and he lets his people off work to go drinking. He hates me now, of course. I should go to do more school, but I'd need a waiver to do the course, and it would have to come from him." She brightened and said, "He took one girl out for drinks, and you know what she said? She said, 'Just wait till he does something else wrong.'"

The women have a new power, whether or not they are aware of it. Sergeant Reilly at Fort McClellan had told me, "When I talk to those male drills about fraternizing with female trainees, I know what can happen. They could be at a very low ebb and confronted with one of these young women, some of whom are immoral little tramps. I've seen what they'll do. So I tell the drills, if they think it's worth it, go right ahead, be my guest. But sometimes the woman will talk, and when she does, there's not a *damn thing* I can do to help you."

I had met an officer at Fort Bragg who was also uncomfortably aware of the threat. He told me that when he was stationed in Germany he sometimes found himself working late at his office with two female assistants, and he was unable to concentrate properly on his work. He could not look up at them without thinking, They are female. He was angry, but not as angry as the women, who feel that too many men, whether they speak out against women or plague them at work or ignore the women's past achievements to revive all the old questions of capability, have forgotten their mission. The young enlisted troops can do little to combat the resentment, but the officers and senior NCOs, although they do not have an easy time of it, are more likely to have resources of defiance or humor with which to defend themselves.

Lieutenant Sanderson, a muscular young woman and an Olympic swimmer who coached at West Point, sat with me in the gym one afternoon watching enormous young men throw each other around in the "close quarters" class, and she grinned a little and said, "Look at 'em. Tubs of lard." Then she told me about the time that a reporter came to watch her and a male colleague giving a class, and the reporter said to the colleague, "Does the young lady ever get hurt?" Lieutenant Myers told me that because she was married, the males felt free to ask her which of the other women were gay, assuming that any woman who was not would be at their disposal. Lieutenant Myers would say, "Elizabeth—oh, she's straight, she's slept with *everybody*, so go *right ahead!*" She would quite routinely ignore the commands one of the male officers gave her, because she knew them to be nothing more than a worthless exercise in showing off. She said, "Of course he never even noticed."

These women are tough and experienced. All that will help today's young soldiers transcend the problems they face is a good unit. PFC Jeannie Fisher is in a good unit at Fort Bragg. Fisher, the shy girl from Florida whose father had noticed her new arm muscles after basic, had become a parachute rigger, going first to airborne school at Fort Bragg and then to rigger school at Fort Lee. Fort Bragg, her permanent post, is a rambling and aggressively masculine post in the North Carolina pinelands, just outside Fayetteville, a typical Army town, with a quiet old center and a sleazy ribbon of pawnshops and used-car dealers and strip joints and bars stretching out into the scrubland past the post.

Jeannie is one of fewer than twenty women in a company of about two hundred. Riggers think of themselves almost as paratroopers. They make regular jumps, for which they get a small bonus in pay, and they wear bright red baseball caps at work as a sign of their pride and status. Jeannie looked very proud and perky in hers and quite different. No longer fragile and bony, she had put on weight, which gave her substance rather than size. Although the shy smiles and shrugs and the blush that suffused her freckled face gave away her youth, she seemed womanly, fit, strong, and sexy, her hair long and a darker red than it had been a year ago. She said she did PT every morning, and, grinning, she flexed her arms so that I could see her muscles.

We sat in a Dickensian restaurant deep in the labyrinthine recesses of a huge shopping mall. Fisher told me, "Fort Bragg is much better than Fort Lee. But still, there's an attitude here that makes me furious. The other week," she explained, "I was dayroom orderly, and something happened that wasn't my fault. The next morning I overheard the sergeant talking about me as 'that stupid cunt.'"

It was, she said, almost impossible to stop the talk, particularly in the ubiquitous Human Relations class, where people endlessly moaned, "Why do we have to have women in the Army?" She said, "Once in a while I do get really mad with all this. A guy one time asked why most office jobs are filled by women and why they don't have to do details [I thought of Jarrell painstakingly correcting other people's scrawled reports], and the officer in charge said, 'Because they're mostly high producers and they do a lot of work.'

This guy in my platoon said, 'I know how Fisher gets her hours off. She walks around and shakes her ass.'" Fisher shrugged, trying to convey her frustration and helplessness. She said, "Sometimes I scream, but often I can't think of the words fast enough, and I end up having to walk away." She mostly puts up with it, especially the dirty talk. "That started in rigger school," she said. "We were rigging up loads and packing cargo chutes, and I'd be with all these men who were talking dirty, and I wasn't going to sit there and *turn red* all day. So I did it too, and some guys didn't like that. One said to me, 'Doesn't this bother you, Fisher?' I said, 'No, I'm used to it.' He said, 'I can't get used to it, that a lady can sit there and listen to all this stuff. Guys are gonna talk.'"

The next day I visited her at work, where the immediately incongruous sight—especially to a stranger who had visualized the rugged man's world of airborne-trained troops— was that of a large, high room full of sewing machines, and young men and women laboring industriously over them, or, with curved basting needles, stitching away at the billowing green folds of the chutes by hand. A sergeant showed me the paper schematic they use as a pattern—a diagram of the chute looking like a mandala. The rips were marked on the diagram, and as the troops completed work on each, they checked it off on the diagram. Fisher smiled in welcome and showed me her sewing. She said that some of the women who penetrated this manly field did not know how to sew when they came in.

It was late Friday morning. Jeannie, twiddling her red baseball cap, said, "You got here just in time. We've almost finished work for the day, and we get Monday off too." There was a system of achievement goals in the shed, and the more efficiently any platoon worked the sooner it could leave. Jeannie introduced me to her two best friends—Mary, a cheerful, noisy and pretty young woman, and Joe, one of the three people with whom she shared a home in the Sleepy Hollow Trailer Park. He was a serious fellow with a swift, gappy grin, and he showed me around the supply office where he worked. Joe put on his baseball cap and pressed the sides of the peak down to form a shadowy cave over his eyes, and, glimpsing Jeannie in a group by the door, he said, "Jeannie is a real good person, you know."

The four of us packed into Joe's car and drove off post a few miles to a small family restaurant for lunch. We sat at a round table, with other soldiers all around, talking about what it means to be airborne. They loved to jump, they said, and were proud to be airborne. The airborne name for the rest of the Army is "legs," synonymous with all that is vile, verminous, and groveling—and they seem to believe that.

Joe said two things diminished his own pride. One was the attitude of civilians who loved to pick fights with people in uniform and insult their girlfriends. The other was the official attitude toward women. He said, "If you're the average enlisted white man, you have less going for you than anyone else in the Army. They're always making sure there's a female—and a black male—in on everything." Jeannie agreed, saying that she was going on a Basic Leadership Course the following week, and it should have been Joe's turn. "The only reason I've been chosen is that they need women, and all the PFCs and above from my company have already been." I realized that the difference between a good unit and a bad might be that in a good unit the men who felt discriminated against would not take it out on the women, whereas in a bad unit they would.

We drove back to the post. It was around two on a balmy, gleaming Friday afternoon in springtime, and while Joe had to go back to his lists and cartons and shelves piled with chute paraphernalia, Mary and Jeannie had until Tuesday morning off. They were happy and rowdy, teasing Joe, trying to intimidate him into letting them have the car that night so they could visit the local music bars. Joe chuckled and broke loose from Mary's bear hug, saying, "I'm gonna file a complaint about female harassment."

The sergeant had said that morning as we walked around the long tables on which chutes were stretched like taffy,

"We try to keep it loose here. That's why you hear a lot of first names used. You've got a number of people in here doing the same work day after day, and you have to make it pleasant for them." It felt pleasant; there was an easy affection between the three that was not sexual. A lot of the ribbing was of the kind that only young males and females can give each other—about dates and sex and whatnot—but it was puppyish, not sexual. It transcended their genders, making them not androgynous or "defeminized" but *fraternal.* It seemed possible because the women were accepted on an equal basis at work, and they were secure in their mission. Jeannie had told me that Joe and the other men in her unit would look after her in their way and come to her defense if men from other units insulted her. I had heard this from Jarrell too, and read about the same phenomenon as it occurred in the course of the Army's Maxwac and Refwac studies in the field.

Men of the old Army, and many other people, talk heatedly about the impossibility of trying to remove the sexual charge between men and women. The more plausible alternative is to live with it, and many civilians and soldiers do. As Captain Whitcraft said about her colleagues at West Point, it takes a while to learn, but men and women can enjoy being colleagues.

One night, when Jeannie was full of dinner and beer, I asked her how she thought the Army had changed her. She said, "I've changed a whole lot. I told you how I deal with guys talking dirty—that's kind of the way I've become. I just don't care so much. If I go out and party with a guy, they say I'm sleeping with him; if I go out with six or seven guys and it's just me, I get a reputation. And I am more casual about sex now than I used to be. But I don't care about the talk." She smiled and said, "If people try to step all over me, I won't let 'em. I say, 'Get lost,' or I'll curse. I didn't used to have that confidence, but now I have, and I *like* it." I thought of Cindy saying, "Everyone at home thinks I'm much more independent and less belligerent than I used to be," and Jarrell, staring at me impatiently and saying, "What's de-feminized? So what if you have short hair and they don't want you to wear lipstick and eye shadow to work? There's no way you're going to look like a man in the uniform, unless you're shaped like one already."

Some women fail as soldiers because they have no models, others because, like Jarrell, they do not have encouragement. Others fail because they are not ready to adapt to the military. One thirty-two-year-old New Yorker who had left a good middle-class job to join the Army wrote to me in fury that she found herself being ordered around by people whom she would never pay to clean her house. It was clear that her career would be short and devoid of epiphanies.

There are real hardships in Army life, and some afflict men and women equally. Money, for example. After two years in the Army these young people were earning somewhere in the region of $500–$550 a month plus allowances. This is why so many people make "contract marriages"—marriages of con-venience—because they can bring in up to $200 more a month for each person. One soldier I know, who has such a marriage, said in resigned tones, "When I first arrived at my unit and they found I was single, everybody said, 'You wanna get married?'" Senior NCOs and officers turn a blind eye, out of sympathy for the financial plight of their troops, and the practice is very common. After all, they may be on food stamps or moonlighting themselves.

Jarrell told me that when she first arrived in Germany she had lived in a barracks where one floor was set aside for the females from several companies. They could wander around half-clad and check on their laundry; they could leave their doors open and relax. "Now," she told me, "they're all integrated, and there's no way the women can unwind or get away from the men. They always have to be fully dressed; if they want to use the latrine for a shower they have to wait till the guys have finished using it. Sometimes the guys use it all night and the girls have to fight for it. They have a hard time." Cindy had said, "We have no privacy at all except for separate rooms. They cut my phone wires the other day; people's rooms get ripped up. There's racial hatred. And of course there's nothing to do. I go and play cards, go to the movies. I have a hot plate in the room so I can eat here without going to the mess hall."

Those who can afford it move to trailer parks, three or four to a trailer. In their evening spare time they might go to a bar or a movie. Usually they just go home, shine their boots, launder their uniforms, and watch TV until they fall asleep. Although they may have made friends with the young men, there is a shortage of men to date because the women find them too young, not intelligent enough. Those who are resourceful date sergeants.

Loneliness and isolation are not confined to the enlisted. A West Point lieutenant told me, "Just because I'm single it doesn't mean I'm weird." She confessed, reluctantly, that she was jealous of Army men. "I've chosen a career that would make it very difficult indeed to have a spouse, whereas my male counterparts all do. I can't find a man who can deal with the fact that his wife gets home two hours after he does, with black boots on, and goes off for six months or to the field for three weeks at a time. A man who would be willing to move every three years would be a gas station attendant maybe," she said, "but I'm looking for the kind of man on his way to a senior executive position." This was the swimmer. She had cut off her waist-length hair when she came to West Point so that nobody could find an easy reason to call her unmilitary.

Women like that lieutenant are philosophical about their chances of finding such a man, but not about the consequences of being single in a family-dominated world—where, for example, they are likely to find themselves living in dismal quarters so cramped that the stove defrosts the refrigerator, with furniture consisting of two straight-backed chairs, a bed, and a flea-infested rug, in a building that is overcrowded, filthy, and noisy. The lieutenant said, "This is

one of the biggest problems women have. The men have
wives who can contend with the problems of no drapes,
storing furniture and taking it out again every three years,
looking for an apartment that they can afford." She added
that she was one of the luckier women, in that the wives of
the men she worked with had come to accept her after her
long and patient attempts to allay their anxieties. "At last,"
she said, "they have begun to invite me over to their
homes."

Paul Revere wrote about Deborah Sampson Gannett,
"When I heard her spoken of as a soldier, I formed the idea
of a tall, masculine female, who had a small share of
understanding, without education, and one of the meanest of
her sex—when I saw and discoursed with her I was agreeably
surprised to find a small, effeminate, and conversable
woman, whose education entitled her to a better situation in
life." We have the same preconceptions today, complicated
by double standards that are expressed at their most damaging in the official attitude toward pregnancy.

Many female soldiers are as Paul Revere would have liked
them to be, others are not. Some of those who get accidentally pregnant are, like civilians, likely to be young, poorly
educated, and single. In the old days they would have been
discharged automatically, whatever their circumstances. This
policy came to be seen as discriminatory, and so pregnant
women in the modern Army may stay in the service—but
they have to pay for their own abortions. They are the
soldiers who live on food stamps and make contract marriages, and it is not easy for them to find the money.
Sometimes they may go ahead with the pregnancy, for the
wrong reasons, and the result is, at the very least, time
missed from work, and most likely a woman who will leave
the service and not justify the money that has been spent on
her. I asked Sarah Lister, the General Counsel for the Army,
what she thought about this. She said, "It was a slap in the
face for the military; a great shame." She told me that

Pentagon officials had fought the decision and then tried to interpret the ruling as freely as possible. Army women or wives overseas are offered free air travel to a military hospital in which the procedure can be carried out. This is intended to protect the health of women who, because they cannot afford to travel far to an expensive hospital, might otherwise be at risk from local facilities. In an outrageous circumstance, they have tried to be humane. Soldiers are also entitled to air travel for abortion counseling, in the U.S. or overseas. However, many women are carrying the babies to term, and approximately 40 percent of the women who have babies leave the service. Others give their children up for adoption because they cannot afford to keep them.

The dilemma thrust upon Army women is unfair and unethical. Women are asked to be efficient soldiers but are denied free abortions. Gays, who do not get pregnant, are persecuted or discharged from the service. The women are not allowed equal opportunity to behave like soldiers, and then they are condemned for their failure. Whatever the official policy toward pregnancy, everyone would rather deal with a female soldier who is not pregnant, or a woman who has no child-care or family problems. Since readiness is the first priority of the military, and since pregnant women are always seen as a threat to readiness, it should be a matter of military necessity to allow soldiers who want abortions to have them quickly, safely, and free. The women are done a great disservice; they are soldiers who are forced into being mothers. Critics of this view would probably say that the women should behave better. Some of the women have said to me, "Nobody ever tells the men that."

I asked Cindy Hopkins what Fort Hood had offered her in the way of a special briefing when she arrived. She said, "The re-up sergeant said, 'Hopkins, our policy here is, Don't get pregnant. Too many females here get pregnant.'" That was it. More usually, so I have been told, the briefing is in two parts: "Don't get pregnant. Beware of lesbians." The only formal birth-control instruction is given in basic training.

The Army policy toward pregnancy defines it as a "temporary disability." There is a maternity uniform for the women, consisting of a green tunic to be worn over slacks or a skirt. Service women who reach their eighteenth week of pregnancy have to be evacuated along with civilians when ordered. Otherwise they are supposed to be treated like everyone else. In fact, they are excused from duties, left behind on field trips, and, in general, tend to be given the opportunity to grow slack in their behavior even if they wish to work hard.

The men hate and loathe seeing the women getting over, as they call it. The majority of women are very uncomfortable with the idea of pregnant officers commanding men, or pregnant troops finding themselves unable to fix the tire on a truck. They most certainly do not want these women nearby. Jarrell said emphatically, "I think to have pregnant women in the Army is just *ludicrous*. Other people have to come in and take over their jobs—people who aren't familiar with the job. And so everyone's effectiveness is impaired." Colonel Hallaren, a small, elderly former director of the WAC who had reviewed the reunion parade, said, "I can't believe that any military commander from the old days would go along with this policy. Ike and the others would never have stood for it!"

One soldier wrote to me, "Attitude toward unmarried pregnant women is bad . . . as if they're automatically promiscuous and dumb enough to get caught. Females themselves promiscuous express a 'how-could-she-do-that, she's-a-bad-person' attitude toward other females who are pregnant." Behind this scorn, which tends to be conveniently vented on unmarried women who may "deserve" it, is of course the insecurity of women who feel themselves judged collectively, resented a little more by each man who finds himself working alongside a pregnant woman.

Most of the women feel that the Army is grievously at fault in not providing adequate birth-control instruction, not fighting Congress over a soldier's right to an abortion, and being too civilian about pregnancy. A young married lieutenant I visited in Germany, who had left the Army when she got pregnant, said, "I hated to leave, but I have to do things properly, and I couldn't split myself between the Army and my family." That was Lieutenant Myers, who is now a full-time wife and mother. Standing in her living room and staring with adoration at three-month-old Charlotte Myers while Ted, the other Lieutenant Myers, was at work flying his medevac helicopter, Lieutenant Myers said firmly, "People think the Army should start day-care centers, but I don't. I hate the thought of a day-care MOS."

The current Army policy on its 16,800 sole parents, 3300 of whom are women, is that they should make suitable and satisfactory arrangements for other people to care for their children in case of an emergency. I asked Lieutenant Myers what she thought about that. She said, "It's quite right. Children and an Army career can be combined—if that's what you choose—but it should not be the Army's responsibility." She continued, "We're too much of a social organization already. We rehabilitate by curing drunks and teaching people to read. The Army should be for the strong, not the weak."

12

In the Line of Duty: Sixty-seven Army Nurses in the Philippines

"I don't know how to march. When they gave us our Bronze Stars I was standing next to a little sergeant at the ceremony and he said, 'Take my hand and I'll show you.' We never had any of that training, you see."

Major Minnie Breese Stubbs (ret.) laughed throatily as she told me this incident. We were sitting in her tiny modern apartment in San Antonio, filled with pictures of her dead husband, Stubby, and the travel souvenirs and knickknacks that you see in most Army homes. A small, plump person with curly gray hair and a friendly expression, she rubbed absently at her thigh and said, "I'd think it was arthritis if I didn't recognize it as a residual from the beriberi I got in the camp."

Minnie Stubbs is a retired Army nurse, one of sixty-seven who survived the World War II defeats of Bataan and Corregidor and endured nearly three years in Santo Tomas, a Japanese prisoner-of-war camp in the Philippines. By devoting the next few pages to the story of the captivity of some American nurses in World War II, I may seem to be wandering from the point of the book. They were not strictly soldiers. Nevertheless their experiences as told here represent a reminder of the countless parallel circumstances the world's women, in uniform or out of it, have endured in all wars, and on the largest scale in World War II.

In any war, nurses are so greatly idealized as angels of mercy that the nature of their sacrifice is overlooked. They die—from typhoid, pneumonia, wounds—and what chiefly distinguishes them from men is their lack of weapons. Their vulnerability makes them a paradigm for all the millions of unarmed women who cannot escape the horrors of war. Their endurance reminds us that ordinary people, men or women, become the heroes of war.

The first official Army nurses served in the War of Independence after General Gates reported to George Washington that "the sick suffered much for Want of good female Nurses." On July 27, 1775, Congress authorized the first Army hospital, with a plan providing for one matron and ten nurses for each hundred wounded. These nurses were to receive $2.00 a month and one ration a day. Large numbers of nurses were involved in the Civil War, many of them in work that was as much housekeeping and cleaning as nursing. In 1901 the Army Nurse Corps was officially established, and the women served in great strength during World War I, with a peak of more than 21,000. Several were wounded by enemy fire, and more than 200 died, most from influenza or pneumonia that they caught in Europe.

It was not until World War II that the nurses were brought up right behind the troops. As a history of the Army Nurse Corps says: "They served on beachheads from North Africa to Normandy and Anzio, in the Aleutians, Wales, Australia, Trinidad, India, Ireland, England, the Solomons, Newfoundland, Guam, Hawaii, New Guinea, New Caledonia, Puerto Rico, Panama, Iceland, Bataan, and Corregidor . . . they traveled in close support of the fighting men, endured relentless bombing and strafing on land, torpedoing at sea, and antiaircraft fire while in flight-evacuation of the wounded." They waded ashore at Anzio only five days after the troops did, and six were killed. In the Southwest Pacific they lived under the same abominable conditions as the men and the Wacs, plagued with disease and fatigue, and there were times in the European war when their field hospitals were surrounded for hours at a time. But it was the nurses of Bataan and Corregidor, especially those who went on to prison at Santo Tomas, who came the closest to combat. Many were young and green when they arrived in the Philippines, and, said Minnie Stubbs, "We were so naïve."

These nurses guard their privacy. Like many POWs, they prefer to talk about their wartime experiences only with each other. A retired general and former head of the Nurse Corps had put me in touch with them, saying, "Some of the others won't talk, and some are far gone; most can't discuss their experiences without being maudlin and sentimental. But I promise you, these two won't cry, and they'll be candid." A handful of the women live close to each other in and around San Antonio, and near Fort Sam Houston, which has been for some years the headquarters of the Army Medical Department and a place where many Army doctors and nurses retire to be near their friends.

Minnie Stubbs told me that Manila was a plum assignment before the war. She said, "We lived high on the hog; we used to go dancing. Hattie and I were mad about golf, so we played a lot of that. We didn't think too much about war," she said, "but then they sent the wives and dependents home, and we knew something was up." Minnie had other things on her mind; she had fallen in love with an artillery-man on MacArthur's staff.

Lieutenant Colonel Hattie Rilla Brantley (ret.) is a farmer's daughter from East Texas, a slim, tall woman with feathery cropped gray hair and elegant clothes. One afternoon she visited me at my motel and sat tracing patterns on the table with a finger, looking out at the people splashing in the pool as she reminisced. She said, "Oh, yes, we were unprepared. That morning of December eighth the chief nurse said, 'Now, girls, war has started, but we will go about our business as usual.' Minnie and I had worked all night," she continued. "We should have been packing our bags, we should have been preparing the hospital, we should have been filling sandbags." She paused, then said in a flat Texas voice, "We should have been doing a lot of things, but we went out and played golf."

She smiled. "That night the bombs fell near us and the firing started, so the four of us who lived in this little bungalow scrambled out and got underneath, I with my red silk nightgown on, Mary Jo, the most dedicated Catholic you ever saw, starting in with her rosary, and I just began to laugh!" That was how war began for the American nurses, under a bungalow with their rosaries and silk nightgowns. Immediately, that day, the casualties came in. The hospitals outside Manila were evacuated and the personnel moved into the city as the Japanese drew closer. On the twenty-fourth, General MacArthur ordered the abandonment of Manila, and the trek began to Bataan, a peninsula across the bay. Nurses, doctors, and patients went there by bus and boat.

The Bataan peninsula is twenty-five miles long and twenty miles wide, an intractable and hellish place choked with jungle, slashed with ravines and rivers and cliffs, and plagued with rain. Eighty thousand troops, American and Filipino, defended it against the Japanese for over three months. This population, and 26,000 refugees, lived on half rations, and then on three-eighths rations. By early March only 4 out of about 100 men in a field artillery battery had sufficient strength to lift the ninety-eight-pound shells up to the breeches of the 155-mm guns. The troops, and the nurses, had beriberi, dengue fever, hookworm, malaria, pellagra, and dysentery. The water was contaminated. People ate roots, leaves, papaya, breadfruit, monkey, chicken, pig, water buffalo—anything they could find. Nevertheless—and both Brantley and Stubbs agreed on this—the esprit was high. "We believed the U.S., greatest country in the world, would send a convoy to get us," said Minnie Stubbs.

The nurses worked, from first light until dark, at two makeshift and overflowing hospitals, one in the open air, with patients lying on mats on the ground. They had outdoor latrines and bathed in the streams. Each nurse had set out for Bataan in white, starched duty uniforms, white hose and shoes, a gas mask, and a tin helmet, c. World War I. These were replaced by Air Force coveralls, size 42. There was no lime for the latrines, which had to be near the wards so that the dysentery patients could reach them, and so there were flies. Hattie Brantley said, "I can remember doing dressings. Starting right after breakfast and continuing throughout the day. I'd not go far along that line of cots before my back would not straighten up, and I'd get down on my knees, finally not even bothering to arise, but crawling to the next cot. My experience in a cotton patch back in east Texas stood me in good stead." They used vines as ropes for the patients in traction, and found out when dressings ran low that gangrenous wounds healed well in the open air with no dressings at all. There were two bombings, the second a deliberate attack, when two nurses were wounded and many patients were left dead and dying. Hattie said, "People were killed and mangled and screaming, and the priest was standing there on the desk in all the dust saying the Lord's Prayer."

On April 8, 79,500 men surrendered, along with the nurses—the largest force in U.S. military history to lay down its weapons. The medical personnel were evacuated, sick with malaria and dysentery, deaf from quinine, and weak from malnutrition. Hattie Brantley had hepatitis. They would not leave their patients until, said Minnie Stubbs, "You could hear the Japs yellin' 'Banzai' as they were coming over the hill," and they fled in buses, with explosions and flashes all around, the roads clotted with the chaos of fleeing soldiers and the wounded, with wrecked cars and desperate refugees. Seventy-eight military nurses headed for the bay. They had cared for about 9000 patients during the months on Bataan.

Corregidor was worse, a precipitous craggy island the size of Manhattan, with a fortress on top, and, underground, the tunnels twelve feet high and thirty-five feet wide, in which about 13,000 Americans were holed up. In the hospital were 2600 American and Filipino patients squashed into triple-tier bunks, cared for by ten nurses. Minnie Stubbs said quietly, remembering, "We were like a bunch of rats in a hole. The shelling shook the whole mountain, and as they closed in we weren't allowed outside for our cigarette breaks." They could not sleep because of the noise of the raids. After each one the broken bodies would be brought down.

Operating conditions in the tunnel were wretched, with the press of people, the dark, the heat, and the noise. The nurses performed surgery by flashlight, often without anesthetic because there was no time for it. At the onset of the final bombardment thirty-two nurses were evacuated. Those left behind toiled on until the surrender on May 6, when doctors passed out tubes of morphine and said, "If you have to, commit suicide." Hattie Brantley said, typically, "I doubt that any of us would have. Anyway"—she looked at me with a vaguely professorial frown—"if you swallow an overdose of morphine it won't kill you, it will make you very sick."

It was the next day before the Japanese came down and discovered the nurses, to their great astonishment. Minnie Stubbs, who has an earthy dislike for them, said, "They were hollerin' and carryin' on and their language sounded like a bunch of magpies. But they didn't touch us."

For six weeks the fifty-four nurses remaining were not allowed out of the tunnel. In the dark and the confused despair of surrender they cared for thousands of patients. The Japanese seemed embarrassed by their presence, wondering if perhaps they were some kind of geisha, since they had taken off their military insignia. Eventually the population of Corregidor was dispersed to different camps, and the nurses were sent to Santo Tomas, the big civilian camp of the Philippines.

Santo Tomas was a former campus that contained about

nine thousand civilians, including executives and their wives, as well as missionaries and at least six bishops. Families were segregated, but in most other ways the camp ran itself like a small town, with government, garbage disposal, meals, laundry, and the other facilities all operated by the internees under the direction of the mayor (a top executive from General Electric) and his city council. The difference was that armed Japanese guards manned the flimsy reed gate, and the guards patrolled, demanding that internees bow from the waist when they passed, or kneel. And fluttering above the compound was the Japanese flag— "That fried egg," said Minnie.

The nurses worked from the first day of captivity until their last, thirty-three months later. They had arrived severely weakened by disease and semistarvation, but they spent a minimum of four hours a day in the hospital, twice as long a shift as the civilians in the compound worked, and on the same amount of food. The rest of the day was spent on chores—laundry, gardening, cleaning, food preparation, and standing in line for hours waiting for food. Food, or the lack of it, was their constant preoccupation. The basic supply was a cup of rice twice a day, supplemented by whatever could be grown or procured from the outside. People formed groups or collectives to tend little plots of vegetables; the nurses were so desperate for green vegetables that they would eat the leaves of the potatoes as soon as they appeared.

Like everyone else, they learned to be resourceful and cultivate their contacts. A British businessman who had workers on the outside conducting business for him lent them money every month so that they could buy vital fruit or vegetables, on the assumption that they would pay him back after the war. A man whittled bamboo into knitting needles, which the women bought, along with grocery string, from which they knitted underwear and socks. They made clogs from wood, with inner tubing nailed across the top. They learned to guard their clothes as they dried on the grass, and to scavenge. Minnie Stubbs told me she had two items always in her pocket, a precious toothbrush and "a spoon, in case I got to meet up with some food. Always carry a spoon with you," she said, laughing, "and remember that salt is very good for toothpaste."

These small gestures of independence kept everybody's spirit alive, and there were even enjoyable moments. In the evening there might be plays or music. A disc jockey would play records in the courtyard and the internees would come out to listen. One night, close to July 4—and everybody knew, somehow, which night had been chosen—musicians played "The Star Spangled Banner," and for an instant a light was shined onto an American flag that someone had managed to hide; then the light went off. On another night, close to liberation, the disc jockey played "Pennies from Heaven" as the planes came over.

Nurses seldom falter, because their mission leaves them no room for doubt and no time to spare. Hattie Brantley told me, "It was a matter of faith; we really believed that if we could get through today, help would be there tomorrow. We would climb a tree in the morning and look out in the bay, which was going to be full of ships. So it wasn't that morning, but tomorrow it would be." But behind the brave words and the attempts to fashion a life from rags and roots, fear of the Japanese was always present. The beatings and beheadings that were commonplace in Japanese prison camps took place at Santo Tomas, but not often. When they did, they were the result of (often imagined) transgressions, such as smuggling, communicating with the underground, trying to escape, lying. Both nurses said, very deliberately, that everyone knew the rules. If you broke them, you had to be ready for the consequences. Toward the end, however, the Japanese became jumpy and the prisoners apprehensive. Hattie said, "They didn't want us to see the planes—they told us that they were holding maneuvers, but of course we could see they were ours. So they made us go inside the building and not look out. Anyone who was caught had to stand outside and look up all the day." By the end the roll calls were constant, twice a day, the prisoners standing there for hours in the sun and bowing in just the right way to even the lowliest soldiers. Finally the Japanese took out some of the camp administrators, including the mayor, to be tortured, beheaded, and dismembered. Whatever happened on any specific day, there was the persistent gnawing torture, a shared knowledge of which holds POWs together and excludes anyone who has not experienced it.

Hattie explained it in this way. "It was, simply, torture to be without our freedom. They did not live up to the Geneva Convention, so we got almost no mail and we couldn't send any out. One time they had five, or ten, or twenty-five postcards that had those little boxes that say 'I am well/sick/dead,' you know"—and she traced her little patterns on the table, well aware of what she had just said—"and they gave them out. The Nurse Corps had one card and I got that card." She sent it to her parents; she in turn had only one card from them, a Christmas card from her mother, which arrived in August 1944 and said that her father had died in the summer of 1943.

She said, "That was torture. You don't have any food or any mail, and you've lost your freedom. You can't pay allegiance to your flag. You can't have the Red Cross packages, and you have to smell the Japanese smoking the American cigarettes and see the Japanese wearing the GI shoes from inside those packages."

I asked the nurses if they felt able to tell whether men as a group or women as a group seemed to hold up better under those circumstances. Both of them said, independently and without a moment's hesitation, that the women managed better. Hattie Brantley looked quite aggressive and said, "It is my philosophy that if you take away a man's tobacco and his liquor and his women, he hasn't much left. Mentally women stand up much better than men do, in war or in peace." She continued, "The women had all these things to do. They had the responsibility for the noon meal for their families or groups, they worked on the laundry and picking the bugs out of the rice. Lifelong habits are hard to break. . . . But how could the men do things like that? They *can* but they don't—and they didn't." She said of the women's work, "It soothed their nerves, and it kept them alive."

There was little that the nurses could do for their patients. They had aspirin and morphine and drugs for the dysentery, but when the Red Cross sent penicillin they did not know how to use it, because it was new to them, and it came without instructions—or else the Japanese had taken them. They doled out vitamin pills to those who were worst off, but mostly it was, as Minnie Stubbs said, a case of "tender, loving care, making the patients comfortable, washing their faces." Hattie Brantley said, very firmly, "The men died, and the women didn't, and that is statistically true." She said, "Since we were the nurses, we *knew*, and as I remember, not one woman in the camp died, except from surgery complications. None of them died from ennui, as the men did—we were burying five and six a day, and a lot of them were the younger men."

There was heroism in the camp. Each nurse told me her story of a dangerous exploit. When Minnie Stubbs came back into the compound from her hospital duty outside the gates, she would smuggle notes from the resistance, stuffed inside her string brassiere. She said the Japanese would ask if you were carrying anything, but they would not search you. If they had reason to suspect you were lying, and you were detected, you would probably be decapitated. Nevertheless she did it.

Hattie Brantley prefaced her story with embarrassed throat clearing. "I have never told anybody this," she said, "and in retrospect it sounds so ridiculous, but it was one of the most horrible experiences of my entire life. When I was working the night shift in the hospital, from seven to seven, some people approached me about smuggling, and they provided me with a rope ladder. I would hang it from the second-floor window ledge, and go down the building to the outside and then to the fence. This was all by prearranged signals. Somebody would pass a bag of food through the fence, I would tie it on a rope, and this girl would pull it up, and we would hide it in the laundry. The next day, when the men carried the laundry out, they would take the parcel too." She said seriously, "I am frightened on a second-floor balcony, but because it was night, I couldn't see anything. However, one night they decided to search the camp. For searches they would sound an alarm, and you would go to your bedside and stay there; then you'd go out for a head count. When the call came, I was in the camp. The rope ladder was in a woven bag under my bed in the hospital. I just sat there, frozen, in a chair. I knew they were going to find it and come and get me and I would be beheaded." It was hard to imagine a woman who looked as if she was on her way to a bake sale as a terrified second lieutenant captive in the Philippines and anticipating decapitation. She paused for a while, laughed shortly, and said, "Nothing happened. They had pulled that ladder out and looked at it, I could tell, because they didn't quite put it back. What would a nurse in a hospital be doing with something like that? There was no mistaking it . . ." Her voice tailed off.

For the most part the heroism was quiet, sustained. The Japanese ordered all written records to be burned, but Josie Nesbitt, the second-in-command, would not do it. She hid all the nurses' records, because she thought it wrong to destroy them. There was heroism also in enduring and working on despite the bouts of fever and the hunger and the menstrual problems. (Most of the women stopped menstruating but experienced monthly tension and pain caused by the extreme, prolonged stress.) There was a doctor who refused to put anything but "starvation" as cause of death on a certificate and was punished with solitary confinement. The women used precious flannelette rags for sanitary napkins and put them to soak in pails. One woman, not a nurse, took them out of the pails, and washed them. Minnie

Stubbs said, "She had cancer, and she knew she wasn't going to live, and she wanted to do what she could. I'm sure she's got a star in her crown in heaven," Minnie added, "because that's a dirty job."

The food ran out at the end of 1944, and more and more patients came in to die of starvation. The nurses would joke about whether the Marines, the cavalry, or the vultures would get to them first, "and we were betting it would be the vultures." The nurses, who had held up the best of all, began to get edema, a symptom of protein deficiency, which causes the body to retain fluid until the patient drowns. This was what killed many of the men.

They knew liberation was on the way because, with the sensitivity caused by deprivation, they had smelled gasoline from the tanks in the distance, long before they could hear them. Hattie Brantley was on duty in the hospital, but Minnie Stubbs was in the compound. She said, "The Japs were busy packing, loading trucks, and they were going to leave us and burn us alive. They locked us in the building with tanks of gasoline with wicks on outside in the stairway, where the Americans found them later. They hadn't had time to light them." She said calmly, "We saw these big searchlights coming in the front gate, and then this huge tank. It just knocked down the gate, and came in with these big tall people marching in front of it, and we said that they must be the tall Texans."

In the hospital, a colleague of Hattie's produced a six-ounce bottle of Coke that she had saved through the war. Sometimes she would bring it out so that people could look at it. This time, she opened it and shared it with Hattie. In the compound, a soldier shouted, "Are there any Americans in here?" and the prisoners locked in the building screamed, "Yes, over here." After some fighting, as Minnie Stubbs told me, "They raised our flag, took down that fried egg, and we all sang 'God Bless America.' Those big soldiers were just *crying;* they couldn't believe how thin everybody was." And then? "They brought their casualties in and we just went to work, worked all night." I asked how they managed, and she said, "Well, one of the doctors fainted, and Colonel Hall said, 'How long is it since you had anything to eat?' We said, 'Not since breakfast,' and he told the sergeant to bring in cases of condensed milk, and he made each one of us drink a can." She added, "We'd all have starved to death in a month or two."

None of the women did starve to death; furthermore, they recovered and their periods returned. Most are still alive today, even though they suffer from aftereffects, just as the male POWs do. Some are psychological. To this day the nurses who were captured and imprisoned do not talk to those who got away, and those who got away still feel guilty for leaving their post. Hattie Brantley told me that while the ex-POWs may find it difficult to talk about their experience to people who did not share it, when they do decide to talk, people may prefer not to listen. "Not long ago," she said, leaning forward and speaking in a low, tense voice, "I was out with my sister and one of her friends, and this lady asked me about what we had to eat. I said we ate cats, dogs, rats, and grasshoppers and that kind of thing, and my sister whispered [here she lowered her voice into a fierce stage whisper], 'Don't talk to her about any of that, it'll turn her stomach.'"

The experiences of POWs evoke feelings of guilt and awkwardness from the rest of us. When the POWs are women—and these are the only American women in recent history to have endured such circumstances for so long—the feelings are even more troubling. Certainly there was ambivalence in the attitude of the authorities. When General MacArthur made good his famous promise to return, he urged the liberating forces to get to Manila as fast as possible, so that the nurses could be freed. He visited Santo Tomas after it was liberated and was, apparently, shaken by the sight of thousands of sobbing, emaciated people in rags coming to crowd around him. The women might have expected a heroes' welcome; there was none. Neither Hattie nor Minnie seemed particularly bothered about that.

The women received an increase of one rank, to first lieutenant, and the Bronze Star. At the start of the war the Nurse Corps had no official rank structure—it arrived only with the Women's Army Corps in 1942—so the women were grateful for the promotion. "I wasn't inclined to mind," Minnie Stubbs told me, "until I bumped into one of the women who escaped from Corregidor and found that she was a major." Hattie Brantley shrugged and said, "They weren't interested in us. They just wanted to get us back to duty if we wanted to go, or else out of the service."

13

The Action of the Tiger: Combat

"Those Wacs in Vietnam were really at a disadvantage. It was not fair for them not to know how to defend themselves. If you were in an area that guerrillas had infiltrated, which would *you* prefer to throw at them—a typewriter or a hand grenade?" Sergeant Reilly, the first sergeant of Alpha Company, was well aware of the paradoxes surrounding the women in Vietnam. Some of them were fighters.

In 1962 a small unit of fifty South Vietnamese women from the Min Top region, under the command of a woman physical education teacher, the daughter of a French Army officer, engaged with the Viet Cong. Through a combination of decoy and ambush, the women killed twenty-two Viet Cong, says the relevant Army document, "picking them off as they ran and clubbing to death those who fell wounded." The famous "Tiger Lady of the Delta" was the adjutant of the 44th Rangers, led by her husband. She was formidable and ruthless; she was decorated three times for bravery and killed in action in 1965.

On the other side, women had been working for the Women's Liberation Association since 1961 in more traditional roles, but in 1965, when the United States began sending troops, the NLF moved women into guerrilla positions at all levels. A Viet Cong woman, Huynh Thi Tan, commanded a company of one hundred men. Her husband also commanded a company, and when he was killed, she defected to the South Vietnamese side. She said during an interrogation, "Discipline? There was never any trouble when I commanded the company. The men knew who was in charge." The Vietnamese women against whom American soldiers fought were smaller than American women.

Only six or seven hundred Wacs in all served in Vietnam over the course of the war, among them Lieutenant Evans, who told me about their compound at Long Binh. "We were overprotected. We had an eight-foot fence around the compound, topped with barbed wire, and we had a male Marine guard. We had to be in at ten. It was like Stateside; we had beds and air conditioning and real food." I asked if she had minded any of this, thinking back to World War II and how bitterly the Wacs in the Southwest Pacific had minded being kept virtual prisoners. She said stoically, "No, those were the rules. We had to live by them. But," she added, "if we had been overrun, we would have been completely helpless, because we had no weapons, and anyway we didn't know how to use weapons. I think we may have had a pistol locked up in a safe somewhere, but those male guards were the ones with the weapons."

Lieutenant Evans worked in an office with ten men in the Engineering Corps, five of them officers and five enlisted. "I was an E-5," she said, "the highest ranking female and the highest ranking NCO, but because I was a woman I could not be the NCOIC [NCO in charge]. Also, every morning I had to be there first, to make the coffee. They all agreed about that; I was a woman, so I made the coffee." Lieutenant Evans was drawing fire pay, just like the men.

General Parks, a former head of the Nurse Corps, told me with relish a little story that neatly illustrated the paradoxes surrounding American women in Vietnam, seven thousand of whom were military nurses. At the time of the war she was in charge of fifty-six nurses in the Qui Nhon hospital, about forty of whom were women. "One day," she said, "the commander of the support command at Qui Nhon needed a new protocol officer, so when he called Saigon he told them he wanted a Wac. They told him they couldn't send a female up there, that was too dangerous. So he said, 'What the *hell* are two hundred and fifty American women doing here in Qui Nhon???' They said, 'WHAT?' We had Red Cross, nurses, Dacs [Department of the Army civilians]."

The hospital was one of two in the country that had a POW ward. It was not particularly secure, and there was a big supply depot next door. There were infiltrators and small-arms fire in the compound on several occasions. Because of the ever-present danger, some of the nurses were given .45s to carry with them. At this particular hospital only male nurses were assigned weapons, but at other hospitals females carried them, and slept with them under their pillows.

The nurses there, and throughout Vietnam, worked night and day with shelling all around them. Some were killed. General Parks told me that on one day during the battle of Dak To, between two in the afternoon and ten at night, they evacuated 106 patients and received 85 casualties. She said, "We had a lot of bad patients, and some of those youngsters were just out of nursing programs and were performing so far above their heads they didn't know it." Nobody collapsed or became pregnant. General Parks told me that occasionally in situations in which there was a great deal of danger, commanders in the rear had been reluctant to send the women forward. She said, "We tried all-male units in Vietnam too. We sent a MASH unit with all-male nurses down to a very dangerous area. Here came all the combat units to help them set up, and then, when they saw the nurses were all males, they just turned around and walked off. And they couldn't get the help and supplies they needed. The commanders just don't like it," she said; "they say it does a lot for men to see the women in the hospital."

The current official status of military women in relation to combat is as follows: the Navy and the Air Force are subject to laws that preclude women from serving in a combat zone—laws that formerly were interpreted so strictly that they kept women from the sea and out of the sky, both of them potential combat zones. Until 1979 the Navy and the Air Force had followed these to the letter. Then the Defense Department petitioned Congress for a change in the laws, which were the cause of assorted problems and resentments. The women were complaining that their careers and promotions were restricted; the men complained that theirs were too—for example, Navy men had to stay at sea longer because the women were filling all the less exacting desk jobs on land. Current policy permits women to serve in peacetime on many ships and planes.

Meanwhile a suit had been brought against the Navy in a federal district court, where Judge John Sirica ruled that the law forbidding women to serve on most ships was discriminatory. His judgment was persuasively worded: "None of the limitations and disadvantages facing Navy women is traceable to any studied evaluation made of male and female capabilities that reveals that women lack the native ability to perform competently in positions held exclusively by men." He said that the legislation suggested "a statutory purpose more related to the traditional way of thinking about women than to the demands of military preparedness," representing "a generalization about women that even the highest defense authorities concede is unsound."

There is no law restricting the deployment of Army women, but there is a policy that excludes women from units whose mission is "to directly engage the enemy" in combat. Close combat seems to be defined as narrowly as possible: combat in which weapons are aimed by line of sight. As a result, women are not assigned to infantry, armor, cannon field artillery, combat engineers, or low altitude air defense artillery. They can work in all billets except those concentrated in or feeding into such units, which currently are estimated at 52 percent of the force. Therefore, even though women can work in over 95 percent of Army specialties, they are excluded from 52 percent of Army jobs.

General Becton, Commanding General of the Seventh Army in Europe, said in a recent interview: "We have a large number of women in my corps rear, and in the division rears, and yet I expect combat to take place there. . . . We also have women in covering forces, as close to the enemy as you find them. They're not there as combatants, but as intelligence experts, in signal units, as drivers and military police and medical personnel. We also have women in missile artillery and air defense units. I'm going to have women throughout the entire battle area, and I expect that, and I have no reason to doubt they will perform like any other soldier." As a recent Army memorandum somberly stated: "Women will share the same risk and hardship as their male counterparts in periods of armed combat. They may be required to engage or be engaged by an enemy with individual and crew-served weapons, experience physical contact with enemy personnel, and experience a high risk of capture." General Kingston, Commander of the Second Infantry Division in Korea, said of his troops, "There's no such thing, if there's a war on the peninsula, as separating combat from non-combat. And we're going to get girls, women soldiers, killed, burned, disfigured, amputees, put them home in body bags. That will happen."

The Army's definition of combat and the definition that forms in the minds of soldiers are the same: ground warfare under strenuous circumstances that approximate those of World War II. The military effectiveness of women in such a battle or in any other kind of battle or war depends on far more than questions of capability. As a male West Point officer said, "Give a tiny woman a rifle and she's as powerful as a quarterback." In a conventional war, when the women present are properly trained and selected for whatever job they are assigned to perform, and present in large enough numbers to give them a chance of being accepted, the attitudinal component will determine their military effectiveness—the way the males and the females regard each other and each other's capabilities. Opponents of women in combat hate even to visualize such a scene, and talk darkly of violating taboos.

There is said to be a taboo against women in combat. The word "taboo" is misleading when used under these circumstances because it suggests that women are never, and have never been, involved in any way in war. There is, however, no taboo against their fighting *when it is felt to be necessary*, usually in cases of the direst need, when everyone must fight. There is, similarly, no taboo against killing women. When women die in traffic accidents, or are murdered, the reporting is the same as it would be for a man. When the first woman police officer died in the line of duty, the event received a great deal of news coverage, but no cries of outrage were heard.

The idea that war and fighting are a function of male biology is deeply rooted in all of us. Because wars and the threat of wars are never absent, people have come to believe that war is natural. Because the United States is such a violent country, we have come to believe that physical aggression, expressed, is just as inevitable. Because it is overwhelmingly the men who have until now initiated and fought in wars, and fought in the playgrounds and streets, we see it as the male imperative. Whatever the context of all this, the sociology as opposed to the biology, the result is a mystique, the myth that fills boys' minds with dreams of soldiering and sends them off to fight. The poetry and novels of war, and the films of our day, are full of it, and they reinforce the mystique in grown men just as heroic tales of the French Foreign Legion or the Crusades suffuse the thinking of boys.

In *The Red Badge of Courage* Stephen Crane wrote about the camaraderie, the rage, the fear, and the bloodlust of the heat of battle. When Henry and his fellow soldiers gained a small victory, "they gazed about them with looks of uplifted pride, feeling new trust in the grim, always confident weapons in their hands. And they *were* men."

The cliché is true. Military service has always been a rite

of passage that turns boys into men. Combat is a deadly, formalized game between men. Bravery and loyalty or ruthlessness and barbarism—all of these traits expressed through war—surviving or dying, are proof of manhood. The mystique is about the most hideous and cruel habits of men on the battlefield, as specific as the foxhole, and the descent into an animal existence. James Webb, an ex-Marine and author of *Fields of Fire*, a novel about Vietnam, has one of his characters say, "There's no tents, no barbed wire, no hot food, no jeeps or trucks, no clean clothes. Nothing. You're an animal. It gets so that it's natural to squat when you take a shit. You get ringworm and hookworm and gooksores. You roll around in your own filth. You forget how bad you smell. Dead people, guts in the goddamn dirt, miserable civilians, it all gets sort of boring."

The intense absorption of soldiers in every detail of their battle is another part of the mystique, midway between passive despair and dark exhilaration. Crane describes untried soldiers on the march: "They were going to look at war, the red animal—war, the blood-swollen god. And they were deeply engrossed." Glenn Gray in his book *The Warriors* describes the thrill of danger so immediate that it gives "communal freedom," in which men are "liberated from our individual impotence and are drunk with the power that union with our fellows brings." This in turn induces a kind of assurance of immortality, an ecstasy of abandonment so extreme that it could lead a man willingly to sacrifice his life. Such feelings and actions not only make boys into men, they make timorous clerks into warriors. There is the impulse to destroy, the discovery and release of secret feelings that in civilian life a man might only have sensed while he watched a building being razed or heard on the car radio about a mugger being caught and beaten by his victim. For all the scrappy misfits there is the final legitimization of the itch to fight. War can liberate as it debases, as it instructs and ennobles and appalls, all at the same time, and the men who have experienced that have a bond that changes them in some way forever and separates them from the rest of us. We know about it, however, and many of us are in awe not simply of the heroism but of the thrill.

The heroic exploits of the past illuminate the humdrum realities of peacetime Army life. Here, from James Jones's *From Here to Eternity,* is the classic description of Prewitt the bugler playing taps on a warm night at a post in Hawaii. "Men had come from the Dayrooms to the porches to listen in the darkness, feeling the sudden choking kinship bred of fear that supersedes all personal taste. They stood in the darkness of the porches, listening, feeling, suddenly very near the man beside them, who also was a soldier, who also must die."

Rugged masculinity in wartime can elicit supreme feats of selfless bravery from undistinguished persons; in peacetime it is an attitude that ennobles. The young soldier who has no comfortable home life and no wife or girlfriend has at least his innocent profanities and his macho pride and his buddies, in the same way that a street kid has his gang. Much of the mystique is a romanticization of the deprivations of military life. There are two problems with this process. The romanticizing may be misunderstood, as when, for example, people insist that male camaraderie is biological and not the result of circumstances. The other problem is, of course, in relation to women. There are 65,000 women in the Army, the majority of whom expect to be able to work as colleagues with the men whose heads are full of images of women that have nothing to do with professionalism.

Enduring stereotypes of women have sustained soldiers through the centuries. So many of those who are young and alone—particularly in wartime, when the large numbers of young men are drafted—have little experience of adult relationships with women, whether sexual or simply friendly. As teenagers do, they divide women into the whores and the radiant, delicate women to be cherished and protected. Their contacts with women confined mostly to infrequent visits to the brothel in town, they stare at the pinups in *Soldier* magazine and *Playboy* and dream.

In wartime the stereotypes grow more exaggerated. On the

one hand, the fleeting animallike sexual encounters and the acts of rape and atrocity committed against civilians are aspects of the fighting man's unleashed control. On the other, there are the piercingly intense and often doomed love affairs that arise, the worship of nurses, and the acts of gentleness toward women and children. To be in a uniform lessens a man's inhibitions and increases his feelings of potency. The sexual symbolism of guns is made known to the lowliest trainee when, in training, he first learns the rhyme: "This is my weapon/ Here is my gun/ One is for fighting/ The other's for fun."

One evening Sue Jarrell and her German Air Force husband, Egon, were sitting side by side in their small apartment in Kitzingen while we talked about combat. Egon said, "When I think about war, I get afraid that Susie's gonna go, and when she gets caught they will rape her." Jarrell's face was wan. She said to me, "Maybe they want to keep us out to *protect* us." Egon added inexorably, "I couldn't stand it if I had to fight with half or one-third of my company female. I couldn't stand it if I am in a foxhole with one and she gets shot or dies. I would get crazy." His English was wavering, but not his powers of expression. Jarrell fell silent and rubbed abstractedly at her cropped hair. Egon said, "A man's death, even if he's your friend—you can get over it. But with a woman"—he paused—"it's so difficult to put into words, but you get involved, and if she dies and you don't really know her, you still think maybe if she were married, you think of your own wife, and in this case she is also a soldier, and I think about her, and then I feel bad." Jarrell stared at him for a moment and said, "I've heard that a lot. Men idealize women more than I thought they did. They think women are really something." Egon said, his voice thick, "The best thing in the world." Jarrell said quizzically, "Are you drunk, schatzie? Imagine, best thing in the world— just for their bodies or for them?" "For them," said Egon, looking into his glass. Silence fell; there was no answer.

Egon said thoughtfully, "I'm not sure that I would control the animal impulse if I was up against female guerrillas. If you know you can destroy her personality that way . . . or you might just do it for fun, to see what you can get out of it." He said he thought violence against Army women would increase, particularly rape, as the women soldiers continued their advance. I was struck by the passionate, unmanageable combination of adoration and threat in his voice.

The Army has carried out no authoritative studies on the use of women as combat soldiers. Attempting to imagine what could happen is as easy as taking up a war novel and trying to imagine half the characters female. Some say that other countries would think any nation that voluntarily puts its women in the front line so morally degenerate and weakened that they would hasten to the attack, assured of their victory. However, the use of women is generally regarded as the bottom line, a sign that the country is totally committed to the war. Other countries might, instead, hesitate before embarking on a war that would be so far from a ritual, or limited, gesture and would from the start be designated as a determined struggle for survival, a struggle that would be taken to the bitter end. There is some speculation that women soldiers, having put themselves beyond the pale, would be treated with terrible cruelty if captured, even though there is no hard evidence to support the notion.

Other concerns center on our own side, and the conduct of our women in battle, especially as leaders. General Goodpaster said to me at West Point, with obvious sincerity, "Some of our women in the Signal Corps will be leading men over difficult terrain, and under terrible conditions of bombing and weather, and I'm sure they will be able to command any unit of any size. Some won't have, just as some men don't, the command force, the strength and assurance that are required." It could be said that women, because of the way they grow up, would make *better* leaders than men in times of crisis, more realistic and down-to-earth, more concerned with the vital details.

If the idea of mass mobilization is losing ground to the idea of a highly professional, skilled, and smaller core of troops, if the old infantry engagement is to be replaced with longer-range technological warfare, if the style of leadership has to change to accommodate the changes in society at large, then the women have much to contribute.

Interested participants in this debate like to generate steam over sex and its potential as a primal force that absolutely could not be controlled, a tidal wave that would sweep away years of training, swamp the deadly fear, override injuries, lack of food, and all the other factors constituting the combat environment, and leave male and female troops locked on the ground in an embrace while the war boomed on around them. The sexual urge is often spoken of as "the real issue." The only peacetime circumstance that resembles the enforced proximity of battle conditions is life on board a Navy ship. However, there are so few women on ships, and they are so recently arrived, that generalizations are dangerous. It is reported that in some instances there has been a great deal of female sexual activity, both homosexual and heterosexual, but it seems to be directly connected to problems in command. For example, when a lesbian scandal broke aboard the U.S.S. *Norton Sound* in 1980, it was accompanied by stories of sexual harassment, loan-sharking, drug dealing, suicide, and attempted murder.

Here, however, the overriding reality is the lack of war. Men and women confined in the same place may behave quite differently when that place is "the combat environment." Some say the women would be dragged into the (male) debasement around them, others say they would diminish it. A recent book—*Women, Sex, and Pornography*, by Beatrice Faust—suggested that rape in war has a distinct biological function, as well as the sociological one described by Glenn Gray. Supposedly it allays fear before battle; it increases testosterone in the rapist and decreases it in the vanquished. This theory may be disproved next year.

Opponents of women in the Army have often stated that the women's presence would bring out the male chivalric impulse, and cause the men to fight over them. Would the women then be raped or overprotected or fought over or seduced? Certainly you could say that in the long, enforced lulls that wreck the nerves of soldiers at or near the front it is quite likely that the thoughts of both male and female soldiers might turn to sex. You could also say that they would not act on such thoughts, or that, working together in a perilous and terrifying situation, they would perhaps think about sex with other people, at home or in their fantasies. They might see each other as comrades, partners in a male/ female bond that would be better than the old bonds, because each of the pair might have special skills or characteristics the other one lacked, and so the possibilities for mutual help and encouragement could be greater. The special feelings men and women have for each other as men and women, far from leading them into perilous sex, might complement and greatly strengthen their comradeship, help them overcome the surrounding horrors. There is no reason why the women's presence should not have a beneficial effect on the men, making them calmer, less rapacious. Whatever that does for the men's testosterone levels, it could make them better soldiers. A homesick male trainee sitting under the pines at Fort McClellan had said, "I like having the women around. It gives you someone to *talk* to."

Margaret Mead suggests that because women have grown up with little sense of the ritual nature of war, they would fight ruthlessly and without scruple, as they always have, fighting like the underdog, paying scant attention to the chivalric rules. They might be less likely to commit meaningless atrocity, because, with a less mystical approach to war, they would not be needing the kind of emotional discharge that men in battle seem to require. Similarly, if they reached positions of real power, and were involved in policy making, they might steer the country away from damaging wars fought for abstract reasons, such as the struggle in Vietnam.

Since most career Army women are traditional and serious, they might be easier to lead, less likely to run. Hence the men too might be encouraged to stand fast. The women's presence might prevent the foolish heroics that turn out to be self-destructive as often as they lead to an undreamed-of triumph; there might be *more* foolish heroics, with or without the triumphs, as the men, even if only subconsciously, tried to impress the women, vying for their favor. As the theories multiply so do the confusions, because we have absolutely no idea what will happen. Furthermore, there is an artificial, luxurious atmosphere surrounding the repetitions of this debate—the result of America's privileged status as a country on whose soil no war has been fought for more than one hundred years.

Mary Wollstonecraft wrote, "Men, in general, seem to employ their reason to justify prejudices, which they have imbibed, they cannot trace how, rather than root them out." Critics of women in the Army trundle out the example of Israel when hypotheses fail, as hard evidence of women's lack of effectiveness in battle. The facts show otherwise.

The Palmach was an elite force of full-time soldiers, formed in Israel during World War II. During the War of Independence, fought in 1948, the Palmach numbered about 45,000 troops, of whom maybe 20 percent were women. Yigal Allon, the general commanding the Palmach, made the following assessment of his female soldiers. He said that the women "blurred and decreased the harshness of military life," that they "lent substance to the Palmach concept of an armed force free of militarism," that they "precluded the brutalization of young men thrown into an all-male society for months on end," and that they "turned the Palmach into a true people's army." However Allon intended his remarks to be construed, they amount to powerful praise.

Israeli women soldiers are an image so familiar that they have become part of a pulpy mythology, an echo of the liberated sixties, with their miniskirts and rifles, ready to die for their homeland or in the embrace of men strong enough to win them. Nevertheless, those who like to argue the case against using American women in the dangerous, nontraditional Army jobs, however capable they may concede women to have been in wars of the past, will point to them and say, "Look, the Israelis tried it, and it didn't work."

The War of Independence was the only war in Israeli history in which large numbers of women were involved in fighting, but the women of Israel have defended their homeland from the time of its creation, in the tradition of their Biblical ancestors, and many died when their settlements were overrun. Through the 1920s and 1930s the expanding Jewish state required a large network of secret militia groups, particularly in the areas of isolated kibbutzim. Women were present in the Haganah, the Irgun, and the Stern Gang, and they were used extensively as the need for numbers grew more urgent. They were trained in the use of small arms, and some became commanders.

The heroic stories of women in combat come from the Palmach women in the War of Independence. Twelve thousand women altogether were in the war, in combat support and at the machine guns. They often worked, as a matter of course, in circumstances of mortal danger, but as soon as the war was over, the women were removed from combat-related jobs. Allon wrote of the impending changes: "the girls stormed at any proposed discrimination, arguing that it ran counter to the spirit of the new society being built in Palestine to restrict women to domestic chores, particularly since they had proven their competence as marksmen and sappers." Although they were still trained for combat, the women were restricted to a separate noncombat corps, known as CHEN, which was established in 1949, theoretically because war statistics had shown higher casualty rates in the mixed units than in the all-male units. The assumption was that Arab soldiers fought to the death rather than be disgraced by surrendering to or being killed by a woman. On the other hand, it is commonly said that the morale of Israeli soldiers plummeted whenever a woman fighting alongside them was killed or wounded.

In the Talmud women are referred to as "temperamentally light-headed." The early Zionists had seen themselves as spiritual as well as geographical pioneers; their state had been founded on utopian ideals of equality for men and women. By the time thousands of refugees from Europe and the Arab countries began pouring into the country—people who did not share those radical views—the War of Independence was under way, a war so consuming that everyone was involved, not just the men and young women but the children and the grandparents and the infirm. The new nation was fighting for its existence, so there were no questions as to who should be involved. But as soon as the war was over, the old attitudes returned, with a vigor that came partly from the tiny nation's need for children.

With fresh wars, the need for qualified personnel has brought the women a little nearer to the mainstream of army life. After the Six-Day War and the October War women moved back into intelligence and communications work, they were used in parachute maintenance, and armor, as mechanics and drivers. This policy is based simply on need. The Israelis have over the last three decades enshrined an attitude to women that has not only held them back in the military but has also resulted in the reinstatement of traditional roles in the kibbutz. Today's drafted Israeli women— currently only about half of those eligible are taken—handle weapons for familiarization, cleaning, assembly, loading, and even firing, but they are given no target practice, no tactical or assault training.

Three types of jobs are closed to them: those involving physical strain, those that "because of environmental or service conditions are not considered suitable," and the jobs involving possible combat. In the category of prohibitive physical strain is included truck driving. (British women in World War II of course drove heavy trucks routinely between Cairo and Jerusalem, Russian women drove trucks in the war, and today, all over the U.S., in civilian and military life, women drive trucks.) The environmental category refers to separate showers.

As for combat, noncombatant women are now trained as combat instructors, which neatly shows that it is not their capabilities that are in doubt. However, if a war were to break out in Israel today, Army policy would dictate that all women at or near the front line be moved to the rear. Male soldiers say that women in the field would create too many problems. Nevertheless they are in the field, all the time, and it is reported from the remotest outposts of the Sinai and the Golan Heights that wherever there are women, morale is extraordinarily high.

Today there is not a single female general in the Israeli army, despite the numbers who serve and have served. As a psychiatrist observed to Lesley Hazelton, author of *Israeli Women*, "Women come out of the army more inclined to the feminine stereotype than when they go in." They are happy to be protected, because they derive no benefit at all from whatever degree of independence they can achieve in the military. They in fact lose their status. Gainsaying their past, which was a remarkable and valiant chapter in the history of Israel and of brave women, today's female soldiers in Israel, caught in the paternalistic embrace of a society that through its protection of them celebrates its own masculinity, readily accept their secondary role, their vulnerability, in a country where attack and invasion are a real, present, urgent threat.

Captain Kathy Whitcraft was the West Point tactical officer whose life was ruined by running, and she said to me, "If serving your country is a responsibility of citizenship, it should fall just as heavily on the shoulders of women. You can make commonsense exceptions. But I get very upset when people on Capitol Hill make rules on what I will do. NOW, for instance, is lobbying for women in combat. I'm a member of NOW, I have no quarrel with NOW, but I wish to hell they'd quit lobbying to get me into combat. Don't lobby to send *me:* if you want to go, lobby for yourself."

Army women feel that combat represents the biggest gulf in understanding between civilians and military people. The proponents of the combat mystique have been so successful in its defense that outsiders often mistakenly think that the entire Army must be ready for hand-to-hand combat day and night. Senators with horrid mien fling around the term "combat readiness," demanding to know why the entire military is not in this state, and wondering whether it does not have something to do with the deficiencies in female upper-body strength. In fact, since very few soldiers expect to experience hand-to-hand combat on the battlefield, the others do not fixate on fighting in the course of their normal working day. Most of the women I met agreed with Captain Whitcraft that they should share with men the responsibility of defending the country. As Lieutenant Myers put it, "I must say I don't see anything wrong with a couple of years' service, even *compulsory* service. I wonder if I've been too long in the military? I wonder if I would have said that ten years ago?"

As for war, the women feel exactly as one would expect them to: phlegmatic. The question of who should be in combat is irrelevant, for they know that many of them will be. Their view is, in a nutshell, that women should do almost anything they are capable of doing, knowing that their contract requires them, in exchange for their opportunities and their careers, to be prepared to give up their lives. What would one expect them to say? Jarrell, in her drafty hangar in Germany, said with a shrug, "We'll be in combat. No doubt. We'll have time to move out but not to get set up." Fisher, cobbling away at parachutes in North Carolina, said, "Sure, I think about war. I'd be in the back lines sewing parachutes, but some of my friends would get killed." They are resigned, hoping—like most people in the world—that they will not be called upon. Occasionally the press will turn up a young woman like the Marine lieutenant who said, oddly, to an interviewer, "Logistically it would be impossible to support women in war. The days when I've had bad cramps and had to go out on foot patrol, it's been tough." This was not a typical view.

Within the general acceptance there are variations. One woman said, "They shouldn't ask us to give up our lives without passing the ERA first." Another said, "If combat is truly open, it will not be on a voluntary basis, and then the *unqualified* women will be in there, as well as the qualified,

and until the Army trains them more equally, every unqualified woman will be a rubber stamp of I-told-you-they-
couldn't-do-it. Women should be drafted *only* for combat
support jobs, and volunteer for the front line." Several
people pointed out that however capable women might be, it
would be wrong to put only a few of them at the front or in a
position of extreme danger. General Parks said, "It's not that
she couldn't do the job. Women can take the field. But one
young female troop out there with a bunch of males couldn't
function because of the men. In the lulls, anything might
happen. There might be harassment, there might be sex."

Elizabeth Brady shyly admitted her traditional views,
which are shared by many of the women, even though they
are prepared to do anything that might be asked of them.
Several years before she joined the Army, Elizabeth had
been married briefly to an Army man and had been in
Germany with him. When I found her a few months out of
basic, she had gone through initial medical training at Fort
Sam Houston and was back in her hometown of Dalton,
Georgia, where she was studying for her practical nursing
diploma and had begun to see her ex-husband again. He had
left the Army, but Elizabeth said of him, "I think he's better
battlefield material. I'd be better at picking 'em up and
taking 'em in. I picture myself as a field medic and him in
the lines firing. But if I had to fight, I could." She continued,
"Women shouldn't have to. We have a different sense of life
and death from men. The men are taught to be aggressive
and demanding. But I'd like to save someone's life." A
lieutenant at Fort McClellan had said, "I didn't join the
Army so I could kill people. I joined to prevent that from
happening." It is very rare to find a woman who desperately
wants to go into the infantry, like the gallant, tearful young
cadet I had watched in collision with General Hoisington.

Capability was not the issue for the women. After the
invariable preamble about the physical strength needed for
some jobs, strength that some men as well as some women
lacked, they would come out with the neat, logical arguments that are part of the current thinking about current

warfare. They talked about the need for intelligence over brawn, about technology and the shifting front line, fluid to the point where it hardly existed, about police actions instead of prolonged warfare. A West Point officer confessed that she felt she would be at a distinct disadvantage if war were to break out tomorrow and she were to be evaluated. She would lose out because she lacked the platoon experience, she said. Otherwise the words were spirited, particularly in regard to leadership over men.

Sergeant Bell wrote from Korea, "Yes, I believe men will follow female leaders in a stressful situation, although the females would have to prove themselves more." She added, "Of course there are some men that will not follow *men*." Lieutenant Myers said, without a trace of a smile, "So what if men know how to swear and holler? Women have icy eyes." And Elizabeth Brady, sitting in a restaurant in Dalton, Georgia, said, "Women may have to prove themselves at first. But whoever's leading *me* doesn't have to be faster or stronger." Pausing to flick the ash off a cigarette, she said, "It doesn't take brains to be strong, but it takes a brain to figure out a problem once you get in it, and if I had a leader, I wouldn't care if he couldn't run but half a foot—get him in a jeep—as long as he can get me out of a place that I didn't want to be in. I mean I'm talking about *warfare*."

Elizabeth was full of good sense. She said, "Men have a tendency to think women break down in crisis, but psychological studies show that in certain emergencies the men will break down sooner than the women." She might have been talking about the prisoners in Santo Tomas, or the women at the antiaircraft batteries in England or at the switchboards in the Southwest Pacific. Whereas older women tended to be worried about sanitary matters and modesty, the younger generation were not at all concerned. As for sex in the trenches, the mention of it seemed to upset them all. They would blush, or look discomfited, and say words to the effect of "I think most of us would be concentrating on survival. Our lives would depend on it." Nobody denied the possibility of sex taking place. After all, there are stories of men turning to each other under such circumstances. But the women's answers seemed to be full of doubt and difficult emotions, not the least of which was a heightened sense of vulnerability.

Combat represents an Achilles heel for the women struggling to be accepted in the Army. They just want to be allowed to do their work and enjoy it. However, being accepted at work on all levels means having to face danger in combat. Since the women will not face equal danger in equal numbers, they feel guilty. They know that the men who will find themselves marching off to the front while the women replace them in the rear do not appreciate their contributions. They know that the men will hate them for interfering in business best left to men, and for forcing them into more danger through their interference, while they, the women, are left with a choice.

Secretly, and sometimes aloud, the women worry about finding themselves in combat with men who would not be adequate to back *them* up. Still, they cannot be sure, because war, and the Army, remain provinces securely under male control; it is men who have fought and won and lost the wars, and men who will organize the next war. Wherever women find themselves in that war, whether at a typewriter in Washington or laying telephone wire through a pitted landscape, they will be surrounded by and dominated by men, and will be in their power. War is a strange land to them in a way that it cannot be for a man, however peace-loving he may be.

The women are vulnerable because they do not know what the connection is between the mystique and success in battle. They are afraid that they will fail, however competent they are. Those who have read any military history may find themselves wondering if women would have come out of the trenches to play soccer with the enemy, as the Germans and the Allies did on Christmas Day 1914. There is very little the women can do to dispel their feelings or to lessen the tension between them and the men. If the rough and violent mystique is not simply unpleasant to them but is forever closed to them, what place have they in the Army? Maybe the men were right after all. To criticize men about the way they run their Army would be self-destructive. Nevertheless there are some independent women able to retain their skepticism, especially on the question of the supposed delicacy of women that makes it essential to keep them out of war.

Colonel Allen, the gentle, rigorous woman in charge of the training battalion at Fort McClellan, said, "I'm a professional soldier, and if as part of my professional commitment I go to an area where I could get blown up, so be it, that's part of the risk. I don't want it, I'm not looking for it, I'm not out to storm foxholes with a bayonet in my teeth and slug it out in hand-to-hand combat, but if I had to do that, I hope I'm trained for it, and I hope I have just as much survivability as my male counterparts." She added thoughtfully, "Many of the people who cry wolf about women dying in combat are men."

Frances FitzGerald, author of *Fire in the Lake*, wrote that the officers she watched in Vietnam, in the rear areas or on the fringe of combat, existed in a state of "horrendous boredom tinged with anxiety." "Apart from the knowledge that they were serving their country," she said, "the one compensation the soldiers had was their sense of superior masculinity." It is well known that in conventional wars, too, the farther away soldiers, particularly officers, are from the front line, the more jingoistic their utterances become. The jingoism is often fueled by women at home, whether they press white feathers on presumed cowards or send fierce and bloodcurdling letters of encouragement to their loved ones at the front.

By the same token, those men who have a great deal invested in their warrior status, real or imagined, are the ones who most resent women soldiers. Even those who are less self-consciously masculine compensate for their loss of individuality in the Army by taking on the group identity; "the more specific that identity, the more compelling." Fitz-

Gerald was writing at the time of President Carter's proposal to register women. She said, "To draft women is to diffuse this collective identity—to change the very idea of what a soldier is." Because women are not as yet eligible for the draft, they are hamstrung in their sensible arguments about their own suitability for combat.

The women readily concede the genuine concern that their colleagues feel for the safety of women, the real chivalry they possess. But, overall, they wonder if the concern is similar to that often expressed about the large number of blacks in the Army. Some black soldiers feel that worry about their disproportionate numbers is motivated less by genuine concern for fairness than by fear on the part of whites, fear that when things turn nasty the blacks will leave them in the lurch or turn on them. The women worry, just as the blacks do, that much of the expressed concern is a mask. Like civilian women, the soldiers are well acquainted with the prevailing realities of male violence against women, in the form of wife-beating, rape, incest, and assault. According to FBI estimates, two million of this country's women are likely to be beaten up by men this year. Some of the women suspect the men of building up the combat mystique, as they did at West Point, not only to prop themselves up but also as a weapon against the encroachment of women. The mystique is added to the arsenal of harassment and sexual abuse and slander and the threat of rape, tactics designed to keep women out of the power centers that are the symbolic peacetime equivalent of combat—the most prestigious or "masculine" parts of the service, not just the Rangers and Special Forces but also the top jobs at the Pentagon or the Army War College and the command jobs that place women in charge of men.

General Parks, from the Nurse Corps, said impatiently, "So *what* if women get killed? SO WHAT? We had nurses hurt and killed in World War Two." She thought for a moment and then said, "My dear, if we have another war, it's going to be of such magnitude that there ain't going to be any question about anybody's role." Lieutenant Myers said,

"At Fort McClellan, just before I arrived, nobody was allowed to take a picture of a woman holding an M-16. It was supposed to be too shocking and alarming a sight. When they finally did permit the women to be photographed, it was when the women had begun actually *using* the weapons, and there was no public outcry of any kind."

In war there is nothing new about violence against women. Tacitus wrote in his *War with the Germans,* "Germanicus divided his enthusiastic troops into four columns. These ravaged and burned the country for fifty miles around. No pity was shown to age or sex." In World War II the men responsible for millions of deaths, whether they ran the concentration camps, dropped two atomic bombs on Japan, or fought in the siege of Leningrad, did not stop to distinguish between men and women. In a nuclear war, whether "limited" or total, civilians will be the first victims.

The debate is not really about women as victims, as a useful historical parallel, drawn from the early years of this century, will show. When London suffragettes began to agitate for the vote, most of the organizers were middle-class women, well educated and taught to behave with gentility and decorum. After genteel, decorous efforts to win the vote for women failed, they resorted in desperation to more violent means—heckling, window breaking, and selected acts of public sabotage. Christabel Pankhurst, daughter of the movement's founder, first spoke up for votes for women at an election rally, and was forced to her seat. As she continued to speak, blows rained on her face. Six men dragged her, bleeding, into the street, and flung her down. She spent a week in prison. That was how it began.

As the movement became larger and more vocal, the level of violence against the women increased. Peaceful demonstrations were broken up by club-wielding police, who punched and hit the women, kicked them as they lay on the ground, and dragged them along by their breasts or hair. Those women who were imprisoned went on hunger strikes and were roughly force-fed. One observer said of this sustained ferocity that it "often turned well-brought-up and conventionally inclined young women into anarchic, fanatical enemies of a society that could permit such brutality." The brutality seems to have been "permitted" because the women, by rushing angrily into the streets of Edwardian England, had gone beyond the pale and broken the chivalric code. They had called down indignity upon themselves by demanding a man's privileges in an unwomanly way.

Sitting in front of the Kitzingen apothecary, with the engine of her car running, Jarrell had said, "I'm going to be real careful with my marriage. But the way it is now, when I come home and I'm so tired that all I want to do is take a shower and lie down on the sofa, Egon gets hurt because I won't talk, and he thinks I'm excluding him." I had heard anger in his voice as well as hurt and concern, and I wondered if he would have been less upset if his pretty young wife had been working in administration and not in a hangar. It was clear that he had no intention of letting her continue in the Army. Cindy, in El Paso, had experienced the same double-edged response: a boyfriend who protectively walked her to work also denigrated women to the members of a promotion board.

I asked Elizabeth Brady what she thought about women's chances of being accepted in the Army, and she said soberly, "The Army is an ego trip for men. They think they're rough and tough and better than average and better than women. You have to live with it, because if you buck their way of life, ruin their ego trip, they'll turn on you." Elizabeth had a vivid example in her own life. She had remarried her second husband, the one who had been in the Army, and the marriage, after a brief attempt, had failed. She told me, "He couldn't watch me put on combat boots and fatigues and go to work. He knew what the other men would be thinking and saying when they saw me. He'd done it himself."

"Men want to be independent of women," said a Washington lobbyist for the rights of military women. "Having women around makes them feel like children again." Simone de Beauvoir wrote about war:

*   *   *

The warrior put his life in jeopardy to elevate the prestige of the horde, the clan to which he belonged. And in this he proved dramatically that life is not the supreme value for man, but on the contrary that it should be made to serve ends more important than itself. The worst curse that was laid upon woman was that she should be excluded from these warlike forays. For it is not in giving life but in risking life that man is raised above the animal; that is why superiority has been accorded in humanity not to the sex that brings forth but to that which kills.

In the current debate, "combat" is a synonym for "power." As long as women remain restricted to those Army jobs that do not depend primarily upon killing or being prepared to die, they are as marginal in the Army as they are at West Point, despite their numbers, because their status is noncombatant (whatever the reality) in an organization the premise of which is combat.

Male soldiers have always thought of women as small and weak, the people whom wars are fought to protect. Female deaths in combat imply a failure to protect, and therefore a failure of masculinity. The combat debate is so fierce not because of reluctance to expose women to the enemy but because men do not want women *on their own side*. The problem is not women's incapability. It is a problem of men's incapability if women are beside them, even leading them, particularly when the women are armed aggressors. Femininity is something that does not have to be proven; the ability to bear children is enough, or the absence of a penis. Masculinity is a much more precarious notion, and, after the upheavals of recent years, one that has dwindled in importance. In peacetime, masculinity is being different from women; in wartime it means going off to war. Women soldiers deprive men of their masculinity by showing that soldiering is not so terribly hard and by usurping the profession. This is why men at West Point and throughout the Army insist on the need to protect women. This is why they emphasize physical toughness and combat. This is why they would rather protect women than teach them to protect themselves or to protect men.

Many male soldiers welcome the women, or do their best to tolerate them. Those who do not, reflect the realities of civilian life, where women, in their grindingly slow advance into government and business and the academic faculties, have met with as much resistance as female soldiers have. The most illuminating comparison is with those civilian jobs that, like the military, depend on traditional ideas of masculine strength and courage.

Recently at a Long Island jail, two female correction officers charged discrimination because they were not allowed to work with the male inmates. "You get a young, good-looking woman, she'd be subjected to abusive language, and some of these men would drop their pants," said the sheriff. The women said that was an excuse to keep women out of jobs. There was also, apparently, concern that the male inmates would feel embarrassment and resentment at being "scrutinized" by the women, and that the women would be unable to stop fights. In this muddy swirl of an argument it is unclear just who needs protecting from whom.

The Iowa firemen who fought so hard their female colleague's freedom to breast-feed in her off-duty time were reacting viscerally against the presence of a woman who seemed vulnerable in her maternity, but, far more than that, against a woman who detracted from the rigors of the job by her action. She was not taking away a man's job; she was demeaning the other men's jobs.

The Detroit police force provides another example. Women on police forces throughout the country have stirred things up, and their presence has been regarded as disruptive. Policemen's wives are not happy with the idea of their husbands out on night patrol with women—not just because of the potential for sex but also because they do not trust policewomen's ability to defend and protect their husbands as well as men might. In Detroit a policeman's safety was the issue; a berserk man attacked and beat him badly while, so it was said, two female officers stood by without coming to his aid. The truth was different; the women, who had radioed for assistance, had been calming the man when their colleague arrived. The policeman, however, swiftly approached the wild man, who hit him and knocked him to the ground, whereupon the two females rushed to his aid, and the wild man, who offered little resistance, was subdued and handcuffed. The total time from the first call until the end of the incident was two minutes. The policeman was not hurt. The women were charged with cowardice. One of them said in a subsequent interview, "The old philosophy was that when anyone hits a police officer, beat him up. My philosophy is, stop the violence."

In the Kitzingen hangar where Jarrell worked, there had been slow morning conversation, the Southern accents thickened with sleep, while Jarrell fretfully shuffled through the reports that were her responsibility. She was in charge of ordering the reports of each flight and repair and service sheets for each machine, a task that consists primarily of neatening other people's handwriting and filing. She said quietly, "Oh, we do those SQTs once a year." An SQT is a test that measures job proficiency. Jarrell said, "You're supposed to work without the manuals. But that's ridiculous! I was raised with manuals, and I know it's stupid to check a helicopter without referring to a manual." She had made a fuss, but it was ignored. It was this aspect of Army life, the pointless bravado, that turned women against the Army; jump school was the place where it became most evident to Jarrell.

Jarrell had prepared to go airborne throughout basic. I had watched her endlessly practicing push-ups between the beds, trying to develop her skinny little arms and strengthen her back. Near the end of her airborne course she was told she had flunked part of a test, too late for her to retake that part without going back to the beginning of the course. She had already retaken a week because of illness, and was not convinced of the need to do it again. Furthermore, she said, at the time of the test they had told her everything was fine. So Jarrell, after pestering for precise details as to what she had done, and not being able to obtain a satisfactory answer, decided to opt out. She said, "At first I wrote on the form that I had decided that, due to unfair circumstances, I wanted release from the course; they got mad and made me erase it. They made me say 'I do not desire to go airborne.'"

I knew Jarrell to be a perfectionist. She told me that after she quit she had stayed on for a few weeks working in the office, and she watched the process closely. She told me with disgust that women who fell behind on runs were not recycled as they should have been. She said, "All you hear is how you have to make those runs. They concentrate on it so much. And then I saw this one girl get jump wings who had made *no runs* in the important week. Sure she was cute," she said. "She had blond hair and all that deal, *but . . .*"

Jarrell told me they trained in such intense heat (at Fort Benning, Georgia) that all those in training—officers, Marines, women, everyone—were hosed down at regular intervals. "Still people kept passing out," she said. "It was *unnecessary*, creating real emergencies for no reason." Jarrell felt that the men were playing games with the macho image. She could never find out what the absolute standards were; they seemed to change all the time.

Colonel Allen said one day at Fort McClellan as we stood watching the trainees practicing drilling for a parade, "Those people who say women are softening the Army have a stereotypical idea of manhood—that tough virility. But it's just a prop. You see that spirit among the Rangers and the Special Forces, an elite whose training is so tough and demanding. They place great store in the cult of the man, but their criticisms of the 'soft' Army are just alibis. I can't put any credence in them." She said, "Women shouldn't be here if they can't function, and neither should males."

Major Nederlander, working grimly behind her West Point pillar, agreed. She told me, "Those Rangers would have you believe it's all incredibly tough, but I wonder . . . stories get exaggerated. There are few things in combat that most women can't do. It takes concentration, attention to detail, the ability to think fast."

Female cadets at West Point were, at the very least, detached about much of the mystique. The third highest ranking young woman in the Corps, a loyal and diligent cadet who would burst into tears if people complained about the Academy, said, "They showed us motivational films—I came out of *Patton* saying, 'If that's what they want me to be like, forget it.'" The cadet who had shown me her fourteen pages of autobiography said, "That business of stripping you down and rebuilding you—it kills you. *I* don't want someone brainwashing me and computing a little program in my head." Whitcraft neatly summed up their feelings when she said, "You know, being a Tac is not nearly as bad as it's cracked up to be. It's a lot easier than running a company of two hundred men. I think that when a guy tells you how bad a job is, that usually means it's a good one or he wants it for himself."

However scathing Whitcraft had learned to be, she was still imprisoned by the mystique when she wept in her room over PT. So are all the other young women commanders, who have to be always visible on the morning runs, and who have to steel themselves to be a little too remote so that young troops do not rely on them as mother figures. They are not at ease in this man's Army. Jarrell said, despairingly—and she might have spoken for them all—"American men are big-time macho. They were like that in high school," she added, "so caught up in the impression they made. These men in the Army think the only way you can be a soldier is if you can hump a fifty-pound pack, a rifle, and a canteen and rations for forty days. If you can do that, you're ready to go, even if you're dumb as a gourd and you can't do your MOS." She said with finality in her voice, "And as for me, it doesn't matter *how* well I do. I'm still a woman, a female, in the Army, and so I can't be accepted."

Army women are victimized by a mystique that, because it is partly built on excluding them, renders them powerless.

However much the women may despise it, it dominates their working lives and assures their inferiority by setting up a double standard that identifies them as unmilitary if they behave in a "feminine" way, and as "defeminized," or "butch," if they behave like soldiers. They are penalized if they get pregnant and if they are gay. If West Point cadets wore skirts, they were harassed; if their officers were not married, they were whispered about. The result is a lack of status in a status-conscious environment.

In the Army, attitudes are facts. Prejudice is quickly learned by the nice, eager, flexible young men just out of basic. Soldiers are polarized into men and women. The combat mystique is strengthened by the artificial division between "combat" and "noncombat" soldiers, which is demoralizing for all those men and women who are classified as noncombat—in effect, inferior. Men blame women for ruining their Army, women blame men for resisting them, and the mutual resentment plays havoc with everyone's effectiveness.

To ridicule the feelings of the men is futile. The old way of life was crucial to soldiering, and it was not simply soldiers who thought so. Everybody did. Still, to a great extent, women who seriously want to make a career out of the Army are thought to have "swerved from the accustomed flowery path of female delicacy," as Deborah Sampson Gannett put it. People who can accept the idea that women perform most Army jobs successfully might nevertheless agree with the general who said at the hearings on women in combat: "We do teach the women soldiers defensive tactics so that they can defend themselves." He did not add ". . . and others." The idea of armed, uniformed women having the power of life and death over men sits uneasily with all of us. Today's Army men are required to accept this idea of female power and at the same time not to resent the policies that move more and more women into combat support jobs, pushing the men out and closer to combat. This is unfair, the men think. The women have equal opportunity without equal responsibility. The men have lost the prestige of their all-male soldier's world and have gained little in return except a closer proximity to the field of battle.

As women have begun to claim more of their constitutional rights, their advance into citizenship has brought them to the front lines. If the All-Volunteer Force is to survive, the morale of the soldiers has to be rehabilitated and become high enough to attract recruits and retain them as effective soldiers. Changes are required, and the policy makers have to decide what will be best for the women, their male colleagues, and for the country. There is no evidence to provide answers to the most problematic questions raised by the presence of the women soldiers—which means that the big decisions will have to be made from a moral point of view, as principles. More than the draft is involved, and more than the extent to which women should be used. Fisher said to me, explaining her decision to leave the Army, "I like these men, but I'll never understand them. The way I see it, if we do our work and we're good soldiers, they should leave us alone. They have to learn to live with *us* too."

14

In Close Formation: Soldiers and the Citizenry

"I love the military," said a West Point lieutenant, the one who had bemoaned the circumstances that made it hard for a soldier to keep a husband or a home. "From the time I went home on my first leave and I got off the plane in my little green uniform, I knew I'd found something that made me feel good."

Other women feel the same. I have watched them at parades, or absorbed in polishing brass, or hearing that they have been chosen for guard duty, and they transparently show all the tremors of pride that men feel under the same circumstances. The intense West Point captain with her green eye shadow was as exercised as she was about everything that was wrong with the Academy precisely because she was so awed by its tradition. She said to me one day, "I feel a thrill at being here because this is a wonderful place. To eat dinner on the Poopdeck, where Presidents have dined, is wonderful. I get a real sense of pride even now just to be here." However much women may be handicapped or distressed by the ways in which the Army works, they are, fundamentally, in sympathy with it. They *like* the Army, and the contract upon which it is based.

Women soldiers are traditional, despite the gleam of intrepid determination that makes them decide to join the Army. They want to be successful, but few want to be the first female Chief of Staff or hold a top job at the Pentagon, even though they know that women must have power. Many of them are happy in the jobs in which they have become accepted. In short, they are neither crusaders nor radicals. Respect for the status quo in a status-dominated society is not, however, the same as passivity. The changes they want have to do with professionalism and fairness and do not, accordingly, emerge from the single-issue thinking that dominates so much of public life today. Military women would not tend to pick out any one of the programs mentioned above and concentrate upon it—except for harassment. All are united on harassment. However, I have not heard them complaining at length about blocked promotion or the quota system. They see things differently from civilians, in ways that people who speak for them often do not fully understand.

Pressed on equal rights, they will talk about equal responsibilities. Asked whether they are feminists or not, they will often say no, but that women should be allowed to do anything they are capable of, and in the Army too, except when it interferes with military necessity. Soldiers, male and female, learn that their individual rights have to be balanced against the national security, and at times relinquished. So the women do not obsessively worry about their rights. They are more likely to speak sincerely about the many opportunities military life has given them. It has. Aware of the over-all realities, they do not fuss about tokenism—instead, they say that there should be one more female general. They may complain about specific things wrong with the Army, but they are very loyal, and, since most are not detached or of an intellectual disposition, they leave the larger issues alone. Whatever their reasons—insecurity, or a too ready acceptance of military customs, or a true understanding of the

Army—they are prepared to live with most Army policies.

On various subjects they speak with one voice, most particularly on harassment. The Army has moved against it by issuing directives and memoranda. Prosecutions have become more common. An outspoken and determined general in Europe has begun to treat sexual harassment by publicizing the names of the offenders and ordering them to research and teach classes on sexual abuse. Women too have been prosecuted—this is an equal-opportunity Army—for behaving obscenely toward men. There is talk of an ombudsman for those people whose chain of command is not functioning properly.

Nevertheless many women feel that despite these labors and good intentions, the atmosphere of the Army remains hostile at any unit with a substandard commander. The women are not satisfied, because they feel that the problem has not been approached in the correct way. They want a serious, consistent, strictly enforced policy against harassment and a shift in thinking to back it. Repeatedly they told me, "Harassment is unethical; it goes against the mission; it means a failure in command." They wanted the Army to cope with it in a more military way.

The same complaint was made about the ways in which female capabilities are assessed. The women are sick of having to bear the burden of proof. They feel that the small, pointless tests that drag on and create phony doubts should be stopped. General Meyer, of the Joint Chiefs of Staff, has said there has to be evidence that women can do it before they are sent to fight from the foxholes. A high ranking woman at the Pentagon said to me, "So why don't they do a *real* study of women in combat? After thirty-two years I still hear them going over the same old things, but they haven't really dealt with the possibility of a substantial female presence in some units. They should test the performance of an all-male unit against an all-female, and all the various permutations. They should test them in simulated combat and in combat support. Why don't they? What if Congress decides to draft women? Have they prepared for an influx of women?" The Army will say only that it plans more consistent and far-reaching tests, but not until sufficient numbers of women are well enough trained.

The women clamor angrily for more sophisticated and gender-free individual testing to determine which person is capable of doing which job. They know that in a large institution precise testing of each person is an expensive fantasy, but that is what they want. For two years the Army research laboratories have been trying to develop a physical test that would establish the actual and potential strength of an incoming recruit. Louis Ruberton, the civilian in charge of the project, told me, "We are trying to get a profile of the stamina and endurance required for each MOS, and the critical tasks that are common to all of them are being established." He said they were using exercise machines, and weight-lifting tests. Ruberton continued, with the wary note in his voice that is used by Army people responding to civilians' questions, "Of course we can't come up with a standard that would cut the females out. What would we gain? And what unit functions without teamwork?" Such remarks provoke mixed feelings in female soldiers, who strongly resist such broad and misleading generalizations as "male" and "female" when strength is being discussed. They want large numbers of women admitted so that their presence can become normal and accepted. However, they know, to their cost, how much inadequate women may harm the cause of the rest.

Lieutenant Myers said, wandering around her German apartment with a hiccuping infant on her shoulder, "Women come in way behind men . . . and we do it to ourselves, of course . . . but they need to be put in two weeks earlier than the men for physical training so that they have a chance to catch up. Women should have had to carry the M-14 just like the men used to, and they shouldn't be babied now. If they're not babied anymore, they're going to respond, and *then* you can start finding out about differences." She said, "I'm not saying you should push people to do things they can't manage. People shouldn't be made to keep on with push-ups, one, two, and so on. They should concentrate on exercises to build up the arm muscles so that next time when they come to do push-ups it's much easier and they can manage quite a few more." She looked at me wryly and said, "That's the way the WAC used to do things. We worked on problems, we didn't just crash into them."

Lieutenant Myers spent much of the time playing with her baby girl and watching from the narrow balcony to see when her husband's chopper flew back over the pines to base, a signal for her to start cooking lunch or dinner, which was an aspect of domestic life that somehow threw her. Still, in a world dominated by tiny plastic toys that crunch underfoot, language problems with the landlord, and a husband's schedule that would necessitate his springing up from a half-eaten steak and dashing off on emergency call, she kept returning to the idea that haunted her even now when she was out of the service. "It's not just women who should be pushed," she said. "More important, the men should be pushed too. Women should not be allowed to 'hold the men back,' which is the complaint you always hear." She said carefully, "I might have a lesson plan that says everyone should carry a forty-pound pack. A few of my women cannot do that—so to make it all equal, are we all to carry twenty-pound packs and then blame the women?" Lieutenant Myers made it clear that in her opinion these were the truly moral issues. She reminded me that the decision to bus the men and women in training out to the ranges instead of having them march was made by men. That decision was wrong. The men had decided that women could not march, and because the women were never offered the chance, the case against them was proved. Subsequently, she told me, the policy was changed at Fort McClellan; the trainees march to the ranges now, without problems.

Career female soldiers are elitist, and it is not just those who are nostalgic for the WAC. I had a long, serious talk one day at Fort McClellan with a captain who had welcomed integration as an advance for the women. She said, with furious irony, "It used to be a Known Fact in the old days

that women were not equal to men. All of a sudden there
came a Great Doubt in our minds, followed by a big push
toward Equality, which is all they can think about. Everybody's afraid now that we might prove that men and women
aren't equal. Therefore, what we in the Army like to do is
find the happy medium, so that we can all be mediocre
together, and then we can all be equal." She added, "Maybe
things will go rigorous again, and we'll start going for the
truth, to find out what the average man does best, and the
average woman, and the superior man, and the superior
woman."

All the women emphasized rigor. They agreed that while
trends in hardware might come and go, and policies might
change, the best available people had to be trained in the
best possible way to meet whatever emergency would face
them. They expressed disillusion, a bitter feeling that when
Army women came under the control of Army men, a
constructive search for excellence had disappeared. I heard it
also from Colonel Allen at Fort McClellan when I asked her
about the supposed shortfall of high quality female recruits.
She put the tips of her fingers together, looking very precise
and intellectual, softly cleared her throat, and said, "Is there
really a shortfall, or are we talking about recruiter compla-
cency?" She continued, "The truly gifted, truly competitive
women are going to have to be recruited for the Army just as
well as they're being recruited by industry and the colleges.
They're not a *given*." She paused and inhaled in exasperation. "This shortfall could have been corrected, given time
and attention, and without lowering the standards."

Special treatment designed to obtain the best women and
elicit their best work is equated with favoritism, but the
women mean something different. I heard from them,
"These young women have uniform violations, and the men
don't know, so they go uncorrected," or, "There should be a
woman looking out for the young females, telling them what
to do and how to behave." One sergeant wrote to me,
"Every female troop should be allowed the option of access
to a female officer or adviser." She wanted a return to

segregated training, with males instructing males and females instructing females. She knew this would set the women back, but she was looking for an atmosphere of female authority.

The West Point women, as they go up through the Army, will make a difference, not simply by augmenting the numbers coming in through OCS or ROTC but because, with the assurance of women who have graduated from that most prestigious and masculine of institutions, they will have a faint sheen of glamour in addition to their expertise. As it is, enlisted women have reservations about female officers, because many of them have experienced lieutenants or captains who are unconfident, or too quick to do what the men tell them to. However, Fisher told me that her company had acquired an effective female lieutenant a while ago, and Fisher said proudly, "I can talk to her, she's cool. Because she's good-looking too, none of the men talk back to her. Everyone seems to get along with her, and it helps just having her around."

Women benefit greatly from knowing that there is someone who will keep them up to scratch or look out for them when they may be one of four or five in a company of a hundred and forty males. Lieutenant Myers said, "Why shouldn't you give an inch, especially with physical things? I *know* I can do thirty push-ups, so I'll do them in front of anybody, but there are so many things in the Army that young women have never tried." Her face thoughtful, she said, "It could even be a man, you know. I can think of men who are especially good with women, the ones with daughters."

The subject at issue is how best to educate women in soldiering. Lieutenant Myers told me she would use her sex in dealing with female troops. "I'd say to them, 'When I came in I could run half a mile in a time I'd be embarrassed to confess, but I made it through, and if I could, you can.'" There are other ways. I watched a young female drill sergeant at Fort Dix urging on her females as they squirmed on their stomachs to set up a Claymore mine. She said, her voice rippling with irony, "Come *on*—make like John Wayne." There was a moment of real camaraderie as the grimy trainees relished the joke.

Lieutenant Myers said, "There's no separatism about any of this, for goodness' sake. They still get the male example coming at them all the time from all sides." As a result the women soldiers in the man's Army seem like poor relations, except when the media are present. They are tolerated; a place is set for them at dinner; but they are not esteemed. However, to a PFC and a second lieutenant alike, the sight of a senior female NCO or field grade officer, immaculate, crisp, authoritative, is a tonic. Just as the women in basic training were crushed if singled out for criticism by a female, so they were doubly thrilled if Lieutenant Myers or Sergeant Bell or one of the female drill sergeants gave them a few words of praise. As Julie Drake said, with her mauve eyes wide, "You feel they really know you, they're *like* you."

I discussed this question with Colonel Lorraine Rossi, who had been the director of the Equal Opportunity programs, and she told me that she was deeply opposed to the idea of any separate treatment for women. She said, "If you have advisers, it makes it too easy for commanders to pass the problems along. You have to make the existing system work—education and training and the chain of command. A leader has to know how to lead men and women. There are not enough role models for the young women, but they should aspire to being senior officers anyway, not female senior officers." She said, "I know that the women have lost a feeling of unity in the process—you see that especially with the younger ones—but it was necessary."

As the women talked, there always emerged a profound wish for unity or connection, between themselves and the other women sparsely dotted across the post, and between themselves and the Army men. Lieutenant Myers said to me, "I often think of Infantry Hall at Fort Benning, with all the beautiful traditions, and then I think how our tradition is hidden and glossed over as if it never happened and now we're all men. But the Army is all traditions, and that is one we have. It's something the troops should be educated in, along with all the other traditions." She, and the others, would not have wanted a return to the Corps, simply a return of the old esprit or something in its place.

I attended a retirement parade very early on a hot summer morning at Fort Sam Houston, in San Antonio, at which four members of the Army Medical Corps were being honored. In the foreground were bleachers, where retired medical officers sat fanning themselves with programs, and in the background the young enlisted troops who had made up the parade wobbled and dropped and were helped into the shade. One of the four was a woman. As is the Army custom, the wives of the retirees were called out from their seats to receive their own plaques of distinction. They stood proudly by their husbands in front of the reviewing stand, and the thin woman with gray hair who had been an Army nurse all her working life stood alone in her mint-green dress and sensible shoes.

She was not pathetic. That retired nurse had made a choice, and her career had undoubtedly been more invigorating and interesting than a civilian nursing career would have been. Since she was working in an approved "feminine" aspect of the military, she had status that could be carried over into civilian life, which is not true for women in most of the regular Army jobs. Captain Whitcraft spoke for them when she said, "The biggest problem for me is wearing a uniform every day and not being appreciated for that by the general public." She said, "We are not compensated financially for the long hours of work and the dedication that is demanded from us. The compensations should come as appreciation. But people don't understand." The women are several times alienated—not just from the traditional rewards of Army life but also from the civilian world, whose customs they have contravened by taking on a life that is generally thought to be inappropriate for women. However, since the Vietnam war, Army men have felt alienated too, and so have those civilians whose wish for a rehabilitated and reconnected Army surfaced so plainly at the time of the public debates over registration.

A black woman in her early thirties, a successful businesswoman and a friend of a soldier I met at Fort McClellan, had a shrewd assessment of the problem. She said, "Those advertisements bring in the wrong people. They just talk about all the things you're going to get, all the benefits." She added that if the Army was functioning properly, people would be proud to be a part of it.

Elizabeth Brady agreed. She comes from the patriotic South, and when asked about her parents' view of her military career she will say cheerfully, "They love it—they're just tickled to death!" She said about the recruiting, "They never mention anything about being patriotic or the honor of wearing the uniform. All they advertise is *money*." She added, "You never hear the national anthem anymore unless the TV is going off at night." Elizabeth said, "Those trainees were very patriotic when they came in to basic; we all believed in what we had pledged. When we got our fatigues, we were excited and proud to wear them, and then when we left and put on our uniforms for graduation, we weren't so proud anymore. After seeing some of the ones who made it through, it was hard to feel proud." She smiled and said, "You remember that Private Littlebit poem when we all cried?" Brady said it would be hard to attract the best people, male or female, unless there was something intangible they could believe in. "People are looking for something," she said. "They want basic to be tough, so they make it more traumatic than it is, just like people do with labor. Women who have simple childbirths dramatize the pain, because it has to meet their expectations."

When I asked Lieutenant Myers her opinion, she heaved a great sigh and said, "If you could follow all the young soldiers around in the service, reminding them of Private Littlebit, you could give them more pride." She continued, "There has to be something—beautiful housing and hula girls to clean it for you, or something to believe in." She mentioned Vietnam, when it was so hard for the young men to hear the Army attacked as they were going off to die for the United States. Myers said, "It's the same with Iran; all that jingoism when the hostages were seized, and then the immediate 'Hell No, We Won't Go' as soon as registration became real." She said, "The trouble with people in the U.S. is that they have no sense of responsibility, or of the luxury in American life. We take appliances and shopping malls and plumbing and TV for granted, and we assume it will all be there for us always."

The most constructive of the sociologists who observe the Army is Charles Moskos, author of *The American Enlisted Man* and numerous studies and articles. In his recent interviews, some prompted by the problems of the AVF, others by the increased role of the women, Moskos has maintained that women will not alter the military very much unless considerably larger numbers are admitted. He agrees with the women about the unfortunate lowering of standards, pointing out that "the 1979 policy change to accept female high school dropouts will only further complicate the utilization of female soldiers." Nevertheless he sees the over-all problem from much the same perspective as the women do: that the Army is becoming less and less representative of society and therefore more estranged from it.

In the Army today there are more than 200,000 blacks, 29 percent of the whole. Moskos points out, however, that 65 percent of the blacks have high school diplomas, as compared to 54 percent of the whites, which indicates that the Army is attracting a representative sample of the black community, but not of the white. There is an obvious reason for this: the military genuinely does offer blacks prospects they are denied elsewhere. Nevertheless, if the white middle class cannot be recruited, and if lower-class youth are the stratum within the military that goes into combat jobs, the balance is all wrong. Moskos describes the advantages of the draft era, when military life had more camaraderie, when the barracks were less of a bolt-hole, and the young enlistees—many more intelligent than their sergeants—created a dynamic and vital mix, which in turn created esprit de corps.

Moskos also blames the misapplication of management techniques, and he says that recruiting will fall off badly because the underprivileged, who still see the military as a bridge to long-term stability and success in the mainstream of American life, will begin to realize that this is no longer true. All those promises in the TV and newspaper advertisements serve only to set up unrealistic expectations that cannot be fulfilled. So, despite all its overdue reforms, Moskos says, the Army is merely filling the holes in a wall that needs rebuilding. This is the point on which soldiers, male and female, and theorists and interested civilians agree.

Various approaches have been proposed. There are those who say that a draft would cure the problem. However, since a nonselective draft would provide too many people, the only useful draft would be the most unfair, and would occasion the same collapse in morale that the draft did at the time of Vietnam. Everyone concerned seems to favor national service, but with the emphasis on service. Forcing people into the military when there is no war is less desirable than bringing them into some form of voluntary national service, not all of it military. Moskos' plan, which includes a GI bill and a two-track career system to differentiate between the long- and the short-term soldier, would rely on federal aid for higher education as a way of involving the nation's young in voluntary service, military or civil. He has offered elaborate explanations of the financial merits of this system, which he insists could be accomplished without any additional expenditure, and which would bring in the required mix.

There have been other attractive schemes for bringing the young people of the country into voluntary service, but whatever their merits and appeals, the schemes are too complex and gigantic to be adopted. Bringing civilians closer to the military involves the creation of new bureaucracies, which is an unpopular idea at any time, and never more so than in the present. However, one expert has suggested a version of national service that operates from another perspective—that the military should be brought closer to civilian life instead of the other way around.

Dr. Albert Biderman works at the Bureau of Social Science Research in Washington, and his idea, which he has proposed regularly over the years, attempts to deal with the core of the military dilemma, namely, that having to bribe people to make them choose the services over civilian life amounts to "a systematic derogation of the communal values." To preserve and restore the communal values, he proposes radically changing the mission of the U.S. armed forces. He would like to see them responsible for coping with natural disasters and emergencies, floods, hurricanes, refugees, power failures, riots. He says calmly, as people turn away, that in most crises the various agencies overlap, and the resulting complications cause chaos and delays that kill people, especially when ambulances or fire fighters are required. Often when the National Guard is called out, the call comes too late for the troops to do more than support, and in some cases add to, the confusion.

Biderman's idea makes sense in the abstract. He points out that an organization that has operated in the real world instead of during an imitation war will be much more efficient when all the military virtues, such as survival in the field, first aid, fitness, discipline, physical endurance, can be learned under transferable circumstances. The communal expertise of the military can be used for the peacetime needs of the populace. Army people know how to "supply, communicate, organize, build, manage, transport, train, heal," he says—all of these functions as applicable to peace as to war. Biderman does not worry about the need for numbers; instead he discusses the new "high purpose" that this force would have, a movement away from ritualized violence and death dealing and toward curbing violence, "the goal of maintaining a peaceful, thuggery-free international order."

In essence, we would have a defensive military, in which more of the Regular Army would resemble the Reserves or the National Guard, while the elite fighting units would be left to concentrate on their ritualized violence. Professor Morris Janowitz, the first sociologist to study the military seriously, had advanced a similar idea more than twenty years ago, in *The Professional Soldier*, when he referred to "constabulary forces," seeking "viable international relations rather than victory." To foster this change, he called for reforms identical to those proposed by General Meyer twenty years later, when the general announced plans to adopt aspects of the British regimental system so that the ties between soldiers and the community off the post would be closer, making a post more like a home than a three-year stopover.

Biderman sees his plan as a possible saving of the AVF. He says the military should be open to the civic and public business of the community if it is to retain its vitality, a reform that would make the military more responsive to the changing world outside. Biderman says wearily that this idea is not popular. The people who run the volunteer organizations that would be challenged regard the military as evil and would see the plan as an ominous step into militarism. The pacifists agree with them. It has never been, in this country of determined individualism, an easy task to rally the citizenry around the idea of a peacetime military, or a draft at any time. Nevertheless, as it says on page one of *The Armed Forces Officer* manual, "The traditional esteem of the average citizen for the military officer is a major ingredient, indeed a prerequisite of the national security."

The Army exists through the will of the people, who may disband it if it falls out of favor. It is pointless to hate the military or soldiers; they exist, like government and its officials, and can be used for good or evil, recognized or passed over. However, this is a two-way process. Career military personnel may disdain close connections with the civilian world. The West Point cadets would talk about young men and women of their own age as "unwashed hippies and students," as if they were an unconscionable and sinister affront to the ordered life. At a parade, where overweight civilians spill out from the bleachers with their noisy children and candy wrappers, the dismay of career soldiers is visible.

Although it is easy to understand the desire of military men to hold themselves aloof, as an elite, their mission is different. On page 5 of the manual: "To think of the military as a guardian class apart . . . rather than as a strong right arm, corporately joined to the body and sharing its every function, is historically false and politically inaccurate." The role of the soldier is called here "trusteeship." The manual cautions soldiers against a defensive manner when aspects of the military are criticized. Officers are too prone to treat national security as "a private game preserve" when they should approach discussion of such matters "with the devotion of the missionary, seeking and giving light."

It would be as unrealistic for the public to expect missionary behavior from the Army as it is for soldiers to look for the placid and unqualified support of their fellow citizens in peacetime. However, it is not healthy for this society to be so fractured, and it increases the country's vulnerability. The Army needs to change in ways that parallel the changes going on in the society that encircles it, in which large numbers of women have moved into the work force at all levels, bringing flextime and day-care centers, and in which the ideal of successful leadership has become less authoritarian, more persuasive, and talk of the quality of life is mixed in with the profit-and-loss index.

If an overlap were to be created between the two worlds, and if the Army adopted a more regimental system, the military community would be less shifting and anonymous. Parents could sit on the school board or become involved in local activities without feeling their involvement was temporary. The present severe shortage of civilians to fill the nonmilitary service jobs would dwindle if the post and the town were more closely integrated. Young soldiers with money in their pockets on a Friday would not be wandering out into a lonely night, feeling aimless, looking for trouble. Junior enlisted troops, who have to endure the thumping noise and communal living and enforced inspections of

barracks life, could, after a specified length of time, move
into more private quarters, while retaining uniforms, drills,
and whatever other attributes of military life were thought
necessary. As the pressures of estrangement, boredom, and
the taxing life of the barracks dwindled, men might lose
some of their frustration and rage at the Army, and hence
they might stop blaming the women. If the morale problems
eased, the men and the women alike would be more likely to
stay.

Old Army types who mourn the passing of the Army's
pride keep searching for a way to bring it back, to return to
the days when people stood to attention at the sound of
"Retreat," and everybody lived on post in a tight group.
That old Army is gone forever. Off-post housing and the
increased employment of civilians are part of the irreversible
change. Even though military life must still be authoritarian,
today, when all soldiers are volunteers, they have to see their
careers as personally rewarding if they are to work capably
and submit to discipline. This is what enlightened commanders have wanted ever since the 1960s, when Vietnam and
the changes in the culture made established systems of
authority vulnerable to the skepticism of the young.

I asked Dr. Biderman how he answers the people who
accuse him of wanting to civilianize the military. He laughed
and said, "It's quite the reverse. The huge, ludicrous
enlistment bonuses and talk of pay raises are civilian. I want
things to be *more* military, in terms of discipline, hardship,
selflessness, challenge. It's more than being professional.
That's why we need uniforms and rules," he said. "The
military needs to be different." Biderman agreed that the
question of women in the military is distorted by the
emphasis on close-quarters combat, a distortion that once had
a purpose but now serves only to pull the military down. He
said smoothly, "I know that people-killing is at the heart of it
all, but my concept is of a core of very highly specialized
people-killers." He added, "We must also recognize the
critical nonshooting roles—what most soldiers do almost all of
the time—and then apply those to the things like natural

disasters. As for the women," he said, "they fit in very well with all this."

Women, through their families, tend to be more firmly rooted in the community than men are, and so women soldiers have immediate legitimacy to offer, as well as a basis for long-term change. Many of them are from the educated middle class, precisely that category of recruit that the Army so badly needs. If the numbers increase and the middle-class women continue to participate, the Army will seem to be a more civilized and humane place to those young men who currently shun it—the middle class, the college-educated from the West and the Northeast. The Army needs its women, just as West Point does, to restore some balance to military values that have become anachronistic.

Women stand to benefit to the same degree that they contribute. Lieutenant Myers pointed out that many of the women's problems could be greatly eased. Those who needed time off for pregnancy and child rearing could be credited with their service and allowed back later. She said firmly, "You could study while you were out, so that you wouldn't lose rank, and when you came back, they would have the benefit of your experience." After all, the Army is quite used to coping with discontinuity, because the junior troops are so transient and career soldiers leave their jobs to attend courses or move from one post to another.

Improvements of this sort would attract and sustain young women who want to be serious about a military career, especially in the Reserves, which today provide perhaps the best indication of what such a military might be like. Both the Reserves and the National Guard have come to rely on women. The over-all percentage of women is just over 8 percent, but in some units it is much higher. Women like the Reserves. Those who want to stay in their community and raise a family are happy to have the chance for adventure, a little more money, an escape from home for a weekend now and then and two weeks in the summer. Women make ideal weekend soldiers. Some Army officials worry that the Reserves are too dependent on the women, who, if war were to break out, would dominate the combat support positions or possibly decide not to attend. Other officials are very glad the women are there, because they are keen, and without them the Reserves would be in far worse trouble. Elite soldiers have little time for the Reserves, male or female, and never have had. Certainly they are not "military" in the traditional sense, as I discovered when I visited Elizabeth Brady at the time when she was a Reserve on active duty.

Elizabeth had breezed through her AIT at Fort Sam Houston, but it had given her a fresh scorn for the low entrance requirements. She had been made acting sergeant of a platoon of seventy people, 75 percent of them male. She told me that some of the men had initially refused to take orders from her, so she wrote them up for reprimands, but they did not care. "The result was that the instructors sat the men down and said, 'This is the way it is, and it will not be changing.' They said if the men didn't do what I said, they would be recycled again and again and again, and made fun of. And after that I didn't have any trouble."

Elizabeth was attending practical-nurse school in her hometown of Dalton, with all her fees and expenses paid by the Army. She was still a recruiter's dream—humorous, flinty, and smart. Very early on a foggy, drizzling Saturday morning she drove me from Dalton through the rolling hills to Chattanooga, where her unit was based. About two hundred people were lounging around outside a low red brick building, apparently waiting for formation. The people were of both sexes and many ages, clad in a motley collection of clothing. Elizabeth still looked as gleamingly neat as she had in basic, her fatigues starched, her boots spit-shined, but some of the others who had not yet gone through basic were in civilian clothing. Most people looked as if they were in their early thirties, with uniforms that had seen service and in some cases had perished.

After considerable flirting and jocularity over the cigarettes and coffee, a somewhat ramshackle formation was dismissed, and the group clambered into trucks for the drive to the firing range. It was the day of the annual weapons qualification on the M-16 and, for officers, on the pistol too. The friendly sergeant major said, "This is a nice bunch. Most of them are specialists in something, but they all put in their six years minimum. Careerists might stay twenty/thirty years. Do you watch *M*A*S*H?*" At the range the chaplain and the sergeant major stood inhaling the sweetish smell from the septic tank and chatting. They told me that Chattanooga was a Bible Belt town and very promilitary. Armed Forces Day is a major event there, and the military has no shortage in any of its Reserve units based in and around the city. The trucks rolled up, and Elizabeth said, "What did we do? We watched the people driving by in their cars and holding up joints at us."

It was becoming a beautiful day, with a bright sky full of puffy clouds and wind. People stretched out their ponchos among tiny blue and white flowers and puddles in the grass. Elizabeth stared at the targets and said, "Good Lord, you'd have to be a real idiot to miss that." She and a handsome lieutenant with a mustache, and her best friend, Sara, a buxom woman who had spent three years on active duty and possessed a sly wit, were to spend most of the day sprawled on the ground waiting to fire or waiting for their scores, and passing the long, boring hours with soldiers' jokes.

Between bursts of activity they planned the social event of the evening. One of the main attractions of the Reserves has always been the after hours. I once spent an evening at the Officers Club at Fort McClellan with a flushed group of male Reservists, most of them lawyers or state senators from Atlanta, who doggedly danced to the jukebox and from time to time broke into rousing choruses of "Alley Oop" or "Tom Dooley," the songs of their schooldays. Elizabeth told me that on such occasions there was considerable fraternizing. However, she was quick to add that because her unit was medical it was different. The sergeant major inspecting their wretched uniforms had said to me benignly, "They're all professionals, you see, and we don't make too much of a fuss about such things unless there's a good reason to."

Morale was, quite clearly, high. On the annual field trip

the unit would go to Fort McClellan and work sixteen hours a day in a field hospital, and then people would relax by throwing each other in swimming pools. Elizabeth said, "I love all the Army scenes and situations. Everyone's so friendly, especially the men." We left the range before the others had finished, and went to sit at HQ, drinking Cokes and talking. Elizabeth confirmed that the friendly sergeant major knew exactly what he was doing, and that the unit ran like clockwork. There was none of the racial tension that might have been expected in the South, and many of the women were making swift promotions.

Because Elizabeth had grown up in a large, turbulent family in a Georgia mountain town, where people were shot in fights or married at fourteen, she had learned level-headedness when very young. She had learned, as Southern women do especially, how to be determined without upsetting anybody, and so the Army men were ready to let her succeed. Since the Army is prevailingly Southern in style, a manner like Elizabeth's, saucy and poised, is immediately understood. The men loved it. They would egg her on just as they had in basic, and talk of her success with a proprietary pride, as if they had in their unit the one woman who could silence the critics. Because she looked good, she was not defeminized, and they were not threatened. Instead there was an atmosphere of affectionate fraternity, as there had been in Fisher's unit at Fort Bragg. The difference was that when I asked Fisher how things were going she said, "I guess life is good, because nothing bad has happened to me. I could be making lawn furniture like my friend, who's bored to death," she added, "but I don't like being so apart from the civilian world."

There can be a place in the military for women who are shrewd, confident in themselves, and tough. Their presence is valued inside the Army and out, especially in the South, where people's warm feelings toward the boys in uniform are readily extended to women. Elizabeth had told me about the pride her parents felt. That feeling, or one like it, was quite apparent in the looks and the repartee she received as we negotiated our way around the Chattanooga airport. She was not looking perfect, with mud all over her fatigues and boots and her cap swinging in her hand until she guiltily glanced down at it and remembered to shove it back on her head. Nevertheless, striding between the parking lot, the coffee shop, and the ticket counter, helping with my luggage, grinning at passersby, she attracted attention. She was not familiar with Chattanooga people, but they felt familial toward her. You could see it in their interest and answering grins, the way the ticket clerk bent his head in a courtly way to ask where she was posted and if she was flying that afternoon. She definitely had a place; she was defending our country, by God, and she was just like our daughter. That was how it used to be for most young soldiers standing stiffly by the boarding gate with coats over their arms and their shaved heads showing at the sides of their caps. Watching Elizabeth show off a little, and noting the pleasure of those watching her, I realized that an Army with roots in the community would give Army women the status they so badly needed. As a result, everyone would benefit, just as the Palmach in Israel had benefited from the women who "blurred and decreased the harshness of military life . . . lent substance to the Palmach concept of an armed force free of militarism . . . precluded the brutalization of young men thrown into an all-male society for months on end . . . turned the Palmach into a true people's army."

Miss Goodall, the former World War I telephone operator, was one of the thirty women chosen to work the switchboard at the Paris Peace Conference. She showed me an official photograph of the "Honor Guard composed of picked men from every division" waiting for President Wilson in front of the Murat Mansion in Paris. At the extreme left of the picture a curtain was drawn back and the dim faces of the telephone operators peered shyly out for a glimpse of the parade. They did attend the dances and parties, and some of them even danced with General Pershing, but there was no official acknowledgment until sixty years later, when Miss

Goodall and her surviving colleagues received their honorable discharges and a World War I Victory medal. Miss Goodall, and the nurses of Santo Tomas, and the Wacs risked their lives, but they were auxiliary, marginal, in a way that today's Army women, however they may be regarded by their male colleagues, are not.

Whether or not the military becomes closer to the community, women will eventually find themselves gaining more power in the Army, as those who entered during the expansions of the 1970s move up the career ladder. The women with talent and determination will find themselves in positions of command, and over men. The techniques that they brought with them and that have been reinforced by the recent changes in policy will affect the hierarchical, authoritarian style of leadership. In closely knit units leadership has always been based on mutual respect and teamwork. The brutalities sometimes practiced in training were never universally held to be the only way of instilling obedience. The harsh and cruel anachronisms of West Point were out of date before the women arrived. Flexible, humane leadership is, as a former Wac put it, something that the good male commanders practiced, while the inadequate ones resorted to bullying. Today the most effective women in command are those who learned in the WAC how to be authoritative without stepping too far out of traditional female behavior. Their undramatic, natural air of authority is appropriate to the times, inside the Army and out. Some predict that this kind of leadership must become the norm if the Army is not to be a dinosaur. The women will set the example.

Women need the Army too. They are not full citizens until they share with men the full duty of defending their country. Citizenship is historically based on paying taxes and being liable for military service. Women collectively, so the theorists say, have no credibility with regard to the use of force, and the ability to be violent is what ultimately determines the distribution of power. Once women have that power, and once they are required to serve alongside men as their strength and capability permit, there will be a balance in the Army, and in society at large.

Such major changes are unlikely to take place in the near future, because the more successful the women become in the Army, the more they raise disturbing questions that rattle at the roof beams of our society, and the more strenuously they are resisted. When traditional definitions of manly or womanly behavior erode, how can they be replaced? The question is pressing in the military because it is the bastion of manliness, generally thought to be the attribute that fights and wins wars. If to become a warrior (however loosely the term is defined) is no longer a rite of passage, what is it? Maybe the role of warrior will come to be defined by age and not by gender. Maybe the profession of warrior will vanish altogether, and the mystique with it, except for those few who make a career in the combat arms, so that the division into combat and noncombat troops will have a more precise, less pejorative meaning, and the heroic ideal will take on a new shape.

Although soldiers do not sit around in their off-duty hours discussing such questions, they are in the air. All the harassment and the rage and the endless surveys and reevaluations of women's role amount to a rearguard action fought by the Army, and supported by the civilian world from which soldiers are drawn, against the upheavals female soldiers threaten to create.

The Times of London carried a picture of a woman officer cadet in the British WRAC learning how to fire a pistol. The caption read: "Officer cadet Peta Dancer, aged 18, firing her 9 mm Browning pistol on the ranges of the Royal Military Academy Sandhurst as 13 girls from the Women's Royal Army Corps College nearby are given their first instruction in the use of firearms for self-defence. The Ministry of Defence has decided that most girls in the WRAC and the Women's Royal Air Force should be taught how to fire a gun so that they can be less dependent on their male colleagues for male protection." There are two points of interest in this short

passage. The first is the familiar obliviousness to the truth
that a woman with a gun has the power to protect not just
herself but her male colleagues too—and also to shoot other
people. The second is the word "girls," used twice, and not
simply about Peta Dancer, aged eighteen. We still live in a
world in which a boy picks up a gun to become a man, but
uniformed ranks of women who know how to kill with
weapons can be called girls. The ubiquitous use of the word
"females" to describe women in the U.S. Army is equally
interesting, in that it is not "women."

The U.S. Army has placed its women in the vanguard.
They have many battles to fight, and most of them are
caused by the assumptions in our society, which happen to
be expressed most forcefully by their male colleagues. The
Army is in trouble because these assumptions have become
untenable, and the women are convenient targets for blame.
Pouring money into pay increases or this year's weapons
system is not the way to solve the military's problems. The
idea of military service has to be refurbished, and the women
provide the opportunity. In the course of the overhaul
already under way the Army will be able to use them to turn
things around. They will have to be seriously recruited and
required to face the same conditions of service as men.
Capable women will have to be used to their limits—if not,
they will leave. Elizabeth Brady, a perfect soldier in that she
is motivated, is over twenty-one, and has had a hysterec-
tomy, has moved over to the Navy, where so few women are
required in her specialty that they are taking only the best
and using them carefully. She said, cautiously, just before
leaving for San Diego, "Everything's terrific so far, but just
wait until I take a good job away from a man."

One afternoon I overheard the following exchange between Lieutenant Myers and her husband, Lieutenant Ted
Myers, as they played with their baby girl on the carpet.
Lieutenant Myers said firmly, "Charlotte's going to graduate
top of her class at West Point, of course." Her husband
looked at her with surprise and alarm and said, "Now hold
it—you can't force her to do that. She might not want to go

into the Army. Suppose she wants to go to Radcliffe?"

By the time Charlotte Myers is of an age to decide between West Point and Radcliffe, military women may have become fully accepted as soldiers at last. There will always be men in the Army like the ones who carried Private Jones in from the march, men like whose who ran Range 17 with such élan. There will be women commanders who are ready to believe that the most marked functional difference between young men and women is in the degree of their familiarity with the workings of the washing machine. And there will always be sergeants like Butler, who said, so carefully, "It's the fellows in the Army that make it great," and added, "and the *ladies*." If Charlotte Myers ever finds herself in the bleachers at the end of a scorching day out on the range, she and her buddies may feel their eyes mist over as the sergeant reads a poem in which Private Littlebit could be either a man or a woman.

Selected Bibliography

Adler, Freda. *Sisters in Crime: The Rise of the New Female Criminal.* New York: McGraw-Hill, 1975.

Binkin, Martin, and Shirley Bach. *Women and the Military.* Washington, D.C.: Brookings Institution, 1977.

Bliven, Bruce, Jr. *Volunteers, One and All.* New York: Reader's Digest Press, 1976. An examination of the All-Volunteer Force and its problems.

Briffault, Robert. *The Mothers: A Study of the Origins of Sentiments and Institutions.* New York: Macmillan, 1927. A classic early work of anthropology that analyzes theories of gender difference.

Crane, Stephen. *The Red Badge of Courage.* The classic novel of the Civil War, written by a young man who had never seen battle; available in many editions.

Douie, Vera. *Daughters of Britain.* Oxford: G. Ronald, 1949.

An account of the work done by 445,000 servicewomen and almost 5 million female civilians in World War II.

Ellis, Joseph, and Robert Moore. *School for Soldiers*. New York: Oxford Univ. Press, 1974. The most sober and sensible of recent books about West Point.

Engel, Barbara Alpern, and Clifford N. Rosenthal, editors and translators. *Five Sisters: Women Against the Tsar*. New York: Knopf, 1975.

Evans, Elizabeth. *Weathering the Storm*. New York: Scribner's, 1975. Women of the American Revolution.

Fanon, Frantz. *A Dying Colonialism*. Translated by Haakon Chevalier. New York: Grove Press, 1967.

Farber, Seymour M., and Roger H. L. Wilson, editors. *The Potential of Woman*. New York: McGraw-Hill, 1963. Fifteen speeches and seven panel discussions from a symposium held in San Francisco in 1963.

Fisher, Elizabeth. *Woman's Creation*. New York: Anchor Press/Doubleday, 1980.

Foot, M. R. D. *S.O.E. in France*. London: H.M.S.O., 1966. An engrossing and factual account of the work done by the men and women of the Special Operations Executive to help the French Resistance movement.

Gabriel, Richard A., and Paul C. Savage. *Crisis in Command: Mismanagement in the Army*. New York: Hill & Wang, 1978. The case against civilian control.

Galloway, K. Bruce, and Robert Bowie Johnson, Jr. *West Point: America's Power Fraternity*. New York: Simon & Schuster, 1973. A scathing critique of the Academy.

Goldich, Robert L., editor. *Women in the Armed Forces: Proceedings of a CRS Seminar Held on November 2, 1979, and Selected Readings.* Washington, D.C.: Congressional Research Service, Library of Congress, 1980. The varied and interesting views of soldiers, academics, and theorists.

Graves, Robert. *Goodbye to All That.* London: Jonathan Cape, 1929. A dazzling and honest autobiography of the poet's youth, in particular the time he endured in the trenches of World War I.

Gray, Glenn. *The Warriors.* New York: Harper & Row, 1969.

Hazelton, Lesley. *Israeli Women: The Reality Behind the Myth.* New York: Simon & Schuster, 1977.

Ibarruri, Dolores. *They Shall Not Pass.* New York: International Publishers, 1966. The autobiography of La Pasionaria.

Janowitz, Morris L. *The Professional Soldier: A Social and Political Portrait.* Glencoe, Ill.: Free Press, 1960.

Jones, James. *From Here to Eternity.* New York: Scribner's, 1951.

Maccoby, E. E., and C. N. Jacklin. *The Psychology of Sex Differences.* Stanford, Calif.: Stanford Univ. Press, 1974.

Macksey, K. *The Partisans of Europe in World War II.* New York: Stein & Day, 1975.

Manchester, William. *American Caesar: Douglas MacArthur, 1880–1964.* Boston: Little, Brown, 1978. This biography contains useful information on Bataan and Corregidor.

Mead, Margaret. *Male and Female.* New York: Morrow, 1955.

——. *Sex and Temperament in Three Primitive Societies.* New York: Morrow, 1935.

Michel, Henri. *The Shadow War: European Resistance 1939–1945.* Translated by Stephen Barry. New York: Harper & Row, 1972.

Montagu, Ashley. *The Natural Superiority of Women.* New York: Macmillan, 1967.

Morris, Jan. *Conundrum.* New York: Harcourt Brace Jovanovich, 1974. A formerly male writer who has had a sex-change operation reflects on male bonding, female vulnerability, and other aspects of behavior.

Moskos, Charles C. *The American Enlisted Man: The Rank and File in Today's Military.* New York: Russell Sage Foundation, 1970.

Oakley, Anne. *Sex, Gender and Society.* New York: Harper & Row, 1973.

Pankhurst, Emmeline. *My Own Story.* New York: Kraus Reprint Co., 1971.

Pile, Frederick. *Ack-Ack: Britain's Defence Against Air Attack During the Second World War.* London: G. Harrap, 1949.

Pomeroy, Sarah B. *Goddesses, Whores, Wives and Slaves; Women in Classical Antiquity.* New York: Schocken Books, 1976.

Redmond, Juanita. *I Served on Bataan.* Philadelphia and New York: Lippincott, 1943. A nurse's memoir.

Rowbotham, Sheila. *Women, Resistance and Revolution.* New York: Pantheon Books, 1972.

Sandes, Flora. *The Autobiography of a Woman Soldier: A Brief Record of Adventure in the Serbian Army, 1916–1919.* New York: F. A. Stokes, 1927.

Smedley, Agnes. *Portraits of Chinese Women in Revolution.* Old Westbury, N.Y.: Feminist Press, 1976.

Thomas, Edith B. *The Women Incendiaries.* Translated by James and Starr Atkinson. New York: George Braziller, 1966. The story of the women of the Paris Commune.

Tiger, Lionel. *Men in Groups.* New York: Random House, 1979.

——— and Joseph Shepher. *Women in the Kibbutz.* New York: Harcourt Brace Jovanovich, 1975.

Treadwell, Mattie E. *The Women's Army Corps.* United States Army in World War II. Washington, D.C.: Office of the Chief of Military History, Dept. of the Army, 1954. This history is definitive, shrewd, and absorbing.

Truscott, Lucian K. *Dress Gray.* New York: Doubleday, 1978. A poorly written novel that nevertheless vividly represents the view (male) West Point cadets have of the institution and of themselves.

Webb, James. *Fields of Fire.* Englewood Cliffs, N.J.: Prentice-Hall, 1978.

Wittig, Monique. *Les Guérillères.* New York: Viking, 1971. A purple novel that attempts, but fails, to create a feminist heroic myth.

Some Army documents are relevant and useful, in particular a survey prepared by the Staff Support Branch of the Center of Military History, Department of the Army, and presented on March 1, 1978. The survey is called *Women in*

Combat and as Military Leaders, and it contains a great deal of information about women in wars throughout the world, particularly in World War II.

I have also taken information from the following studies:

Vaught, W. L. *A Brief History of Women in Combat and War.* Industrial College of the Armed Forces, 1973.

Fox, Lt. Col. Eugene A., et al. *Women in the Army.* Office of the Deputy Chief of Staff for Personnel, Dept. of the Army, Dec. 1, 1976.

Women Content in Units Force Development Test (MAX-WAC). U.S. Army Research Institute, Oct. 3, 1977.

Women Content in the Army Reforger 77 (REF-WAC 77). U.S. Army Research Institute, May 30, 1978.

Report on the Admission of Women to the U.S. Military Academy (Project Athena), Vols. I–III. Dept. of Behavioral Sciences & Leadership, United States Military Academy, West Point, N.Y., Sept. 2, 1977, June 1, 1978, June 1, 1979; also two other surveys undertaken by the Office of Physical Education at the Academy: *Project 60* (May 3, 1976) and *Project Summertime* (Oct. 1976)